THIRD-WORLD
DEVELOPMENT

THIRD-WORLD DEVELOPMENT

Aspects of Political Legitimacy and Viability

Tri Q. Nguyen

Rutherford ● Madison ● Teaneck
Fairleigh Dickinson University Press
London and Toronto: Associated University Presses

Associated University Presses
440 Forsgate Drive
Cranbury, NJ 08512

Associated University Presses
25 Sicilian Avenue
London WC1A 2QH, England

Associated University Presses
P.O. Box 488, Port Credit
Mississauga, Ontario
Canada L5G 4M2

The paper used in this publication meets the requirements of the American National Standard for Permanence of Paper for Printed Library Materials Z39.48-1984.

Library of Congress Cataloging-in-Publication Data

Nguyen, Quoc Tri, 1929–
    Third-World development.

    Bibliography: p.
    Includes index.
    1. Developing countries—Economic policy.
    2. Economic assistance—Developing countries.
    3. Legitimacy of governments—Developing countries.
    4. Vietnam—Economic policy   5. Economic assistance—
    Vietnam.   6. Legitimacy of governments—Vietnam.
    7. Korea (South)—Economic policy.   8. Economic
    assistance—Korea (South)
    9. Legitimacy of governments—Korea (South)
    I. Title.
    HC59.7.N44   1989   338.9′009172′4   87-45959
    ISBN 0-8386-3327-7 (alk. paper)

PRINTED IN THE UNITED STATES OF AMERICA

CONTENTS

FIGURES

FOREWORD

IT HAS LONG BEEN DEBATED WHETHER ADMINISTRATIVE DEVELOPMENT can be achieved ahead of political development or whether political development is a necessary precondition for successful administrative development. As one who has struggled with such issues again and again over the past thirty-five years and has seen more than one major administrative improvement program swept into the trash bin of history in the wake of political upheavals, I have found Tri Q. Nguyen's analysis of the processes of Third-World development a welcome contribution to the continuing discourse on this matter. He firmly supports the proposition that political legitimacy is the essential key to creating a viable polity capable of sustaining national development and that without it, development efforts are likely to be futile and their achievements in administration or any other field are apt to be short-lived.

In focusing on the issue of legitimacy, its nature, achievement, maintenance, and relationship to power, Tri joins Fred Riggs and others concerned with the critical interplay between bureaucrats and other political and economic elements, both internal and external, which affect governmental systems in the real world of national development. He goes well beyond the discussion of administrative versus political development, however. His concern is for the very viability of Third-World nations and their prospects for any form of development in a complex and highly conflictual world environment. Most important for the international development community, his analysis and findings suggest why the technical and financial assistance efforts of Western donor nations and international banking institutions have all too frequently failed to produce the desired benefits, but instead have often undermined the polities they have sought to strengthen and prolonged in power regimes lacking in legitimacy and therefore incapable of making enduring progress.

Tri deals with three key cases: Vietnam, South Korea, and Singapore, with a nod as well to Taiwan. Each is analyzed in depth, but with particular stress on Vietnam, both pro-West and Communist. His analyses are penetrating and his conclusions highly instructive. One wishes, however, that he had examined in similar detail cases in other parts of the world, particularly Africa and Latin America. Would the same conclusions have been reached? It is to be hoped that Tri's work will stimulate others with specialized knowledge of those areas to make similar analyses of the development history of key African or Latin American nations.

Unlike so many who have sought to blame the failure of international development efforts primarily on an attempt to impose allegedly Western concepts and values on non-Western cultures, Tri demonstrates far greater knowledge and employs a more balanced, critical, and therefore realistic approach. He is wise enough to recognize Chinese and other Eastern origins in many of the ideas of contemporary professional administration. The root problem, he feels, has not been imposition of alien management practices, but the inability of most less-developed countries to establish and maintain viable polities. They have been unable to cope with crises of legitimacy, and for this inability they themselves must accept the major responsibility.

Exposure to many of the negative aspects of Western mercantilism, which, unfortunately, Tri does not distinguish from capitalism, has nevertheless eroded the fabric of traditional societies and left them extremely vulnerable to external pressures and negative internal forces. Tri strongly asserts the critical importance of social order and tradition in a world buffeted by far too rapid change.

Educated in both South Vietnam and the United States, and with highly significant professional experience in both countries, including the directorship of the National Institute of Administration in Saigon, the author is strongly versed in both Oriental and Western thought, as well as the fundamental Confucian values that underlie the cultures of each of the countries he has studied. He is an ideal person to undertake a critical evaluation of their nation-building efforts.

Tri argues strongly for cultural renewal as a means to build legitimacy. This has very significant meaning in Eastern Asia and some other parts of the developing world. Renewal may be difficult, irrelevant, or indeed impossible for nations whose cultural traditions are rooted in shallow soil, reflect strongly contradictory elements, or provide little or no guidance for building a viable polity in the contemporary world. There are, unfortunately, many such countries, whose identities derive more from historical accident or colonial power struggles in the last century than from a community of common experiences and values.

The truly significant parts of Tri's work for the development community are his analyses of the causes of development failure on the one hand, and his recommended changes in development assistance policy on the other. There can be little doubt that Western developed nations have for over thirty-five years tried to solve critical development problems with purely technical answers. It matters not at all whether the technology involved was administrative, economic, educational, or even agricultural, positive results have again and again proved ephemeral, transitory, or short-lived because they failed to survive political upheavals or even mere political transitions. Today, many billions of dollars later, that is, after assistance programs were undertaken in the postwar era, most Third-World countries are in serious depression, head-over-heels in debt, and burdened with vast burgeoning populations, living in abysmal poverty, while a small elite class enjoys the benefits of modernization. The world banking community totters on the brink of collapse because of huge, uncollectible loans made to Third-World borrowers. The analysis of how this dismal state of affairs has come about and how a few key countries have avoided it is certainly instructive. True to his thesis, Tri offers no technical solutions to social and political problems in his recommendations. He calls for coordinated efforts by the Western democratic powers to promote political development through open political support for anti-Communist, prodemocratic and proindependence forces in less-developed countries. He correctly notes that covert political efforts to undermine and overthrow undesirable regimes have scored short-termed successes on a number of occasions, only to have these countries fall into even less desirable hands, including those of the Communist powers.

Western democracies have shown very little skill in fostering political development, perhaps because, in contrast to the Communists, they don't know how. In Communist countries, there has never been any doubt as to which came first, political or economic or other forms of development. The first priority has been firm political domination by the party apparatus, even if enormous purges and economic disasters ensued from this political imperative. Stalin understood this well in the 1930s. The recent cases of Ethiopia and Nicaragua are similarly instructive.

Democratic political leaders and scholars with legal scruples continue to worry about principles of noninterference in the internal affairs of other countries, a precept embodied in the UN charter. This concern never seems to have bothered those bent on fomenting Marxist "struggles for national liberation." Opposition is to be crushed. When confronted with the inability to cope with political footdragging in administrative or economic arenas, Western democratic development assistance people turn to infrastructure creation, agricultural research, or attempts to help the poor through nongovernmental organizations. Political problems are simply bypassed.

The United States can point to examples of successful democratic political development only in the cases of its former enemies of World War II. These achievements in West Germany and Japan came about through extended military occupations, purges of the former leadership on a massive scale, and vast inputs of economic assistance. These are hardly formulas for ready application today. Long years of U.S. occupation of Nicaragua in the early years of this century produced no viable democratic polity there, and no one would point to the Philippines as a shining example of democratic nation building.

There may be other factors at work. West Germany and Japan, as well as India, Sri Lanka, Barbados, and a number of other former British colonies employ a basically parliamentary structure of democracy and have achieved viable polities, avoiding the endless pattern of coups and military takeovers that one of Tri's major examples of a successfully developing country, South Korea, has failed to escape. Fred Riggs, in some of his recent work, has taken particular note of the possible structural flaws in presidential systems that make for marked instability.

We have much yet to study and to learn about the processes of nation building and their relationship to economic and social development. Tri has made a major contribution, in both terms of concepts and analysis, as well as in his critical appraisal of the costly consequences of over three decades of effort to resolve what are basically political issues with rational administrative and economic techniques.

Wendell G. Schaeffer, President,
International Association of Schools and Institutes of Administration

PREFACE

THIS BOOK IS THE PRODUCT OF NEARLY TWENTY YEARS OF THINKING, reflection, and meditation about ways to improve the lot of my native country, Vietnam, in particular, and of other so-called less-developed countries (LDCs), in general. The central concepts of "legitimacy" and "power," used in this book have captured my attention since the late 1960s, when I was working on my Ph.D. dissertation at the University of Southern California on the impacts of cultural values on international development assistance. The hypothesis I have developed since then is that for a country to survive and grow, it must have a government capable of commanding obedience on the part of the subject people in matters of public concerns. This obedience can be secured by the use of government authority, which is commonly accepted as legitimate and thus taken for granted, and of government power, which is imposed through coercion, manipulation, or other means. The proportion of authority or power used may vary depending on the situation, but added together, the two must generate enough internalized and externalized motivation to serve common interests so that stability and order can be maintained while growth is fostered. The ideal polity, to be sure, relies more on authority than on power.

The dual political institution of Le Kingship and Trinh Regency, which existed in Vietnam from the second half of the sixteenth century to nearly the end of the eighteenth century is quite revealing in showing this balanced exercise of authority and power. During this period, the Le kings reigned, while the Trinh prince-regents ruled. Breaking all precedents firmly established by a long history of absolute monarchy, the prince-regency established by the Trinh family through hereditary successions became legitimated to such a point that it constituted a rival institution that overshadowed the monarchy itself. The successive Le kings instituted as figureheads by the Trinh regents provided some nominal legitimacy for the political system, while actual power was exercised by the Trinh regents.

Externally, this balance of legitimacy (authority) and power helped the dual regime accommodate the demands of the country's big brother from the north, China, which was ready, as it had been in the past, to intervene on behalf of a dynasty that they had recognized and to take advantage of such an occasion to reimpose its domination upon Vietnam. Internally, retaining the Le kings as figureheads allowed the Trinhs to coopt the Confucian literati who remained loyal to the Le dynasty. With the support of the literati, the Trinhs succeeded in restoring control over the kingdom by suppressing a rival dynasty, founded by Mac Dang Dung, who had usurped the Le throne. Dung managed to obtain Chinese sanction as a governor by bribery and by a humiliating surrender to Chinese troops, and by the same token, he destroyed his dynasty's legitimacy and its chances for survival. In contrast, Nguyen Hoang, a governor of the remote south (now part of central Vietnam) and his offspring succeeded in building up their own legitimacy by claiming to serve the Le dynasty, and they consolidated their power by rallying the literati alienated by the Macs and Trinhs. The Nguyens later became a rival regency; they founded their own dynasty after unifying the whole of Vietnam. This politicoad-ministrative institution, odd by Vietnamese standards, in which power was balanced with legitimacy, helped the country to survive and grow for over two hundred years.

I believe that, however much the content and form of legitimacy and power may change through time and space, integrating them for effec-tive governance constitutes a universal problem confronting polities throughout human history. It it also my belief that development efforts deployed in South Vietnam and many other LCDs have been rendered futile due to their inability to deal with this issue. I have presented this theme for discussion to a variety of audiences over many years. Third-World events heretofore have appeared to confirm the validity of the hypothesis. Encouraged by colleagues, friends, and former students, I started to write this book three years ago.

In this work, I attempt to demonstrate that sustained growth cannot occur where there does not exist a polity capable of securing enough obedience through a balanced exercise of authority and power; to propose a development strategy for the LDC leadership aiming at building up political legitimacy and authority by an effective exercise of power in the service of the public good; and to suggest ways for donor countries to support the LDCs' efforts in this direction.

The study starts with an examination of Third-World polities that are generally characterized by either a shortage of both legitimacy and power or by an ineffectual use of power that ends up destroying legit-imacy and the powerwielders themselves. Difficulties confronting the LDC leadership are pointed out in light of today's world environment, which is dominated by the Western alliance, which puts heavy stress on legitimacy and authority and the Communist bloc, which empha-

sizes the use of power. An analysis is made of the effective neutralization of development efforts by the political vicissitudes that have
resulted from the inability of many Third-World polities to achieve a
balance between authority and power. The key role played by this
balance in the success or failure of development endeavors is illustrated by case studies of Vietnam and its earlier divisions, of South
Korea, and of Singapore. A development strategy is proposed for de-
veloping-country leadership aimed at reinforcing the polity's legitimacy and power basis by leading a movement for cultural renewal;
mobilizing positive, i.e., uncorrupted, dedicated, forces for leadership
positions; integrating traditional and modern democratic political elements in building political institutions; and removing the bottlenecks
created by past erratic, uncoordinated development enterprises. New
directions are suggested for foreign assistance in support of this development strategy, which aims at integrating East-West interests by
helping the LDCs become capable of contributing to world trade and
prosperity on an equal footing with industrialized countries and by the
same token, creating a legitimate world order.

This book is intended for a wide variety of readers. It is addressed,
first, to top political policymakers in donor and recipient countries,
who alone can provide leadership for the radical policy changes proposed; second, to working professionals, whose alertness to interac-
tions between their work and their sociopolitical environments and
whose support for the political leadership are crucial for the success of
these changes; third, to academicians, scholars, and students whose
research on Third-World development can provide valuable guides for
policymakers and working professionals; and last, but not least, to the
public at large in both developed and developing countries, whose
interest in, and understanding of, these problems can exert a balanced
and positive influence on policy decisions.

The issues being raised here are of interest to students in many
disciplines concerned with development. I hope that the book can
serve as a text or supplementary text for undergraduate or graduate
courses, especially in development politics, development administration, development economics, development sociology, and development anthropology.

As the work is addressed to a wide variety of audiences, an effort has
been made to satisfy their divergent needs. As far as possible, the main
text has been kept brief and free of technical jargon to make it readable
for people with different experiences and backgrounds. Indeed, such
words as Third World, LDCs, developing countries, capitalism, communism, colonialism, West, East, legitimacy, authority, power, and so

on, may convey different meanings to different people, connote different value judgments, or appear controversial.

Those who have more time or are interested in further research can refer to the extensive endnotes at the back of the book. These notes not only provide sources of reference but also help me expand on some important points in the text, which I intend to keep brief and concise enough to convey the basic theme of the book. Readers who do not have much time can concentrate on the reader's guide section in the introduction, which may serve as a kind of executive summary.

The book is critical of development assistance systems, approaches, methods, and participants. Having been involved myself in many development endeavors as a professional from both the recipient and donor sides, I fully share in the blame. I am sincerely convinced that it is high time to recognize our mistakes and to explore new ways of proceeding. If the book succeeds in provoking dialogue, discussion, debate, and research in this direction, I will have fulfilled my purpose.

ACKNOWLEDGMENTS

I WISH TO SAY, IN BRINGING THIS BOOK TO COMPLETION, THAT MUCH IS owed to many who cannot possibly be named here. My intellectual debt is first to all the authors to whom I have made reference. My most sincere gratitude goes to Janice H. Hopper, one of my family's sponsors, who has been long associated with me as a colleague at the Institute of Public Administration (IPA), Washington, D.C., in the late 1970s, and as an IPA adviser to the National Institute of Administration, Saigon, Vietnam, in the early 1970s, when I was professor and rector of that institute. Janice not only inspired and urged me to undertake this study by offering me a new typewriter and putting her personal library at my disposal, but she also spent considerable time reviewing the drafts and offering constructive suggestions on both content and form. In retrospect, it is fair to say that this book could not have seen the light of day without such dedicated help, which included her typing and editing the rough draft and purchasing new materials for my research.

I want to thank particularly Randolph L. (Mike) Marshall, another colleague at IPA who has virtually devoted his whole career to improving public administration in the LDCs and who headed the IPA's international programs for many years. Mike has sacrificed a great deal of his valuable time to review and improve the successive drafts of this manuscript all along. My special thanks go to Lyle C. Fitch, chairman of the board of IPA and my family's prime sponsor, and to Eldon E. Sweezy, another colleague at IPA, for having reviewed the second draft and offered very useful comments.

I am most grateful to Chester A. Newland, professor, University of Southern California (USC), and editor-in-chief, *Public Administration Review*, who has carefully reviewed the entire first draft and the text of the second draft and has offered invaluable comments and suggestions for improvement. My deepest appreciation goes to my former professors at USC—Richard W. Gable of the University of California at Davis, Henry Reining, Jr., dean emeritus of the school of Public Administration, USC, and Frank P. Sherwood of Florida State University—who despite their busy schedules have reviewed the second draft and offered most helpful comments.

A great debt is owed to Wendell G. Schaeffer, president, International Association of Schools and Institutes of Administration, who introduces this publication to the readers. The foreword provided by Wendell, a reputable scholar who has practically devoted his entire professional life to teaching, research, and consulting in the field of international development administration, constitutes, indeed, an important addition to the book.

My special gratitude goes to Fred W. Riggs, professor emeritus, University of Hawaii, who has made a generous evaluation of this book. As a matter of fact, Fred's pioneering works on Third-World politics and administration, which I found insightful, perceptive, and fascinating, have not only strongly influenced my thinking in this book but also have been a major source of inspiration in my teaching, research, and consulting work.

A helpful role was played by Harry Keyishian, chair of the editorial committee, Fairleigh Dickinson University Press (FDUP), and Julien Yoseloff, director, and Beth Gianfagna, managing editor, of Associated University Presses (AUP) who have responded promptly and positively to my queries and requests for assistance throughout the publishing process. The book in its final form has been vastly improved thanks to an anonymous FDUP reader's evaluation and recommendations for change as well as the professional expertise, conscience, and linguistic ability of Marilyn Buckingham, my AUP copy editor.

I wish also to thank: Stuart S. Nagel of the University of Illinois at Urbana-Champaign, and my colleague, Charlotte D. Gillespie, director of communications, American Society for Public Administration, for their professional advice on book publishing and editing; and my longtime friends in the defunct government of South Vietnam—Buu Vien, former executive minister at the Office of the Prime Minister, Chau Kim Nhan, former minister of finance, and Do Quang Toa, former chief, Administrative Service, Rach Gia City Administration—for their inspiring responses to the second draft.

Loving thanks are extended to my children—Chi, Thang, Chau, and Khanh—and their spouses for their encouragement and help in my research. I am particularly indebted to my son-in-law, Phuoc T. Le, for his technical assistance in computer wordprocessing. Last but not least, my dear wife, Hong, deserves special recognition for remaining, with only a few unavoidable exceptions, patient, understanding, and caring throughout the long years spent on this work.

I regret to say that time does not permit me to utilize all the inputs provided by those indicated here as well as many others who are not mentioned here. They can, nevertheless, deservedly share in whatever positive contribution the book may offer, while I am solely responsible for all of its mistakes, errors, and failings.

INTRODUCTION

ALTHOUGH THE DEBATE CONCERNING DIFFERENT APPROACHES TO DE-velopment is as lively as ever among numerous competing schools of thought, students of Third-World affairs have at least been able to share some kind of consensus: Those on the Left and on the Right as well as those in the middle tend to agree that the rate of growth achieved by most less-developed countries (LDCs) after four decades of foreign assistance is less than satisfactory, if not disappointing. Indeed, as has been abundantly documented in the literature, today many LDCs that have received substantial amounts of aid from bilateral and multi-lateral donor institutions are not even now capable of designing and implementing development plans, programs, and projects. Many lack the ability to operate and maintain installations and institutions fol-lowing project termination, improve their people's standard of living, or to service their international debt.[1] It is high time to rethink the whole development assistance mechanism and set new directions for development efforts.

WHAT THIS STUDY IS ABOUT

This book assumes that the inability of Third-World polities to deal with the crises of legitimacy generated by an indigenous culture, de-cayed after centuries of contact with capitalistic culture through colo-nialism and world trade, is the root cause of development failure in non-Communist LDCs. It also proposes a strategy for dealing with the problem at its source. An attempt is made in the following sections to:

1. Analyze the crisis of legitimacy as the overwhelming constraint confronting Third-World polities.
2. Demonstrate that the inability to deal with this macro-level con-straint has negated development efforts deployed at the micro level.
3. Use country case studies to show how success or failure in over-coming this kind of high-level constraint makes the difference at lower levels.

4. Propose a strategy that may help establish viable polities and macro environments to support rather than hamper development efforts.
5. Recommend consequent changes for development assistance policy.

A READER'S GUIDE

Most non-Communist LDCs lack a viable polity capable of supporting development efforts; this failure is discussed in chapter 1. *Polity* is understood in the usual meaning as a political or governmental organization of a sovereign nation-state. The polity sets norms, rules, and regulations and issues orders that must be obeyed if the nation-state is to function effectively. When the exercise of these means of control is seen as legitimate by people who are subject to them, compliance will be more or less automatic, consensual, and voluntary. These means of control, which may or may not be gratifying to those subject to them, are accepted as morally justifiable because they conform to the values to which the citizens are committed. Control, in this case, is said to be internalized by the subjects, and the ability to induce such self-control is referred to as *authority*. The sources of *legitimacy* serving as the basis for authority can derive from the forces of tradition, from charismatic leadership, or from an institutionalized rational-legal system of government.

When the polity lacks legitimacy and thus authority, it must resort to other means of control to maintain discipline, such as manipulating rewards and sanctions, or coercion. These are referred to as externalized means, because subjects are not self-motivated to obey but do so only as a result of the pressure of outside forces. The ability to induce compliance through externalized means of control is here called *power*. It is assumed that for a polity to be viable, it must be able to use both authority and power to achieve a level of compliance that is high enough to allow itself and the nation-state under its control to survive and grow in the world environment.

The inability to enforce compliance by integrating internalized and externalized means of control is identified as the root cause of the nonviability of political regimes. Unlike most Western industrialized countries, Third-World polities suffer from inadequate legitimacy. It is difficult therefore for them to rely on self-compliance with laws and norms on the part of the governed. Communists LDCs have dealt with this phenomenon of delegitimation through the determined use of forced compliance. Benefiting from a ready model to follow as well as from the unfailing support of the whole Communist bloc, most, if not all, of them have been successful in establishing and maintaining viable polities.

Developing countries that opt for the non-Communist model in general have failed miserably in this attempt. Many remain the so-called "soft states," which possess little legitimacy to generate self-compliance or the power to enforce it. Others, perhaps lured by the Communist successes, have relied heavily on coercive power to make up for their lack of legitimacy. This reliance on forced compliance has usually been exploited by competing corrupt forces for the benefit of parochial, factional, and selfish interests at the expense of national interests. Such negative power use has been widespread in countries where the indigenous culture, often already decaying, has further deteriorated after centuries of contact with capitalistic culture through colonialism and world trade. Negative use of power further undermines the regime's legitimacy, necessitating resort to an ever-increasing injection of power beyond the rulers' capacities and the limits tolerated by world opinion. Political and social instability result in coups succeeding coups, in situations characterized by either lower or higher reliance on power.

Indeed, it is not uncommon for a reform-minded LDC political leadership to be confronted with an exceedingly difficult situation: a society controlled in practically all areas by negative power, led by spoiled and corrupt elites. With the deterioration of local values and institutions and the selective importation of negative rather than positive aspects of Western civilization, the behavior of Third-World people tends to be directed toward the pursuit of selfish interests at the expense of both traditional institutions and national interests. By declining to use power to force compliance, the leadership cannot hope to change anything. Softness denotes weakness, making the regime even more vulnerable to coups by opposing or competing groups. When determined to use power, the leadership has no choice but to rely on one negative force in dealing with others and thus can hardly expect to improve its regime's legitimacy. In either case, it finally falls into a vicious cycle. The difficulty is further complicated by the interference of international forces competing for influence within the LDC.

How these sociopolitical vicissitudes undermine development assistance efforts is analyzed in chapter 2. Foreign aid has been manipulated by LDC regimes as a means of prolonging their survival. It tends to strengthen the desire for creature comforts, and to strengthen the forces of corruption, which dissipates, distorts, and finally neutralizes most development assistance efforts. Attempts by the professional development community to bring about solutions to supposedly non-political, neutral technical and administrative problems have, in general, failed. The transfer of capital is usually matched by capital flight; the transfer of knowledge, by brain drain. Neither foreign advisers nor trained participants can help improve governmental performance in a bureaucratic environment where personal loyalties and confidences override technical and managerial competence.

Institution-building efforts have fared no better; they end up being submerged by the negative power that controls the environment. As long as the fundamental polity, which provides leadership for the whole system, is deficient, little can be done to build institutions at other levels. Attempts to create organizations isolated from the bureaucratic mainstreams to take care of development enterprises, such as independent project units, and autonomous agencies usually referred to in development parlance as "parastatals," have added more problems than they solve. Instead of serving as "islands of excellence" to lead the development movement, these entities have become burdens for the public sector and the whole society because of the subsidies they permanently require. In the same vein, large-scale cross-sectional reforms, decentralization, debureaucratization, and local empowerment can hardly escape being negated by individuals and factions vying for power and wealth within the government bureaucracy. It makes little sense in this situation for foreign aid to try to seek out isolated cases of success at the micro level except perhaps to rationalize the continuation of aid failures and to perpetuate the waste.

It is more meaningful to learn from successes and failures at the global level, a subject that is treated in chapter 3. Cases of Western aid to the anti-Communist regimes in Vietnam are analyzed in order to illustrate the successive historical failures there to build up viable polities that resulted in the eventual loss of this country to communism, rendering all the many incremental successes useless. The pro-French regimes are shown to have suffered from a serious shortage of both legitimacy and power. When the power supplement provided by the French failed, these regimes instantly crumbled. The Ngo Dinh Diem government fared much better on both counts in its earlier years, but it failed to keep up the momentum by a negative use of power in later years. The regime was finally smashed by a military coup when its legitimacy fell to its lowest mark and power could not be increased to compensate for the loss of legitimacy. The post-Diem regimes were low on both legitimacy and power, but they survived thanks mainly to U.S. power supplementation. As soon as the latter was withdrawn, they automatically disintegrated.

In contrast to pro-West Vietnam, Communist Vietnam has established and maintained a viable polity throughout its history by resolutely and consistently using whatever dosage of power was needed to close its legitimacy gap. By adopting the most ruthless methods of terrorism and coercion while covering them up with a sophisticated strategy of deception, the Communist regime managed somehow to improve its legitimacy by monopolizing the leadership of the war of resistance against the French colonial conquest and defeating the French expeditionary troops at the decisive battle of Dien Bien Phu. In these machinations, Communist Vietnam had the unfailing support of the entire Communist bloc.

Resorting to the same methods and strategy, but this time claiming national legitimacy in a war of resistance against "American imperialism," the Vietnamese Communists succeeded in conquering South Vietnam after two decades of war of attrition. With their occupation of pro-Chinese Kampuchea and their ongoing quarrel with China, their former ally and benefactor, and their continued resort to oppressive methods, the North Vietnamese have run into deep trouble since the late 1970s. Nevertheless, as long as the Soviet Union continues to provide them with the power supplements required, they will be able to survive by increasing power to fill the gaps caused by decreasing legitimacy.

In the non-Communist Third World, cases of viable polities remain scarce. South Korea is considered one. The Syng Man Rhee regime, like that of Diem in South Vietnam, started with a fair amount of legitimacy and managed to increase it during its first decade with liberal support from the United States. Its success in establishing an internationally recognized new and independent national government, implementing urgent social programs, repelling the armed invasion from Communist North Korea, and achieving the tasks of recovery after the war were pluses enhancing the regime's legitimacy.

Rhee's reliance on questionable means to consolidate and expand his personal power in later years, together with abuses and excesses committed by his followers, later substantially decreased his government's legitimacy. As he was aging, power escaped his hands, leading to his downfall following a students' revolt.

Issuing from an honest election, the succeeding Democratic administration possessed relatively high levels of legitimacy but low levels of power. Engaged since the beginning in an internal struggle for hegemony, the new government destroyed whatever legitimacy and power it had and was toppled by a military coup after only nine months of existence.

These regimes of the first and second republics of Korea illustrate the failure to cope with the crises of legitimacy common to most non-Communist LDCs. The Park Chung Hee era represents an unusually successful case in which power was used to increase legitimacy. Suffering from a serious shortage of legitimacy at the beginning of the regime, the leadership unsparingly used power to neutralize the negative forces and mobilize the positive forces in the service of national development. Park's authoritarian methods of government were sometimes controversial. In general, however, his leadership was enlightened, effective, and dedicated to the public good. It has helped to break the vicious cycle that had confronted previous regimes and to establish and maintain a relatively viable polity. Capable of using power to achieve an economic miracle that benefits all segments of the society, this polity has by the same token improved its legitimacy in the eyes of its people and the external world.

Given the exceedingly difficult situation facing the Korean leadership—a divided country threatened by an imminent invasion from North Korea with the support of the Communist bloc, a disintegrated culture in decay controlled by negative forces, and the interference of Western allies concerned for the respect of democratic values and human rights—the progress made under Park was no small achievement. Thanks to him, the Chun Doo Hwan regime of the Fifth Korean Republic has had an easier time maintaining what had been accomplished. Despite some turmoil and setbacks after Park's sudden death, South Korea has been moving toward further economic prosperity. Economic development helps increase legitimacy further, allowing for decreased reliance on raw power. It may be a long time before legitimacy prevails over unchecked power, but the foundation has been laid, and the country appears to be on a hopeful track.

Another non-Communist LDC that has succeeded in dealing satisfactorily with the issue of delegitimation is Singapore. The Singaporean People Action's party (PAP) under the leadership of Lee Kuan Yew is known as one of the very few nationalist parties in the Third World that has not been destroyed or absorbed by Communists while cooperating with them during the struggle for independence. Instead, PAP was able to subdue and neutralize the Communists and has become stronger and more effective on the political scene. Power has been liberally used to maintain discipline in a multiracial society torn by internal dissensions. A resolute attempt to achieve a meritocracy within the government as well as within the party has helped overcome the many adverse circumstances confronting the infant republic at its independence, and direct the use of power toward the realization of national rather than factional and selfish interests. Unprecedented economic progress and prosperity whose fruits have been shared by the whole people rather than a privileged minority have greatly enhanced the legitimacy of the polity, making it possible to decrease the use of sheer power. The downward cycle of legitimacy decrease and power increase was thus reversed to allow for a steady upward spiral in terms of legitimacy enhancement and power phasing out.

A strategy of development for non-Communist LDCs based on the analysis provided in previous chapters of issues of delegitimation and cases of success and failure in dealing with them is proposed in chapter 4. This strategy includes four mutually supportive components: cultural renewal, positive leadership, polity institution-building, and the resolution of basic constraints. Cultural renewal is needed to re-establish a moral basis for the LDC society in decay, where negative behavior tends to be rewarded and positive behavior penalized. Daily negative behavior should not be viewed as reflecting cultural values but rather as manifestations of their violation. Ways must be found to revive and renew local ideal values and induce people to live up to them instead of introducing foreign values or justifying negative local behavior in cultural terms. Given the culturally conditioned moral urge in people to live up to cultural ideals, the use of power to create an environment that encourages and compels the deployment of efforts to that effect will help the LDC subdue and neutralize internal negative forces. And assuming the existence of core values common to all human cultures and of democratic elements inherent in each culture, this way of exercising power will allow LDC regimes to cope with the pressures of international forces for respect of democratic values and human rights and to gain world acceptance. Internal and external legitimacy will rise as a result of this positive use of power, which in turn allows for less and less reliance on brute or negative power.

Cultural renewal is first and foremost the job of top political leadership. Cultural values should be exemplified by top leaders to provide supreme examples for others to follow. They should possess the moral and physical courage and integrity to deal with the corruptive and destructive forces that lure or challenge them and the intellectual capacity to develop and implement a strategy of cultural renewal. The strategy should aim at surrounding top leaders with other uncorruptible and dedicated leaders and extending the number of these leaders all down the line, ultimately giving upright forces control over the environment. This is the way to break the vicious cycle and lay a firm foundation for a government based on legitimacy and consensus.

Exemplary leadership behavior should be sustained by an institutional framework that supports that behavior and facilitates performance. With cultural renewal and upright and respectable leadership, conditions are now favorable for polity institution building through a happy integration of ancient and modern institutions. Given the predominance of capitalism and communism in today's world, the model advocated for LDC's that do not want to fall into the Soviet orbit is that of Western democracies.

This model is so familiar that it has become the norm for the non-Communist Third World. It is broad and flexible enough to be meaningfully adapted to the specific circumstances of each LDC. Assuming a convergence of the democratic spirit in all cultures, this model can lend itself to an integration with traditional institutions to form a meaningful whole that permits the LDC to articulate with the world environment. The basic conditions at the macro level that are required for the model to work are the symbiotic relationships between the party and government and between the public and private sectors, and a legal framework that defines these relationships as well as the function and operation of institutions in each system and sector.

The party should serve as an integrating mechanism that unifies the disparate elements in the nation-state and facilitates the effective exercise of government power. A national ideology should guide and inspire the party's programs and activities. The private sector should be liberalized and developed as a means of enhancing governmental legitimacy and facilitating the exercise of power. The public sector should support but not substitute for the private sector. In keeping itself lean but effective in providing a favorable environment for the private sector to develop, the public sector can in turn benefit from an expanded economic base provided by the private sector.

Capitalization on the country's comparative advantages and foreign capital investments can help the LDC speed up economic development through a more active participation in world trade. The free enterprise system does not prevent a country from realizing its social policies in a way congruent with its local culture. Moreover, economic prosperity will make it easier for the government to take care of the poor and the weak.

Given the pervading problem of noncompliance in Third-World countries that hampers development efforts, an effective legal framework is badly needed. Legal compliance can be improved by top leadership's law-abiding behavior, by improving the quality of the laws, by dropping arbitrary, unjust, and absurd rules so that laws are both enforceable and enforced.

Because development efforts have been exploited, distorted, and neutralized by corrupt forces and dictated by short-run political expediencies on the part of both recipient and donor countries and institutions, many LDCs are now overwhelmed by formidable constraints: heavy foreign debt; deterioration of constructions, equipment, and materials left over from foreign aid; a corrupt and ineffectual public sector constituting a burden for the whole society; a backward private sector; alienated rural masses devastated by misery and famine; land turned into a desert, deforestation, and soil erosion; and an urban population frustrated by unemployment and inflation. These accumulated problems constitute a vicious cycle defying all uncoordinated, incremental solutions. Their resolution requires a dramatic improvement in the polity's performance. The proposed strategy provides the framework for a comprehensive, long-term national policy to enhance that performance. Cultural renewal, charismatic leadership, and political institution building join forces to ensure societal compliance in overcoming these constraints. They create a favorable atmosphere for a consensus on the basic rules of the game to be developed and observed among participants in politics, so that politicization and professionalization can coexist harmoniously within the public sector work force and public and private sectors can complement and support each other in contributing effectively to the development of the country.

Once the downward trend has been reversed, the upward spiral may nourish itself to sustain the momentum. Domestic and international confidence may be restored, facilitating the mobilization of foreign and local capital and expertise for development purposes. The country may also be able to tap its reservoir of local capital and human resources abroad.

Consequent changes recommended for foreign aid policy are discussed in chapter 5. The vicious cycle entrapping many recipient Third-World countries has created real dilemmas for Western donor nations and institutions. No amount of military, economic, social, and humanitarian aid has been able to reverse the situation. The continuation of costly interventions has aroused increasing internal opposition and division within donor countries, while stopping it has resulted in disasters. A good number of LDCs have already joined the Communist side. Ambivalence about continuing or withdrawing aid has only made the problem worse by precipitating the vicious cycle. Ineffective aid feeds on itself by generating ever-increasing demands for aid. Given its dismal results, aid agencies, which have proliferated and expanded instead of putting themselves out of business, have become bureaucratized, emphasizing rules, procedures, conferences, and seminars for the sake of their own survival, regardless of results. Recipient LDCs have fallen into an ever-deepening cycle of dependency on advanced countries, incessantly requiring more and more grants and loans to avert bankruptcies. In the meantime, wave after wave of refugees from the Third World keep pouring into Western countries, with no end in sight.

All these overwhelming problems defy piecemeal technical solutions and require a common political answer: assistance in building up viable polities for the LDCs—polities capable of enforcing societal compliance in the service of national interests through an effective use of power to increase their legitimacy. In joining forces to help establish Third-World polities able to trade and compete with the West by adopting its own game, for example, Singapore and South Korea, Western countries will be working in their own long-term interests. This means that the neocolonialist policy of nurturing "liaison elites" or puppet regimes to serve core economic centers at the expense of the LDC masses should be abandoned. Support should be directed to non-Communist nationalist movements for independence led by uncorruptible and dedicated nationals capable of serving as an antidote to communism. Political legitimacy can be much improved by the popular confidence enjoyed by such leadership and its exercise of power on behalf of the public good.

These overall policy changes in turn require drastic changes in current aid policies. Much more emphasis should be given to the development of well-rounded political leadership cadres capable of relating many different kinds of knowledge to mobilizing resources in different areas and sectors for the achievement of national objectives. Experts and specialists trained by the West for economic development, without intelligent indigenous political leadership, are no match for hard-core revolutionaries trained and supported by Moscow.

In the same vein, development assistance institutions should develop the capacity to view development as a whole in synthesized, strategic terms to work with the generalist policymakers. This generalist capacity, which is rather weak due to the compartmentalization of knowledge, can be remedied by concentrating research efforts on macropolicy studies. The latter should aim at finding the best development alternatives available for each LDC and the strategic elements that may help cultivate symbiotic relationships between developed and developing countries. To that effect, such research areas as strategies of cultural renewal, country studies, studies of charismatic leadership, value systems, comparative advantage, the role of multinationals, the conditions for self-help, and legitimation are proposed.

Aid should concentrate its resources and efforts on helping develop a public sector confined to, and capable of, assuring law and order and providing a favorable environment for free enterprise to operate. Economic development should be left in the hands of local and foreign private sectors. A redefinition of missions and a reallocation of resources among aid agencies is needed to implement the new policies: increasing support to private investments and voluntary help in the Third World; creating politically neutral institutions to provide assistance in sensitive areas; scaling down the two economic giants—the World Bank and the International Monetary Fund—to devote more resources to institutions concerned with the noneconomic aspects of development; and strengthening the capacity of donor country institutions concerned with foreign affairs, defense, and external security.

The concluding chapter points out that the underlying causes of development failures are thus not those commonly advanced in the literature or current political debates, but rather the neglect, reluctance, or inability to deal with the issue of legitimacy and power in developing viable polities. This final chapter emphasizes the important role of political leadership and the professional development community in both the developed and developing worlds in contributing to the solution of the problem and expresses the hope that they will concentrate their efforts to that effect.

1

THE ROOT CAUSE OF
DEVELOPMENT FAILURE:
POLITICS

TO SHORTEN A LONG AND COMPLICATED STORY, THE FAILURE OF DEVELOP-
ment efforts is assumed to be due basically to the weaknesses of the
political systems of LDCs. Given the paramount importance of the
political system in providing leadership and direction for all other
systems—economic, social, and administrative—the political system's
inability to fulfill its role adversely affects the performance of all other
sectors.[1]

The cardinal error of donor institutions thus far is their reluctance or
inability to deal with this political dimension in their development
assistance policies. To be sure, a lot of informal talks have occurred
among development experts about the political situation in developing
countries and its impact on development programs and project work.[2]
Expert reports have sometimes made indirect references to politics,
but only in passing and without further elaboration.[3] There is also no
dearth of literature on the politics of the Third World or the overall
socioeconomic environment of LDCs.[4] Admonitions abound about the
need to take that macro environment into account, but little systematic attempt has been made to improve that environment or devise
strategies to fit development efforts into that overwhelmingly important macro picture.[5]

The reason for this omission is well known. Western development
institutions and staff conceive their role as professional, technical, and
as such, apolitical. They are not supposed to, and do not want to,
meddle in politics. This study argues that reluctance to deal with the
politics of development has contributed to the current critical situation in the Third World and the time is right for an open and candid
discussion between donor and recipient countries and institutions to
find a way out of the present dilemma. Given the danger of collapse of

the world order created by the current international debt incurred by LDCs, it is not only useful but necessary to stop considering politics as taboo and try to deal head-on with political constraints that have hampered development efforts to date.

Understanding the cause of low performance by LDC polities in general and how this weakness creates obstacles to development efforts is thus crucial for formulating strategies to deal with the problem.

THE POLITICS OF THE THIRD WORLD: CRISIS OF LEGITIMACY

Throughout human history, it appears that a country or polity can survive only if it succeeds in preserving its integrity against external aggression and in keeping its people under control or facilitating self-governance. The mechanism of control over the governed can be internalized or externalized. *Internalized control,* or self-governance, is self-induced through acculturation, customs, usages, mores, and traditions. *Externalized control* is imposed by other means, including legal actions, material incentives, manipulation, and coercion. If the degree of internal control is high in a polity, there is less need for external control. Where internal control is low, more external control is required to maintain stability and order. Wherever both internalized and externalized control are weak, instability and chaos result.

Western countries, in general, are characterized by a high degree of internalized control and a low degree of externalized control. The reverse can be found in Communist countries. All these polities—Western and Communist—enjoy stability and order, the prerequisites for steady progress. In most non-Communist developing countries, both internalized and externalized controls are low, making it excessively difficult for the polity to maintain stability and order as a condition for development.

Legitimacy, Authority, and Self-Compliance in the West

The higher degree of internalized control, or self control, on the part of people in Western countries results from a common consensus on the basic rules of the game. These are well-established polities in which norms for selecting political leadership, assimilated through a long process of socialization and institutionalization, tend to be taken for granted by participants. These norms, usually referred to as "rational-legal" in Weberian terminology, are based on democratic values of individual freedom and equality, which derive in part from a dominant Judeo-Christian heritage. Political leadership in Western countries, having been chosen and exercising their functions in accordance with these rational-legal procedures, can enjoy a high degree of *legitimacy*. Compliance with their directions in the form of law, decree, and executive order becomes more or less automatic through the internalized norm or self-control on the part of the subject people. In this way, legitimacy generates *authority*, which in turn generates *self-compliance*. And because self-compliance is high, the use of *power* to enforce the mechanism of external control becomes less necessary.[6] One factor that clearly distinguishes Western democracies from other polities is that their political leaders need not worry about being humiliated, executed, put in jail, or forced into exile after an overnight coup. Removal from office through constitutional due process or assassination are the major and constant risks to their political survival.

The Problem of Delegitimation in LDCs

There are, on the other hand, other polities where little consensus exists about the rules of the game. These are Third-World countries where neither traditional local norms nor imported Western democratic or Communist norms can provide a basis of legitimacy for political leadership. Traditional norms have been eroded, or have failed to grow and adapt, through centuries of contact with the overwhelmingly dominating Western civilization. Newly imported norms, introduced only at the formal conscious level and to educated, urban people, can hardly penetrate the informal, subconscious level to replace old norms. The combination of the old and the new systems results in normlessness or anomie for the whole society and a *crisis of legitimacy* for the polity.[7] The lack of legitimacy leads to the lack of authority on the part of the political leadership and the lack of self-compliance on the part of subject people. A high degree of power is needed to force compliance through the mechanism of externalized control in maintaining stability and order.

Power as a Substitute for Legitimacy in Communist LDCs

Less-developed countries that have opted for communism benefit from a ready model for this crisis of legitimacy, which consists in a full and determined use of externalized controls to make up for the lack of self-internalized control. And in its effort to fill the legitimacy gap with power, LDC leadership can always be sure of receiving unfailing support from the Communist bloc. The model has reached such a high degree of sophistication and perfection that no well-established Communist regimes have been overthrown so far. The resolute and effective use of *power* to enforce the mechanisms of externalized control has helped Communist countries keep their people under the regime's firm grip and maintain stability and order. Whether or not Communist regimes can increase internalized control in order to decrease externalized control is open to discussion. After six decades of experimentation, it appears that the use of externalized control in the Soviet Union has become more sophisticated than in new Communist regimes, but it is in no way less pronounced. Something in the system seems not to be congruent with human nature, making it impossible for people to comply without outside controls. The truth remains, however, that as long as enough externalized control is fed into the system to compensate for the lack of internalized control, the system remains secure and stable (except for possible threat of foreign invasion).[8]

Frustrating Trial and Error by Non-Communist LDCs

In dealing with the same political crisis of legitimacy, most non-Communist LDC polities have tried and failed miserably to achieve the stability essential for an acceptable level of development. The only non-Communist model available for them to follow is basically the Western democratic model, which needs to be adapted to local conditions. Given all the pressures—direct and indirect—coming from the free-world environment, which is overwhelmingly dominated by Western norms and values, adapting some form of this democratic model is a necessary condition for the survival of a non-Communist LDC polity. Unfortunately, this model, as previously indicated, assumes a consensus on the rules of the game and a high level of internalized control that does not exist in LDCs. In the absence of this basic condition, the sincere application of the model by true believers in LDCs has led to coups after coups. Other leaderships, while preserving some appearances of democracy, have resorted more or less to different means of externalized control along the Communist or Fascist lines to make up for the lack of self-compliance. This has helped some regimes last longer than others, but overall, none has reached the degree of stability enjoyed by Western or Communist countries. Indeed, most if not all have failed to restore and maintain an appropriate balance between legitimacy (internalized control) and power (externalized control); a majority remain very unstable with a low level of both legitimacy and power.

The difficulty of achieving this balance can be more easily explored if one bears in mind that ruling an LDC is like riding a tiger. If the rider cannot control the tiger, he or she will be eaten by it. The rider is surrounded by Communist tiger riders who are expert in the art of achieving control through coercion and highly disciplined in combining their forces under one "big boss" to keep all their tigers under tight control. They also attempt by every means to help the LDC tiger revolt against the non-Communist rider and replace him or her by one of their own.

On the other hand, Western riders want to help the LDC rider remain or become one of their junior partners. Since Western riders are used to riding horses and not tigers, they expect and assist the LDC rider to apply horse-riding rules. By adopting such precepts, the LDC leader can barely control, much less tame the tiger, and is in constant danger of falling off and being eaten. This danger is all the greater since each non-Communist rider, concerned for his or her own interest, seeks to back his or her friendly party against any leader who sides too closely with other rival non-Communist riders. If the non-Communist rider copies Communist tiger riders' techniques—administering electric shocks; removing finger nails, teeth, eyeflaps—he or she will draw criticism from the Western world and run the risk of seeing its help withdrawn or reduced as persuasion to terminate such measures.

Moreover, to adopt Communist riders' techniques without the conditions necessary for their effective application is to isolate oneself from both the Communist and the non-Communist world. These necessary conditions are not easy to create. Requirements mandate subjection to the rules and discipline of Communist powers in order to obtain their help and protection, a theory to justify the means adopted, and an elaborate apparatus to implement them. Indiscriminate application of these measures tends to become so clumsy and inadequate that it ends up doing more harm than good to the rider. On the one hand, it destroys whatever minimum respect and affection with which the tiger regards the rider (legitimacy). On the other hand, it does not inspire enough fear and awe on the part of the tiger (power) to make it comply with the rider's will, but it makes the tiger more determined to destroy the rider. To make matters worse for the rider, the tiger's effort to overthrow him or her is usually supported by Communist riders ready to capitalize on chaos and anarchy and also by Western riders who compete with each other in defending human rights as well as their own interests. This Catch-22 situation confronting non-Communist LDC polities is shown in figure 1.

NEGATIVE POLITICIZATION OF THE BUREAUCRACY

In such a precarious political environment, survival becomes the overriding and daily preoccupation of LDC leadership. Every conceiv-

Legitimacy: Capacity to induce self-control among the subject people.
Power: Capacity to induce control among the subject people through external means.

Polity Viability Index

9.5–10 : Extremely viable polity
9.0–9.5 : Very viable polity
8.5–9.0 : Moderately viable polity
8.0–8.5 : Somewhat viable polity
7.0–8.0 : Somewhat nonviable polity
6.0–7.0 : Moderately nonviable polity
5.0–6.0 : Very nonviable polity
0.0–5.0 : Extremely nonviable polity

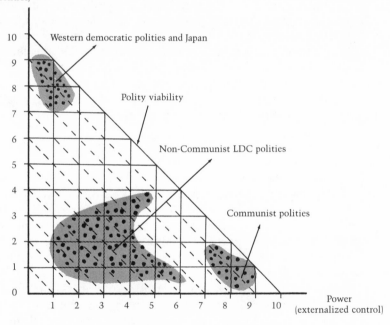

Figure 1. Polity Viability Chart

Note: Any index number given above can be any combination of "legitimacy" and "power," for example, 9 may result from 8 (legitimacy) + 1 (power) or 7 + 2, 6 + 3, 5 + 4, and so on. Of course, index 10 and index 0 can hardly be found in real life situations. These indexes, which are assigned impressionistically by the author, can conceivably lend themselves to quantification.

able means must be used to achieve this first and foremost goal.[9] The main and ready instrument for this purpose everywhere is the bureaucracy, civilian and military. The bureaucracy, especially the military and paramilitary sector, is, however, a dangerous tool to operate. If not expertly and carefully used, it can become a threat to leadership. A need exists therefore for key bureaucratic positions to be distributed on the basis of personal loyalty and confidence rather than technical or managerial competence. These position holders in turn have to use the same criteria for appointing people at the next lower level and so on down the line. Political survival often dictates that a potentially dangerous general be rendered harmless in a diplomatic post overseas or as head of a public enterprise. In the same vein, the leader of a rival faction can be given a newly created portfolio with resounding prestige but no real power. The leader and his or her followers can enjoy all the "perks" deriving from their positions in the new agency as long as they abstain from causing trouble to the regime. To make sure that no individuals or groups can become a threat to the leadership, they should be played off one against the other, with real power assigned only informally according to personality, and not by formal position. In effect, the polity is managed for survival of the leadership rather than for equitable development of the polity.

Corruption as a Means of Leadership

The need to preserve at least some appearance of democracy is also costly. Threats have to be combined with material incentives in order, for example, to influence candidates and voters or change election results. Since the amount of money needed to play these various games cannot be derived from the official budget, some other source of funding is required for the leadership. This further adds to bureaucratic corruption, often in the name of the government party. Lucrative positions are therefore reserved for faction members or regime supporters who are willing to participate in the game. Holders of these positions in turn have to surround themselves with those willing to do the same. Bureaucrats refusing to take part in this informal network are relegated to positions without power.

Negative Political and Administrative Consequences

Despite all efforts to use the bureaucracy as a means of maintaining and strengthening political stability, the regime sooner or later falls and is replaced. The regime that takes over, facing the same situation, must resort to some variations of the same scheme, and ultimately it will see itself overthrown. And so the vicious cycle continues, making the bureaucracy an arena where political factions and groups take turns in controlling power and wealth.[10]

The long list of bureaucratic pathologies that are basically similar in LDCs and well documented by students of the Third World are a consequence of this politicization: self-serving, authoritarian, over-staffed, corrupt, inert, ineffectual, top heavy and bottom thin, lacking qualified managers and professionals, irrational salary schemes and incentive systems, excessively centralized, hamstrung by inefficient rules and procedures, accustomed to selective rule enforcement, process rather than results oriented, and so forth.[11]

All of these problems can be traced directly or indirectly to the recruitment and allocation of public servants along personality, family, ethnic, religious, regional, and factional lines. These factors constitute the power base of the political leadership and prevail over technical and administrative competence for the job.

THE UNBREAKABLE VICIOUS CYCLE: CULTURAL DECAY

The cause of this vicious cycle has been discussed: non-Communist LDC leaderships have been unable to use power (externalized control) to elicit enough external and internal support to establish a viable polity. Why has it been so difficult or even impossible for them to do so? The answer is found in the decay of LDC cultures resulting from several centuries of contact with the Western world through colonialism and mercantilist trade. Capitalism as a way of life, with its values of material comfort, free enterprise, political democracy, individual freedom, and equality has flourished since the Industrial Revolution and dominated much of the world. Wherever it goes—and there are few places in the Third World that it can not and has not penetrated—it has destroyed, changed, and eroded many LDCs' ways of life.[12] It has no difficulty introducing its material assets—car, television, refrigerator, air conditioner; these are valued and desired everywhere! Freedom, equality, and democracy are also enthusiastically welcomed everywhere.

Perverted Adoption of Western Values

What capitalism has failed to bring to the Third World is its spirit, in other words, its moral foundation derived from Judeo-Christian and constitutional heritages. Lacking these spiritual and civic bases, capitalistic behavior adopted by LDC countries has produced over-whelmingly negative results.[13] In the United States, for example, material comfort is accepted by the middle-class culture as a spiritual or social reward for those who practice the values of hard work, thrift, and civic responsibility. Material possessions are a way of showing quality and worth, and giving away or sharing material possessions is a way of living up to this cultural ideal. Imported to LDCs, materialism itself has become a virtue, glorifying the acquisition of material assets by whatever means and their egotistical use.

Many westernized people, long subject to rigid social conformity, are also quick to adopt the value of equality. But here again, the import has lost its ideal feature and tends to become a desire for equality in rights and privileges, but not in responsibility. *Everyone wants to be boss; nobody wants to take orders.*

Foreign pressure to accept the value of human freedom meets little resistance, especially from victimized elements in LDCs. Fed up with poor relatives and friends who continually ask for help, money, and favors of all kinds, people trained in the Western tradition are also quick to become individualistic. Their self-imposed isolation does not, however, go along with a readiness to cooperate with others in serving communal or national causes; it results merely in egotistic individualism.

This one-dimensional internalization of capitalistic values, borrowing the mere forms but not the substance and ideal features does not appear to lead to more socioeconomic development. Rather it appears to foster greater corruption, anarchy, inertia, and selfishness.

Deterioration of Local Values

At the same time, traditional cultures that served as the moral base for LDCs have deteriorated. Social hierarchy and mutual dependence and solidarity within the framework of the extended family, clan, village, tribe, kingdom or sheikdom, empire, inculcate values that help institutions survive, grow, and prosper. These assume reciprocal relationships in terms of rights and duties among institutional members, between king and subjects, elders and juniors, patrons and clients. Everyone according to his or her position is expected to contribute to the welfare of the institutions of which he or she is a part. The higher the position in the hierarchy, the higher the privileges, but also the greater the responsibility. Whenever superiors emphasize the former at the expense of the latter, subordinates follow suit. If superordinates seek their own interest by abusing and oppressing instead of helping and protecting their followers, the latter withdraw their loyalty and support and turn to cheating, deception, or rebellion. The ideal relationship based on mutual trust and support to serve the institutional cause (the well being of all institution members) is destroyed. However, mutual dependence remains rather strong among those members who can get along with one another to divide the spoils at the expense of the majority. Since this kind of coalition is based on selfish interests rather than service of a common higher cause, it tends to last only as long as there are interests to share and agreement on how to share them.[14]

Since this coalition cannot rest ultimately on mutual trust and confidence but has to rely mainly on games played among its members, it tends to be momentary and constantly responds to changes in the political environment. Coalitions of this sort prevail in most Third-World countries. They are created, disbanded, reformed, recreated among the informal networks provided by traditional institutions—clan, tribe, village, region, religious sect. By taking advantage of these informal relationships to further individual selfish interests, these coalitions have corrupted and destroyed modern as well as traditional institutions, including the highest national institution, the polity.[15]

Triumph of Negative Forces

In short, LDC leadership is confronted with a society losing its moral foundation; a society without agreement on values and norms, without viable institutions; a society where the negative aspects of both the homegrown and imported cultures concur to direct people's behavior. Such a society rewards negative behavior—lying and cheating—and penalizes positive behavior—honesty, service, dedication, and loyalty. In such an environment, the combined forces of evil triumph, making survival very hard for those who attempt to live up to the ideal of the culture.[16]

It has been all the more difficult for LDC leaders to deal with this environment because they themselves are its products. Most LDC leaders come from the middle class, which has been most exposed to the Western way of life through education, travel, contacts with westerners and Western commodities. They are, in other words, the people most heavily influenced by the free world. This westernized middle class, in which Western donor countries and institutions put so much faith, is in no way the counterpart of the Western bourgeosie that led the Industrial Revolution.

Instead, it is a class created and supported by the spread of capitalism in the Third World. Unlike the Western bourgeoisie that fought hard to bring about the Industrial Revolution, this westernized middle class is made up of the offspring of kings, mandarins, conquistadors, caudillos, bureaucrats, compradors, local importers and exporters, and multinational firms' employees who have become wealthy and powerful in supporting the spread of capitalism. Serving as puppets at the lower level, they were trained to take orders from their foreign masters and to receive bribes from their countrymen to fullfil their own interests. Making a good life the easy way, they tend to emphasize "perks" but not responsibility. Their accumulated wealth and power in turn have helped their offspring produce more wealth and power the easy way. In the meantime, members of the traditional elite who, to preserve their integrity, refused to collaborate with foreigners were oppressed, persecuted, and reduced to poverty. Lacking wealth and power, their offspring have been absorbed into the poor and weak masses.[17]

The problem is further complicated by the presence in many LDCs of an economic elite made up of the so-called "pariah" foreign entrepreneurs—Chinese, Indian, Lebanese. They usually serve as agents, subcontractors, or suppliers for foreign firms and are supported by cohesive and informal networks. In turn, they control a major part of the local trade and excel in using bribes, kickbacks, market distortions, and the black market. This "economic elite" has generally succeeded in staying strong and stable by using corruption to get along with successive leaderships.[18]

Destruction of the Polity by Negative Forces

As products of a declining environment, LDC leaders themselves are apt to be corrupted and destroyed by the same environment. All the means of externalized control that they employ to make up for the lack of internalized control tend to be distorted and used to the advantage of individual, selfish interests. These means include coercive measures against those who oppose the regime—physical torture, jail, starvation, even assassination; economic measures to buy off opponents— high but powerless position in the government, sinecures in the civil service, financial subsidies as a means of buying votes, import licenses; and other types of manipulation to neutralize the opposition— black mail, character assassination, sowing discord among supporters of the opposition. Such measures can hardly be justified, even by arguing that the end justifies the means, because these tend to serve the interest of only the coalition in power, and not the nation.

Indeed, power wielders in LDCs have to rely on intimate confidants to exercise control. Those willing to serve in this way can, of course, be found mostly among the ranks of supporters motivated by the desire to acquire power, position, and wealth by whatever shortcuts available.

Moreover, leaders and followers involved in this game have to think of the day power escapes their hands when they fall off the tiger's back. Experience tells them that wealth and the most dynamic version of wealth, the U.S. dollar, can help assure their futures. Thus, the more dollars one has, the more likely one is to avoid jail or escape to enjoy life in Western countries, perhaps continuing the struggle overseas and even regaining power at home. Therefore, one must accumulate as much wealth as possible and in the shortest possible time both to exercise power and guarantee one's future. But where does wealth come from if not from the exercise of power itself, from those means of externalized control mentioned earlier? Indeed, such use of power to accumulate riches has become so obvious in some parts of the Third World that the phenomenon is described as "privatization of the state."

What makes these matters worse is that the processes hardly escape the scrutinizing eyes of the public. In a society ridden with intra- and intergroup conflicts, it is difficult, if not impossible, to keep all questionable schemes secret. Communication inside the country and with the outside world cannot be cut off completely. There are always enough local opposition leaders and foreigners—press correspondents, diplomats, aid experts, donor agency staff, human rights organization officials—to expose and denounce. The scheme that can hardly be justified by any end of public interest tends to decrease the legitimacy (and the degree of consensus and self-discipline) of the regime all the more.

This ever-increasing injection of negative power, which is impossible to tolerate indefinitely, given all the internal and external constraints, makes it possible for the regime to be overthrown. Another coalition takes over, has to play the same game, and then eventually falls. So continues the vicious cycle.[19]

The issue is further complicated by the overt or covert interference of foreign powers—the USSR, China, the United States of America, Great Britain, France, Germany, Japan—each competing with the others to install the coalition that is the most congenial to its interests and to discredit and destroy the one that works against it.[20]

2
NEGATIVE IMPACT OF THE CRISIS OF LEGITIMACY ON INTERNATIONAL DEVELOPMENT ASSISTANCE

INTERNATIONAL TRANSFER OF RESOURCES, IN TERMS OF GRANTS AND loans for developing LDCs, has reached massive levels since World War II. If one takes into account international and national public and private organizations responsible for this transfer, the cost of the development effort becomes much higher. Results, however, have been mainly unsatisfactory, if not disappointing. While a handful of shining successes were registered, growth appears to have stagnated in the majority of aid-recipient LDCs. The least development progress was sometimes recorded in those countries receiving the most support in proportion to their national income, whereas substantial improvements were found in countries receiving hardly any assistance at all. As far as Africa is concerned, per capita income is expected to decline in the next ten years according to the most optimistic recent projections. At the same time, the gap between developed countries and LDCs has been widening. Worse yet, development assistance has mostly helped not the LDC poor, but rich and selected elites. And the debt incurred by the Third World has reached an alarming total capable of creating dangerous periodic worldwide financial and economic crises.[1]

Where U.S. aid has dominated, the failure is even more obvious. The losses of China, Cuba, Vietnam, and Ethiopia to communism and of Iran to an inimical regime speak for themselves. Some U.S. aided LDCs, for instance El Salvador, are desperately struggling against overt armed insurgencies supported from the outside. Most, if not all, non-Communist LDCs are either extremely, very, moderately, or somewhat politically and socially unstable. Many appear to have a slower rate of economic growth than Communist LDCs.[2]

LDCS AS BOTTOMLESS PITS FOR FOREIGN AID

Foreign Aid As Contributing to Regime's Short-Term Survival

The incapacity of LDCs to deal with their crises of legitimacy appears to be the basic cause of this failure at the macro level, which in turn generates direct or indirect failures at the micro level. Because they are struggling to survive, most LDC power wielders have to use all forms of aid overtly or covertly to assure their survival. Military and economic assistance in any form—material, technical, or financial—can be employed as a means of externalized control—coercion, manipulation, corruption.

Foreign Aid and the Revolution in Rising Expectations

These means subsequently strengthen the already strong desire for creature comfort and conspicuous consumption exerted on recipient countries' population, which in turn increases the likelihood of diversions of outside assistance to individual and factional interests at the expense of the national interest. No extensive research is needed to confirm this widespread phenomenon, which has been referred to as "revolution in rising expectations." In this vicious cycle, methods of control initiated by donor and recipient organizations on the technical level tend to increase the cost of development all the more, but they can hardly eliminate or even reduce the evils, for reasons previously explained.[3]

The Return of Aid to Donors

In the final analysis, where does this huge amount of international aid for development go? To be sure, part of it has been used to construct highways, power plants, dams, and administrative buildings, many of which have deteriorated with time, due to poor operation and maintenance.[4] A major part of the funding appears to have somehow entered the private sector through the pockets of successive LDC power wielders and their followers. A greater proportion has been returned to donor countries and institutions in many forms: deposits in Western banks; investment in Western corporations; properties in Western countries belonging to LDC political and business leaders;[5] salary and benefits to Western bureaucrats and experts working overseas or at headquarters in the West;[6] and the well known brain drain.[7] How much of the total funding actually goes to the masses in poor LDCs cannot be known for sure but to some extent of course can be estimated. The free world institutional basis for international development seems to have reached a rather dangerous equilibrium where the vested interests of the powerful—politicians, bureaucrats, contractors, professional experts and technicians—tend to converge at the expense of the neglected weak and underprivileged masses of the Third World and taxpayers in donor countries.[8]

All the impressive efforts to correct past mistakes in development programs and projects, the many changes in focus and approach made thus far, seem to have missed the mark because of their narrow professional and technical orientations. None of them has been able to reverse the downward trend. All of them have been swept aside and destroyed by the encompassing vicious cycle. In other words, all these technical and administrative questions that exist at the micro level require political answers at the macro level. Technical solutions alone will not suffice as long as the basic political answer to the vicious cycle created by the crisis of legitimacy and the demonstration effect is lacking.

FAILURE OF THE PROFESSIONAL APPROACHES

The following brief review of development efforts will demonstrate the impact of this vicious cycle on the solution of technical and administrative issues. China under Chiang Kai Chek, South Vietnam, and Iran received large amounts of military and economic aid from Western countries, especially the United States. Because of the failure to break the vicious cycle at the macropolitical level, all technical solutions attempted at the micro level, no matter how well intended and technically sound, were inadequate to prevent the total system from collapsing. Moreover, the political leadership could not be restrained from manipulating foreign aid to expand its control over the polity.

Since these control measures could easily be taken advantage of by dominating negative forces produced by a culture in decay and the population's overwhelming desire for material comfort, what was done at the leadership level directly or indirectly contributed to oppression, corruption, and the failure of the entire system. Indeed, even the most respected institutions and agents in Western countries have been accused of having supported oppressive and corrupted regimes despite all their good will and sincerity in providing help for development in technical fields.[9]

How the forces in the LDC environment have prevailed to distort and destroy any technical solution provided by the aid expert community since World War II is discussed below.

The Transfer of Capital

The capital-based approach assumes that LDCs remain poor because they are too poor to afford enough capital for development investment. Following the Marshall Plan model, capital was transferred to LDCs in the form of grants and loans. This was found not to work well because, according to "expert" opinion, LDCs did not have the technical know-how to make use of the capital.[10] This is true, of course, but only partially so. If one takes into account the amount of foreign exchange deposited in Western banks and invested in Western countries by wealthy citizens of LDCs, as well as their properties overseas, the assumption of capital shortage due to poverty becomes questionable. Indeed, according to the principle of self-help, LDCs ought to make use of this capital before relying on foreign grants and loans. Moreover, the success with which this capital has been transferred and invested overseas presupposes a good deal of technical know-how on the part of LDC political and economic elites. Had these elites used this knowledge for the public good, development could have occurred much more rapidly.[11]

The Transfer of Knowledge

The knowledge-based approach, which started with President Truman's fourth point in his inaugural address in 1949, advocated transferring know-how to LDCs because development requires modern technology and the professionalization of the work force. This transfer of knowledge and skills takes many forms and has reached a rather high degree of sophistication: from adviser to counterparts, through participant training and interchange programs, and through the creation of technical/professional schools. Experts have concluded, however, that this approach met with several obstacles: The successful application of Western know-how and skills requires the existence of complementary and supporting knowledge and systems that do not exist in the LDC environment; moreover, Western techniques and processes are culture bound and cannot be applied successfully without changes in attitudes, values, and behavior of LDC people.[12]

This belief prompted the expert community to provide the famous slogans "adapt but not adopt" and "appropriate technology." While these principles are too broad, general, and obvious to lend themselves to any useful application, and can be interpreted in so many different ways that they cover almost any situation, it is to be noted that some countries, for example, Japan, have successfully adopted the most modern and sophisticated technology without concurrently adopting all related Western values, attitudes, and behaviors. Interestingly enough, there is now rather a reverse movement in the West for the importation of Japanese managerial and behavioral techniques.

Other countries do not seem to follow any technological stages of development in their successful modernization programs. China managed to produce atom and hydrogen bombs and intercontinental ballistic missiles early in the game; South Korea boldly and successfully embarked on the development of heavy industry very shortly after starting her industrialization program.[13] This is to say that the lack of complementary technical systems and modern Western values and behavior identified by professional experts is only the symptom, but not the real cause of failure and solutions provided to cure the symptom will not solve the problem.

Negative and non-Western behavioral tendencies spotted by Western observers often do *not* reflect the *ideal* of the recipient country's culture, but rather the negative side during the period of decay resulting from contact with the dominating culture of capitalism, as described earlier. It is the presence of this negative side that hampers application of modern technology; the solution lies in reviving the positive side of the local culture rather than in the wholesale introduction of Western culture. In fact, direct adoption of Western culture is impossible given the subconscious nature of cultural values, as asserted by most cultural anthropologists. Where positive values prevail, there can be enough motivation to think through technical requirements before introducing a new technology and to make the necessary changes in the complementary support systems. In the final analysis, the cause of failure should be traced back to the incapability of LDC leadership to make positive use of its means of control to serve the positive ends of the culture.[14]

Other problems related to transferring knowledge can be traced to this same deep but hidden cause. For example, the relationship between adviser and counterpart has proved most frustrating. In a bureaucratic environment that emphasizes personal loyalty and confidence at the expense of technical and administrative competence, how can skills be successfully transferred between foreign and local professionals? It is not easy for an expert to find a counterpart capable of learning his or her skills. If luckily an expert manages to find someone with the proper qualifications—usually not without using the necessary leverage—the counterpart, being competent, honest, and neutral in a politicized civil service, may not have enough time to learn due to the many moonlighting jobs that help him or her survive on a meager bureaucratic salary. If the counterpart can devote full time to the job, he or she may not be able to make use of what is learned due to a lack of support from superiors, peers, and subordinates or because he or she is hamstrung by the rigidity of civil service rules and regulations.

Thus it is not unusual for an adviser, thanks to his or her prestige and power, to devote a large amount of time and effort to overcoming these obstacles. An adviser may have to do a greater part of the technical job him- or herself to avoid seeing the project drag on forever and being penalized by a superior, thereby sacrificing the role of teacher. Until the adviser leaves, adviser and counterpart may manage to accomplish something; however, once the adviser leaves, whatever has been accomplished will deteriorate over time. The powerless counterpart may, in fact, be transferred to another job that has nothing to do with what he or she has learned from the adviser.

Once in a while, an adviser is lucky enough to find the ideal counterpart, one professionally qualified and politically active, who will succeed in moving the project ahead effectively. After some time, when the project is in full swing, the counterpart may be replaced for some unknown political reason or put in jail as a consequence of a change in the political regime.

It is well known in the development community that the best adviser is someone who "works him- or herself out of a job," that is, imparts skills to a counterpart so that the adviser is no longer needed and this, the sooner the better. Given bureaucratic realities, this criterion is at the very least unfair to advisers. In their search for solutions to these frustrating dilemmas some experts have quit the profession altogether after one or two overseas experiences, abandoned the job midway, not renewed the contract, become more cautious and selective in accepting other overseas assignments, or taken advantage of the situation, that is, accepted and continued in any job whatsoever.[15]

Participant Training

Disenchantment with the adviser system appears to lead to participant training. The technical rationale for this approach is that participant trainees, unlike expatriates, serve their own country, know the local situation better, and cost less. Participant trainees, however, cannot escape the impact of political vicissitudes engulfing the LDC regime in the absence of legitimacy and power.

A number of trainees remain overseas after taking their degrees in Western universities; others return, but not to the jobs for which they are trained. Still others find themselves unable to perform, either because the bureaucratic environment offers no support or because their long stay in a foreign culture has left them unable to adjust and cope with the local environment. The latter returnees prefer to work for Western firms or international organizations where the pay is forty or fifty times higher than the civil service rate or to remain in the West with its greater material comforts, individual freedom, and equal opportunity.

Those who return home because their immediate families are not able to join them overseas still prefer to work for autonomous agencies that offer considerably better pay than the civil service. If the agency that sponsored the trainees' overseas training require them to rejoin that staff, the trainees may have to yield. They then seek another position in an autonomous agency, affording them two full-time salaries. Another option involves holding simultaneously several appointments to different development projects. The obvious result is that none of these jobs is performed effectively. Only the job holder benefits, and his or her gain is at the expense of all organizations concerned.

Measures taken by LDC governments and donor agencies to deal with these issues tend to create more problems than they can solve. On the one hand, LDC governments often blame Western countries for harboring foreign participants or at least for not being vigilant enough in forcing them to return home. On the other hand, Western governments find it impossible to comply fully without violating human rights. The LDC rules forbidding spouse and children to accompany a participant add further complications, as do similar USAID rules, to enforcing travel laws and regulations in both participant-sending and participant-receiving countries.

Pledges to return and reimburse all training costs in event of violating commitment add more red tape but prove unenforceable due to the lack of an organized information system in the civil service, different ways of enforcing regulations, and political interference. Preferential treatment—higher pay, perks reserved for returnees—creates resentment on the part of the majority of civil servants but in the absence of appropriate working conditions fails to motivate returnees to perform at their best. Raising the pay of civil servants proves impossible in light of available financial resources and the sheer number of civil servants. There is also a great risk that such pay increases will create inflation.

Increasing pay scales without undertaking concurrent reforms in the problem-ridden bureaucracy can hardly lead to significant changes in performance. In the final analysis, increasingly elaborate control measures tend to add more work to an bureaucracy already overextended and inept, making their enforcement even more difficult. As a result, the bureaucracy is unable to prevent clever participants from circumventing rules that finally can only make life more miserable for honest people.[16]

Institution Building

These difficulties in human resources development are interpreted by the expert community as resulting from the absence of a complementary element, the institution. Arguing that individuals cannot do anything alone, but only in the framework of organizations or institutions, experts postulate the needs of developing organizations capable of using human and other resources—financial and material—to fulfill development purposes. Hence, the emphasis on institution building and the emergence of the role of the foreign expert or specialist in manpower and institutional analysis. While *institution* can be defined in many ways depending on one's descipline, viewpoint, and purpose, the definition of this concept in Third-World development has concentrated mainly on creating and/or strengthening formal bureaucratic public or parapublic organizations. Attempts to build institutions do not appear to fare better than those made under the know-how approach. Confining themselves to technical and professional areas, these efforts made at the micro level hardly fit into the macro bureaucratic environment and end up being submerged by the overwhelming abuse of power, loss of legitimacy, and repetition of the vicious cycle previously described.[17]

The Project Unit

Thus, development assistance provided to a bureaucratic agency, whether a division or department within a ministry or a ministry, often leads to creating a project unit isolated from the bureaucratic mainstream so that it can overcome the rigidity of the regular civil service and the budgetary rules applicable to the whole bureaucracy. Placing the project units under the foreign-aid-funded development budget with more flexible rules permitting higher pay and per diem and mandating less complicated and burdensome controls has normally been the solution.

This solution alleviates some problems concerning the internal structure of the unit in charge of development. But it cannot deal with problems related to cooperation needed from other regular (non-development) organizations if development objectives are to be fulfilled. At the same time, the development budget creates a host of new and complex problems for the whole bureaucracy. Any development unit at least needs the support of other agencies to import equipment and materials; repair and maintain them; provide logistical support to its foreign advisers in terms of travel, passport, visas, and housing; and approve their purchasing contracts. As long as this support is cumbersome and slow in coming, project implementation necessarily suffers from interruptions, delays, cost overruns, or outright failure. This dependency of development units for support services is, of course, in addition to the interdependence of many development programs for achieving and sustaining development objectives.

To overcome these obstacles, an alert and experienced foreign adviser must often serve as broker between the development unit and these nondevelopment agencies. At the same time, the local project leader must usually resort to the widespread bureaucratic game of sharing spoils through the mutual exchange of favors. General civil service behavior thus invades and pervades the project unit.

The flexibility provided by the development budget must be compromised, at least partially, to implement this bureaucratic tradeoff. Lucrative project positions must be shared with other factions in the bureaucracy. More liberal personnel rules must be created: base salary double and triple that in force in the civil service and special allowances of all kinds. It is indeed not unusual for allowances to be higher than the base salary itself and for civil servants to earn special allowances simultaneously from several projects while holding down their main civil service jobs. After all, even with these raises, the total pay cannot compare favorably with private sector salaries, especially foreign private sector salaries, and indeed is next to nothing when compared with the compensation of foreign experts and public employees in Western countries.

Project units, of course, enjoy some autonomy. Their needs vary and therefore so do their pay systems. Many factors combine to affect needs and salary/allowance policies: the nature of the project, the project leader and his or her supervisor, the policies of the sponsoring donor institution (AID, World Bank, UNDP, Ford Foundation). Uniformity and standardization are avoided because this is precisely what makes the civil service and operational budgetary rule so rigid that they hamper successful project implementation.

The proliferation of different pay systems leads to gross absurdities and inequities in the total government system, adding more red tape to the development process and defying all efforts of control on the part of local government and donor-auditing agencies. The lack of control leads to more abuses, waste, and corruption and in turn requires some rationalization to achieve a minimum of order and thus uniformity and standardization for the sake of control. Uniformization requires leveling all divergent pay systems, which for equity and financial reasons cannot differ much from the civil service's general scale. This return to equal misery hampers development and requires exemptions and exceptions that must be submitted to more complicated and rigid clearances. And so the cycle continues. The project unit is thus an inherently unsustainable ad hoc solution for serious long-term systemic malfunctions in the development process. For this reason, its use often creates more problems than it solves by deferring effective treatment of these basic malfunctions.[18]

Large-Scale Cross-Sectoral Reforms

The failure of institution building attempts with regular civil service units has been attributed by the expert development community to the piecemeal, incremental approach used. It is rather naïve, the argument goes, to expect small, isolated bureaucratic units to work against, and succeed in, a degenerating bureaucratic environment. Something should be done at a higher level and on a larger scale. So position classification, performance-budgeting, planning-programing-budgeting systems, and Organization and Method have been introduced to many LDC bureaucracies through projects aimed at establishing and/or strengthening central personnel, budgeting, and planning agencies.

Most if not all of these projects have failed. Many were rejected at the outset by local authorities or were discontinued in midcourse. Determined efforts to introduce new systems have led to their existence on paper at the formal level while informal practices continued as before. Other newly established systems worked as long as foreign aid continued to pour in its support but died when foreign aid was terminated. While many reasons can be found for these failures at the technical level, it is clear enough that transferred management tools, techniques, and processes whose successful application requires the existence of a rational-legal service and a professionalized bureaucratic work force could not fit into a bureaucratic environment overwhelmed by the negative forces of factional politics.

Indeed, the application of rational management techniques that rely merely on the job to be done and the qualifications required to do it would leave no room in a bureaucracy for powerful individuals having more political than technical or administrative competence or for a large number of others who consider their sinecures a matter of vested interest protected by the laws and regulations of a life-time civil service system. Where should they go without creating social and political disturbances? The political leadership would be cut off from its main means of manipulation, control, and survival and from its ability to service a significant element of its constituency.[19]

The "Parastatals"

The unsuccessful attempts to improve the civil service bureaucracy have in no way disarmed the expert community. Its recent thinking runs as follows: If LDC leadership does not want foreign experts to tamper with existing civil service systems, why not leave the latter alone and create brand new, autonomous organizations apart from the bureaucratic mainstream. With appropriate operating rules and progressive staff, the new entities will be able to fulfill the purpose assigned to them, contribute to development, and perhaps even help change the whole environment by their shining example. These public organizations, which are granted administrative and financial autonomy, are usually referred to as "parastatals." They are employed by many developing countries to accomplish a variety of governmental functions (for example, research) in addition to commercial and economic activities.

These so-called "islands of excellence" or "institutional enclaves" differ from project units run by regular bureaucratic organizations previously discussed. Unlike the latter, which are created on a temporary short-term basis to fulfill some specific objectives, the former are there to stay, like civil service agencies or commercial firms. The official rationale for their autonomy is usually the commercial, industrial, or specialized nature of the service they provide. Those parastatals that are public enterprises are expected to become self-sufficient and show a profit within a certain predetermined period.

This rationale has been welcomed by donor agencies as a way to bypass inept established bureaucratic channels. In fact, autonomous public enterprises now abound in LDCs. It is not unusual for a developing country to have from one to two hundred such enclaves supported by external funding sources. Instead of changing the environment, they have been submerged by the environment. They suffer from the same problems that plague the project units discussed earlier. Their work has been hampered by slow and ineffectual support from civil service organizations and by general government policies dictated by the requisites of political survival rather than by economic and technical considerations (for example, price setting to subsidize the more politically vocal urban population at the expense of the rural masses). Their liberal personnel and financial rules render them vulnerable to exploitation for political and bureaucratic expediency. Attracted by high salaries, exceptional perks, and flexible operating rules, many public servants, civil and military, have managed to infiltrate and control the parapublic sector, more and more obscuring its differences from the public sector.

With the proliferation of autonomous agencies encouraged and funded by foreign assistance, the parapublic sector has become almost as strong as the civil service in terms of total personnel and budget, constituting a heavier and heavier burden for the latter as well as the entire society. Draining personnel from the public sector, it weakens the latter, rendering it more ineffectual. Rather than developing self-sufficiency, parapublic sector agencies seek more and more funding from external sources, requiring more and more matching funds, recurrent costs, and debt service to be recovered by the regular operational budget at the expense of funding for regular bureaucratic agencies.

It is not necessary to send an expert in manpower and institutional development to the field to find that in a specific LDC civil service salary scales and productivity are too low; the main item of expense in the budget is personnel salaries, leaving next to nothing budgeted for operations; and the obvious recommendation from the expert standpoint is civil service reform and an increase in salary and per diem rates. Where does the money come from, if not again from external sources, under some form invented to suit the purpose, as perhaps a "structural adjustment" loan. As long as money is available through such loans, the situation can be somewhat improved. It will deteriorate again once loan funds have been spent. In the meantime, the amount of external debt continues to rise, requiring an ever-increasing percentage of export earnings just to service interest on the debt. And thus the vicious cycle deepens.[20]

Decentralization

Bitter experience in building institutions at the central government level in the public and parapublic sectors appears to lead to a major change in donor institution policies. Recognizing that the trickle-down approach has not worked well, they opt for helping build institutions at the grass roots level to take the benefits of aid directly to the masses, especially the rural masses.

Arguing that excessive centralization hampers the development effort to meet basic needs, donor institutions concentrate their resources on improving regional and local administration. Decentralization, deconcentration, devolution, delegation down to the grass roots, even debureaucratization and empowerment of local communities have been advocated, encouraged, or imposed as a condition of aid. Here again, projects designed to these specifications have failed due to

insurmountable obstacles created by negative forces of the sociopolitical environment. It is Catch-22 all the way.

It is a well-known fact that half or almost half of the total number of
civil servants in LDCs are concentrated in the capital city, seat of the
central government. The majority of the remaining civil servants serve
in large cities where state, regional, or provincial government offices
are located. A small minority are scattered in small cities and towns
throughout the country. This top-heavy and bottom-light bureaucratic
system is strongly reinforced over time by the migration of the population to urban centers and especially to the capital.[21]

The basic explanation of this phenomenon can be found easily in the
general issues identified in this study: the deterioration of all local
values and institutions, including those at the grass roots, as a result of
contact with the capitalistic system, which makes people care primarily for the economic, material aspect of life; and leadership's lack
of legitimacy as well as power to avoid or mitigate this deterioration or
substitute viable values and institutions. The capital city, and perhaps
a few of the larger cities, can offer the amenities of life, good health
care, and educational services. With the presence of many westerners,
the local intelligentsia, and with the anonymity of urban life come
some relative freedom. Therefore, no matter what decentralization
measures may be taken, civil servants will find some way of remaining
in, or transferring back to, the capital, or at least to one of the larger
cities. If forced to stay in remote areas, they spend their time pulling
strings until the sought for transfer materializes.

In short, civil servants who remain at the local level consist of those
who lack connections and are thus alienated, those who have been
disciplined, and the very few dedicated individuals who do the job for
all these others. The dedicated few who get bogged down in the downward spiral finally become the "suckers." How can local administrative
reforms succeed under these conditions?

Successful decentralization or devolution presupposes mutual confidence between authorities at different levels of government, between
superiors and subordinates, and delegators and delegatees. Superiors
are motivated to delegate when they are assured that the delegated
authority will be exercised by delegatees in accordance with the former's wishes. Delegatees are motivated to exercise their authority in
compliance with the delegators' will when they respect or fear delegators.

In polities enjoying high legitimacy, like the Western countries,
these conditions are established by the respect superiors enjoy as a
result of common consensus on the rules of selection of political and
bureaucratic office holders. This respect is all the easier to obtain since

the delegators' will is expressed in general and impersonal rules designed to serve the public interest. Moreover, in these polities, services and amenities have been more equitably distributed, further reinforcing the willingness of competent staff to serve in the localities. Thus, delegators as a rule can trust delegatees to observe self-discipline in exercising the delegated authority. It is rather exceptional for delegatees to violate this trust. In the unlikely event of a violation, delegators can always resort to the mechanism of externalized control, such as disciplinary or legal action, to correct the situation.

In polities characterized by low legitimacy but high power (totalitarian or Communist regimes), the fear inspired by superiors substitutes for respect. The monopolizing, ubiquitous, and overwhelming party apparatus is always there to help delegators check and control delegatees.

In LDCs where both legitimacy and power are low, little respect or awe can be inspired by delegators to control delegatees. Authority in this case can be delegated only to those who are personally loyal to delegators and willing to use the delegated authority to enhance the regime's survival, that is, contribute directly or indirectly to the leadership's effort to buy support for the regime and to disarm or destroy opposition groups. Because loyal individuals do not necessarily qualify for positions they fill, the exercise of delegated authority suffers.

Moreover, it is extremely difficult for position holders exercising power in this way to resist pressure from negative forces dominating the environment. The result is more corruption, greater abuses, increasing oppression, and greater inefficiency, all of which reduce the legitimacy of the regime.

It is hard for the leadership to deal with these problems by taking disciplinary actions against those who are loyal to the regime without cutting its power base. New regimes, with usually a smaller inner circle and power base, are reluctant to decentralize, because decentralization without effective means of control, either internalized or externalized, leads to anarchy, attempts at secession, and challenges to central authority, as well as widespread and blatant corruption, oppression, and abuses by local leaders. These inarticulated fears on the part of top political leaders could hardly become the subject of discussion among those involved in decentralization schemes. Foreign public administration specialists and their LDC counterparts, given their professional backgrounds, political sensitivity, and concerns for survival, usually do not think that these are appropriate issues to consider in their "technical" roles; nor are foreign specialists appropriately informed, trained, or oriented to address these issues.

Thus, it is not unusual for these reform proposals to be assigned a low priority by the ultimate decisionmaker or even to be forgotten with time. Should these be implemented as a condition for the LDC government's receipt of other project loans or grants, implementation tends to create more problems than it solves, as indicated in earlier discussion. Such negative results make it necessary to revert to centralization, which in turn feeds bureaucratic inertia, inefficiency, and incompetence.

With or without decentralization, the situation in outlying areas, especially the countryside, tends to elude the reach of the central government. Whatever control is exercised by the latter is confined to preserving internal security by the military and security forces and to collecting taxes. The lot of the people at the grass roots level remains in the hands of local power wielders: village elders; landlords; leaders of tribal, ethnic, and religious groups. Cultural values and norms and social institutions have also deteriorated at this level as a result of contact with urban centers and the external world. Negative forces predominate everywhere.

Little can be achieved at the grass roots level, since local leaders also suffer from the same shortages of both legitimacy and power. Thus, it is no surprise that attempts by donor institutions to bypass central agencies and work directly with grass roots groups have also generally failed. Such efforts have met with a host of unsurmountable problems: nonperformance by landlords and tenants; use of loans for purposes other than project implementation; refusal to pay debts; indifference, apathy, or revolt on the part of the poor; intra- and intergroup conflicts over rights of ownership and use of land, pasturage, or water; inefficient operation and maintenance; and sabotage of project works.[22]

From Program to Project and Then from Project Back to Program

The evolution of foreign aid from the general program form of assistance of the earlier period to the tighter and tighter project format of the 1970s and then back again to the recent assistance of a general program nature can also be seen as another significant example of the Catch-22 situation created by deteriorating cultural environment in many LDCs. Indeed, until the mid-1960s, grants and loans had been offered mainly in the form of general support to broad programs or sectors. Although donors were more involved in decisions on how aid monies were spent than had been the case with the Marshall Plan aid to reconstruct Europe, recipient countries retained considerable latitude of choice. The role of foreign aid consisted mainly in supplying resources and technical knowledge within the framework of macro-development models designed to increase aggregate production, improve macroeconomic planning, and encourage investment in technology. Development assistance was not tied to specific project activities but instead directed at large-scale infrastructure investments as well as use of modern technology and equipment, including agricultural extension and community development techniques, institution building, and participant training.

Such supports of a general program nature was criticized as too loose and thus ineffective in preventing aid monies from being diverted by recipient governments to other nondevelopment purposes: It did not provide a donor with an effective way of controlling how aid monies were spent in order to avoid abuses and corruption; neither did it permit donors to know the impact of the aid program on the country's development except in a very general manner.

The project was considered by many as the tool with which these goals could be achieved because it connotes purposefulness, delimitation in time and space, and predetermined results as well as ways and means of achieving them. From 1965 to 1980, project assistance gained more and more popularity and became the main form of aid by practically all donors except the Scandinavian countries. Since the early 1970s, manuals and textbooks have abounded prescribing rigourous norms for project identification, design, appraisal, implementation, and evaluation. Considerable time and energy have been consumed in project development and approval: It takes an average of almost two years for a project to be approved, and an ever-increasing number of expatriates have been involved as project identification teams, design teams, appraisal teams, implementation teams, and evaluation teams.

The art or science of projectivization appeared to reach its highest degree of sophistication in the mid-1970s with the "log-frame" (logical framework) developed by the now defunct consulting firm, Practical Concepts, Inc. (PCI), and incorporated by USAID in its *Project Assistance Handbook* to provide guidelines for project design. According to this scheme, designers should show the project's contribution to a program (purpose), which in turn should contribute to a national development plan (goal). The design should include an "end-of-project status" (EOPS), the inputs needed to produce the outputs that ultimately lead to the EOPS, and should provide for each objectively verifiable indicators by which progress can be measured and evaluated. Also required is a feasibility study consisting of economic, financial, administrative, technical, and social analyses. Additionally, important assumptions made by designers about each aspect of the project that might affect implementation and an analysis of the project background as well as an implementation plan including detailed blueprints for monitoring, reporting, and evaluation should be provided.

This rational-comprehensive approach, which increases the cost of assistance manyfold, has not fared well in many LDCs and has been widely criticized for its rigidity, lack of concern for the needs of the beneficiaries, and incapacity to build sustained development action. As pointed out by Morss and Gow, constraints to project success were overwhelming. They include macroeconomic and political policies that impede development, such as low prices paid to farmers for their produce; institutional inadequacies—from poor management to destructive bureaucratic dynamics; human resources problems, ranging from shortages of skilled personnel to the reluctance of available staff to spend much time in rural areas; failure of projects to make effective use of foreign technicians; difficulties in implementing two concepts consistently correlated with project success: decentralization and participation; timing issues; "monitoring and evaluation systems . . . [that] have not lived up to expectations"; differing agendas of all the important actors in development projects; and sustainability: the likelihood that when outside aid terminates, project benefits will cease.[23] In these authors' words,

> the project era has introduced greater concern for the details of what development monies are intended to do and how these goals are to be achieved. Unlike the earlier days of program support, the project era has set the stage for detailed evaluative work. Did the project follow the steps outlined in the planning documents, and has it achieved its stated objectives? Many evaluations have been carried out, and they all point to a similar conclusion: regardless of their degree of success, almost all projects encountered serious problems during implementation.[24]

To remedy these problems, critics of this blueprint model advocate the process intervention or social-learning approach, which emphasizes flexibility, experimentation, learning, and adjustment through some kind of people-centered planning and management. Some propose such alternative process strategies as the elevator model, quick-step model, low-step model, which attempt to combine both accountability and flexibility to deal effectively with issues of recurrent cost and capacity building for sustained action. Others argue for the empowerment of project beneficiaries through a process of coalition building that would in turn require a revolutionary mechanism of bureaucratic reorientation not only in recipient government bureaucracies but also in donor bureaucratic systems.

Still others challenge the value of the project instrument itself, especially its too-narrow perspective, and recommend going back to the previous general program approach. It is, however, not easy to revert to the latter because

> it will take time for large donor agencies to wind down the project generation momentum that has built up over the last decade, because projects tend to be "expatriate technician intensive," and with the worldwide unemployment rates as high as they are, any attempts to "bring the boys home" will meet with resistance in donor nations [and because] donors will be reluctant to give up on the project approach because it gives them the feeling they have greater control over how monies are spent than is the case when more general support is provided.[25]

The dilemma confronting donors in controlling aid monies can be summarized by the recent observation in the *Washington Post:*

> Shortly after he seized power, Babangida put the question of whether to accept the IMF package to a national debate. The debate made it clear that Nigerians felt signing the IMF agreement would amount to an abrogation of national sovereignty. There is also a strong sentiment, after years of corrupt government in Lagos, that any large outside loans would be stolen by politicians.[26]

and by the comment of the Committee on African Development Strategies that "corruption has often distorted and sometimes replaced economic management. Governmental and private sector elites have drained off a substantial percentage of national resources as well as outside aid."[27]

It is to be noted that similar observations are made not only for Africa alone, but also for many other parts of the developing world. Otherwise, such a generalized shift from program to project support would not have occurred. The fact remains, nevertheless, that neither program nor project as a form of assistance has been effective in controlling the use of aid monies for development purposes. Indeed, as pointed out by Morss and Morss:

> Among all the donors, perhaps the Scandinavian countries come closest to offering the types of foreign assistance most desired by developing nations. They provide assistance to a select number of recipients that appear to share their socialist philosophy of development. While aid usually goes under programmatic headings, recipient countries are given considerable latitude to spend the money as they see fit.[28]

But they hasten to add in a footnote that "interestingly enough, untied aid is frequently criticized by the Scandinavian technicians working in the recipient developing countries. They feel the aid would be more effective if the uses to which it was put were clearly specified."[29]

The inconclusive debate about program versus project notwithstanding, ways must be found somehow by donors to stave off the worldwide financial crises created by the worsening economic situation in many LDCs in the last decade. Thus, since the late 1970s, a quiet but consistent return to the program strategy has taken shape. To assist LDCs in improving macroeconomic policies that the development community considers the basic obstacle to development efforts and to meet specific needs of recipients, flexible instruments of assistance had to be invented for the circumstances. These instruments, which are of a general program nature but sometimes given new labels, include the IMF's standby arrangement; the World Bank's structural adjustment loan, sector adjustment loan, and Special Action Program; and bilateral donors' direct financing of local and recurrent costs.

Indeed, since 1981, the IMF has considerably increased its financial assistance under the standby arrangement to help a growing number of LDCs deal with severe balance of payments problems. Short-term financing from the fund has been complemented since then by the World Bank's long-term concessional and nonconcessional financing under its structural adjustment loan (SAL) program. Other donors have often encouraged and reinforced the bank's efforts with their nonproject bilateral programs. Since 1979, the Development Assistance Committee (DAC, which comprises most donor countries) has agreed, contrary to its traditional policy, to finance the local and recurrent cost component of projects. A Special Action Program was adopted in 1983 by the bank to accelerate disbursement for rehabilitating and maintaining existing projects.

Under these nonproject forms of assistance devised to meet specific and urgent needs of the recipient and officially claimed as a means of supporting policy reforms, aid monies can be used for practically any purpose, including financing needed imports, disaster relief, food aid, and debt servicing. Some sacred principles governing project aid aimed at local capacity building—fund matching by the recipient government to cover local costs, recurrent cost financing by the recipient—thus had to be abandoned. Project aid itself has been increasingly supplanted by general program aid. By the mid-1980s, already a third of official development assistance had been for nonproject aid. In the meantime, with the addition of nonproject loans, many LDCs, including the poorest countries in sub-Saharan Africa, are now facing large and growing repayment obligations.[30]

In short, the project strategy, which replaced the program approach considered too loose and ineffective in controlling aid monies, has been criticized itself as too rigid and too narrow and gradually discarded by the instrument whose place it was called on to take two decades ago. Both program and project support can, of course, be seen as complementary, or part of a spectrum of assistance, as often claimed by the development establishment, if they contribute their fair share to Third-World development. This does not seem, however, to be the case for a majority of recipient developing nations. What appears more obvious is the contribution of both instruments to the ever-increasing Third-World debt that has entrapped donees and donors in an ever-widening vicious cycle.

The bottom-line explanation for this vicious cycle may run like this: In dealing with rampant corruption and mismanagement resulting from the sociopolitical vicissitudes pervading many recipient LDCs, the project instrument became surrounded with more and more sophisticated rules and procedures to ensure its integrity and success. Rule elaboration, complexity, and rigidity made it more and more costly in terms of time and effort to design and implement a project. This high degree of sophistication required that an increasing proportion of expatriates be involved to make sure that the project succeeds. In this way, at least a number of difficult projects aimed at building physical infrastructures—dams, highways, power plants, factories—managed to be brought to successful completion at international market prices. Of course, the tangible and at times impressive results of the projects remain there for the recipient countries to enjoy. Aid monies, however, went mostly to donors in the form of compensation for expatriates—aid officials, project technicians, contractual firms' employees—and purchase of imported equipment and materials. Operation and maintenance of project results became more and more difficult as time went on. Dams, highways, and factories gradually deteriorated or if well maintained and run, constituted heavy burdens for the whole society. At the same time, the amount of debt resulting from successful as well as unsuccessful projects kept mounting and needed to be repaid. The program strategy had to be resorted to, regardless of, or thanks to, all of its defects in order to save debtor countries from financial bankruptcy.[31]

From Infrastructure to Basic Needs to Adjustment with Growth

Difficulties in choosing an effective form of assistance has been paralleled by those donors encountered in selecting the content—sectors or areas—of aid. Following the impressive success of the Marshall Plan, which helped Western Europe realize an average PCI increase of 37 percent from 1948 to 1951, it was believed that a similar transfer of capital, coupled with technical assistance, would achieve similar results in LDCs. Nearly total emphasis was placed, therefore, on building physical infrastructure as a way of increasing production and income. This meant not only investments in Western machinery, equipment, and materials, but also large-scale infrastructures—roads, railroads, ports, power plants. The Western model of development was followed with overall growth as its objective, and industrialization using Western technologies as its prime instrument. Income distribution was of little concern, and little attention was devoted, therefore, to agriculture or the social sectors. It was simply expected that economic growth would trickle down to the poor.

In the early 1970s, a number of economists and supporters of foreign aid began to question this conventional wisdom when some systematic studies as well as casual observations revealed that the major beneficiaries of development efforts were upper- and middle-income groups in many recipient LDCs. These findings were in no way startling, given the predominance of the westernized bourgeois class in the decaying culture of most LDCs, as described in chap. 1. Despite the fact that these conclusions were disputed by others who cited evidence to the contrary in a number of countries, the trickle-down approach represented by the earlier conventional model of development was repudiated and replaced by a new development strategy with the passage of the 1973 Foreign Assistance Act by the U.S. Congress.

Since that time until the early 1980s, this new strategy, which is directed at improving the well-being of the impoverished, was almost universally accepted by bilateral and multilateral donor agencies under several different labels: basic human needs, rural modernization, integrated rural development, new directions, new style, or growth with equity. Development efforts thus targeted directly the poor and addressed basic needs. Three key sectors enjoyed particular attention: food and nutrition, population and health, and education and human resource development. Debates now centered on whether or not there were conflict between equity and growth, that is, between projects that sought to help the poor and those that sought to promote growth. As a result of this debate, poverty alleviation was given greater attention. At the same time, project design, implementation, and evaluation became more difficult than ever with the additional attempt to introduce ways and means of preventing predatory local elements from usurping the benefits of aid to the poor and of quantifying improvement in the "quality of life" of the poor. Efforts aiming at decentralizing, delegating, involving the poor in project design and implementation, and at debureaucratizing and empowering local communities were often fraught with frustrations and failures, as discussed earlier.

With an increasing number of developing countries reaching the threshold of bankruptcy as a result of mounting international debts, the focus began to change, but this time with less fanfare than had been the case with the radical shift toward the basic needs approach. "Flexible instruments" had to be devised to meet the specific needs of the recipient country regardless of sector or area or their potential effects on the wealthy or the poor. Specific needs include closing the balance of payments deficits, debt reimbursement, meeting recurrent costs, maintaining and rehabilitating existing capital, and adjusting to policy reforms. To avert worldwide financial crises that increasing and generalized debt defaults by Third-World countries might generate, donors had no choice but to fight the fire. The label for this new strategy has been "adjustment with growth." The fire-fighting instruments, old and new—standby arrangement, structural adjustment loan, local cost financing—have been discussed earlier in conjunction with program and project approaches. Since experience of the last two decades appears to demonstrate the superiority of the free enterprise model of earlier development strategy, adjustment with growth has been coupled with "development of private sector."[32] In short, the vicious cycle entrapping donors and donees seems well summarized in the following comment by the Council on Foreign Relations and the Overseas Development Council: "Most donors, including international institutions, have jumped from one fad to another to justify development expenditures—from the support of infrastructure, to a concern with basic needs, to the most recent heavy focus on agriculture and encouragement of the private sector."[33]

The Paradoxically Negative Side of Success

This cursory assessment of development assistance appears to be enough to demonstrate how different technical approaches adopted by the professionally oriented development community have failed to fit into the sociopolitical environment of LDCs, and negative forces in their environments. It can be argued that this is a deliberate attempt to paint the darkest possible picture of Third-World development, while neglecting its bright side. Instead of discussing failures of which the development community has heard enough, why not emphasize successes?

There have been, of course, cases of success: Factories well run, highways or dams properly maintained, training institutions well operated. And, to be sure, credit should go to international aid for the Green

Revolution resulting from the discovery and dissemination of the so-called miracle rice. Also, the eradication of several dangerous tropical diseases in many parts of the Third World constitutes no small achievement. In addition, Western countries, the United States in particular, have excelled in saving and aiding millions through emergency humanitarian help following natural and other catastrophes in many Third-World areas. More importantly, foreign aid has contributed significantly to the spectacular economic development of a small number of LDCs that appear to have succeeded in breaking the vicious cycle caused by the crisis of legitimacy. Some of these countries will be analyzed in the following chapter. It is to be noted, nevertheless, that successes are distressingly few and far between when compared with cases of failure. Thus, it is inappropriate for successes to characterize the overall macro picture, and it is easy for them to be negated in the long run by the uninterrupted operation of the vicious cycle. However, if these few LDCs have indeed succeeded in breaking the vicious cycle, then their experience should be closely studied to isolate techniques or approaches for other developing countries.[34]

It also remains to be seen whether individual project successes cause failures in other sectors. It may be that well-maintained highways and parastatals that fare well constitute a burden for the whole government or hamper the civil service's development as a whole. In the same vein, successful health and education projects, if not matched by success in economic projects allowing for increased production, employment, and productivity, create serious imbalances in the society and insoluble problems for other sectors.[35] In other words, successes or failures have to be evaluated not in isolated individual cases but in systems terms, in relationship to the survival and growth of the general system. If one looks at individual cases, there is no dearth of successful projects in South Vietnam or Iran. But where did all of these successes lead after the general system crumbled? What good is it to have a few isolated successful economic projects and professional heroes here and there when the country's economy has been sapped by a continuous exodus of capital in search of a safe haven in Western countries? How could a successful participant training project enlarge the reservoir of human capital when 600,000 professionals from the Third World have chosen not to settle in their native countries in the past quarter-century; when the number of doctors and teachers in Great Britain and France from the latter's former colonies exceeds that of British and French doctors and teachers working in these countries; when the estimated saving in training costs for the United States, Canada, and Great Britain as a result of professionals' immigration is even higher than the amount of aid provided by these countries to the Third World?[36]

What is considered to be a positive lesson at the professional level may ultimately lead to negative results from a broader perspective. On the one hand, successful projects tend to be exceptional, resulting from a concurrence of events and circumstances that are hardly replicable in the wider environment: show cases, dedicated and competent leadership that is tolerated as a means of attracting foreign aid in other areas. On the other hand, these exceptions are likely to serve as life preservers to which development aid bureaucracies can cling to justify their approach, increase their futile work, expand their ranks, and thus to perpetuate the waste and deepen the vicious cycle.[37]

3
EVALUATING DEVELOPMENT: TO WIN THE WAR OR THE BATTLE?

SINCE SUCCESS AT THE MACRO LEVEL IS THE PREREQUISITE FOR MEAN-ingful success at the micro level, a focus on the former appears crucial for development policymakers. While most development efforts have failed at the general systems level, there have been, fortunately, a few cases of success. It is good to learn from the failures to avoid repeating past mistakes and from the successes for the sake of replication. The reason for failure is the incapacity of development efforts to build up viable polities, that is, polities capable of exercising adequate control on the society through a balanced use of legitimacy (internalized control) and power (externalized control). Thus far, development assistance has failed in polities that take two main forms: (1) those where the political leadership possesses both low legitimacy and low power and is incapable of increasing either to deal successfully with the negative forces dominating the environment; and (2) those whose political regimes attempt to increase power in such a negative way that it decreases legitimacy and is finally overthrown.

Development efforts appear to have succeeded in polities that manage both to use enough power to make up for the lack of legitimacy *and* to use it in such a positive way that it enhances legitimacy and decreases reliance on power in the long run.

PRO-WEST VIETNAM

A review of the successive non-Communist regimes in Vietnam from 1945, with which this author is most familiar, provides some illustrations of failure.

Regimes Installed by the French: 1945–1954

Vietnam was a French colony from 1884 to 1945. On 9 March 1945, the French government in Vietnam was overthrown by the Japanese; about six months later, the Japanese surrendered to the Allied Forces. After World War II, French troops reconquered most of the main cities of Vietnam and installed puppet Vietnamese regimes in three regions, north, central, and south. Later, a central government headed by former emperor Bao Dai was added to these regional governments. While the Vietnamese Communists led the resistance, Vietnamese officials who had served the French well during the earlier colonial period ran these governments.

LOW LEGITIMACY AND LOW POWER

Bao Dai had been well known as a playboy and puppet king. It is obvious that these regimes supported by the French, who were attempting to reestablish their domination over Vietnam, enjoyed extremely low legitimacy. Moreover, local officials, trained to serve their colonial masters and rely on the latter for all important decisions, possessed very little power; they were unwilling power wielders, incapable of exercising whatever power the French delegated to them to deal with the resistance movement. Yet they were adept at using their power to serve their own interests through bribery and corruption, further undermining the legitimacy of the regimes.

RELIANCE ON FOREIGN POWER

It was the French military and civilian bureaucratic apparatus that provided the quasitotal amount of power to make up for the lack of these regimes' legitimacy and to help them survive until the French defeat in the battle of Dien Bien Phu in 1954. Overwhelmed by well-trained Viet Cong troops equipped by the Chinese and Russians, the French asked the United States to intervene directly with U.S. air combat support to save Dien Bien Phu. The United States refused. Baffled by the ever-increasing cost of the war and unfavorable domestic and international opinion, the French signed the Geneva Accord with the Viet Cong in 1954 to end the fighting.

COLLAPSE OF THE REGIME AFTER WITHDRAWAL OF FOREIGN SUPPORT

The accord resulted in dividing the country into North Vietnam under Communist control and South Vietnam under Ngo Dinh Diem, to whom Bao Dai had delegated authority. In terms of this model, the instability and final collapse of the pro-French regimes in Vietnam resulted from their lack of both power and legitimacy. The power provided by the French tended to decrease their legitimacy, so that an ever-increasing power became necessary for their survival. When the French were no longer able to supply the necessary additional power to deal with the resistance, these regimes collapsed. This dynamic balance of power and legitimacy is represented in figure 2.[1]

The Diem Regime: 1954–1963

LEGITIMACY WITHOUT POWER

Bao Dai had appointed Ngo Dinh Diem prime minister with fully delegated legislative and executive power sometime before the Geneva Accord was signed. Diem had an outstanding record as an incorruptible mandarin and a dedicated patriot. He had spent most of his life as an underground revolutionary leader fighting for national independence.

After seventy years of French domination and nine years of Viet Minh (Vietnamese Communist party) terrorism and monopolization of the resistance movement, Diem's return from overseas was warmly welcomed by a few of the many divided nationalist groups and a sizable portion of the people. Initially, the regime enjoyed a fair amount of legitimacy thanks to Diem's past record and personal charisma. But he had very little actual power, since the situation remained practically under the control of the French and pro-French forces.

USE OF POWER TO FURTHER LEGITIMACY

With the support of his followers, patriotic elements in the armed forces, public opinion, and some U.S. groups, Diem managed to dismiss those who challenged him, especially the pro-French chief of staff of the armed forces and regional governors. Thus, Diem was able to assert his authority and establish his control over the military and civilian bureaucracy.

With the armed forces behind him, Diem succeeded in destroying the independent paramilitary forces that had refused to submit to government control. He also more or less neutralized the underground

Legitimacy

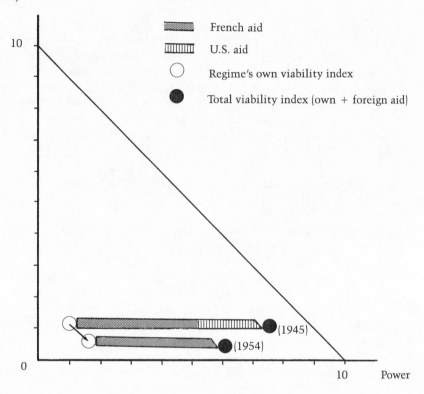

Figure 2. Pro-French Regimes in Vietnam, 1945–1954

(For further elaboration on conceptual framework, see Figure 1, Polity Viability Chart, and the section that precedes it in chapter 1.)

Communist infrastructure in South Vietnam. Over a million refugees from North Vietnam were brought to the South and successfully resettled. Out of an anarchic situation created by the departure of the French occupation forces and the division of the country following the Geneva Accord, peace and order were restored throughout South Vietnam.

The legitimacy of the regime was substantially enhanced by Diem's charisma combined with an effective use of power to deal successfully with so grave a national crisis, as well as his insistence on genuine independence vis-à-vis all countries, including the United States of America, which provided substantial military and economic support to South Vietnam. Indeed, it can be said that from the time Diem took over in 1954 until 1958, the Republic of Vietnam was moving in a positive direction with a balanced use of power to increase its legitimacy.

FAILURE TO ENHANCE OR MAINTAIN EXTERNAL AND INTERNAL
LEGITIMACY

Unfortunately, this positive tendency did not continue during the remaining years of his government. His resolute attempts to expand his power base from 1958 onward became more or less controversial. The way Diem used power during his first four years was justified by national interest and thus was perceived as just and right by the people. The destruction of pro-French groups who plotted to overthrow him, and the placement of his followers in key positions in the bureaucratic machinery could be explained by the need to deal with a national crisis, to regain independence for the country, and to provide a legitimate nationalist government capable of safeguarding the southern part of the country from the northern Communist aggression.

Once the crisis was over, however, his power consolidated, and the situation stabilized, the unfortunate use of Diem's power began to surface and be exposed, especially by the foreign press. Neither the U.S. press nor U.S. officials felt comfortable with his traditional dictatorial family rule. The French, unhappy over the loss of their former colony, resented his anti-French, pro-U.S. stance and were ready to find fault with his regime.

To be sure, Western pressures made it difficult for Diem to survive by increasing his legitimacy and/or power. It is worth noting, however, that Diem himself was also responsible for his own loss. His basic mistake was failure to revive the ideal of the Vietnamese culture, which would have helped continue to move the regime in the positive direction of more legitimacy and less power. Cultural revival or renewal was indeed badly needed after a long century of decline and decay.

As a Vietnamese leader, Diem represented both the best and the worst of the local value system. As a man with a high sense of integrity, probity, responsibility, and dedication, he refused to serve as a puppet premier in a French- or Japanese-protected local government or a ceremonial adviser in the Ho Chi Minh government. Leading an austere life, he had no wives, no children, and no fortune. He vowed to, and did, devote his whole life and time to saving his country and people.

At the same time, however, Diem was much too authoritarian, condescending, patronizing, and uncompromising. It was these latter characteristics that led him into trouble. Since he did not want to hear arguments or comments that did not please him, he ended up surrounding himself with sycophants and yes men. Those who had supported Diem during bad times but did not want to be subservient were discarded by him little by little or tended to shy away from him. "He just wants 'serviteurs' [sycophants] but not 'collaborateurs' [cooperators]" was a popular comment on Diem's way of using people. As a result, many of the obedient bureaucrats who had served well under the colonial government became puppets for the power wielders— Diem's relatives—who remained behind the scenes.

Diem's somewhat weak intellectual capacity was complemented by that of his brother Nhu, who served officially as an adviser to the president. For all practical purposes, however, Nhu and his wife, as well as the three other brothers—Can, Luyen, and Archbishop Thuc— kept a tight control on the whole governmental and party machinery. With opposition groups neutralized, they became all powerful by using yes men and playing off different factions of henchmen one against the other.

All assets and liabilities taken into account, Diem and his brothers might belong to the category of superior men in terms of the local culture. They were firmly committed to the national cause and strongly determined to fight for national independence against communism as well as against any form of Western domination. Their ambition for power was more likely to be directed toward the service of a higher cause than selfish, personal, or family interests. By adopting the policy of using puppets to divide and rule, however, they were encouraging their subordinates to behave as "small men." Rather than attempting to break the vicious cycle by reviving the positive culture, they were instead perpetuating its negative aspects, capitalizing on them for political purposes.

Nominally during this period, there was a modern, democratic form of government with division of power among the three branches. In practice, however, the election and appointment processes were controlled in order to select officials in the three branches of government who would serve as rubber stamps for the ruling family. With the expansion of the regime's power base, the government apparatus as well as the local private sector ended up being controlled by henchmen who enjoyed the confidence of the ruling family but had little technical competence, and by yes men who were ready to implement mechanistically any orders coming from the regime's éminences grises.

In this highly politicized bureaucratic milieu, it was no surprise that the Michigan State University Advisory Group failed to introduce public administration techniques that fit a professionalized bureaucracy, such as position classification and performance budgeting. Foreign aid recommendations that were adopted and worked well were those that supported leadership's policies, such as centralizing government by abolishing regions; or those measures that were more or less neutral or inconsequential, such as mechanizing accounting for the national budget or preservice public administration education.

DIEM'S FALL: INABILITY TO INCREASE POWER TO MAKE UP FOR DECREASING LEGITIMACY

The expansion of power permitted continuity of leadership, peace, order, and stability and allowed the leadership to accomplish some development programs it cherished. But because power was overly concentrated in a small family circle, inertia and inefficiency set in. Moreover, there was no way for Diem to prevent abuses, corruption, and frauds committed by his henchmen and yes men without destroying his own power base. These realities tended to make a mockery of the official ideology of personalism proclaimed by the regime as well as the party apparatus created to help implement this ideology. Taken altogether, the regime's success in increasing its capacity to impose compliance through external constraints (power) did not occur without harming its capacity to induce self-imposed compliance on the part of the people (legitimacy), thus necessitating the resort to more and more use of power.

Increases in power have their limits, especially in non-Communist regimes. This applied to the case in point, even though Communist North Vietnam was trying by all means and at any cost to conquer South Vietnam, acting with the unstinting support of the two Communist giants, the Soviet Union and China. Support from other nationalist parties and the masses as well as assistance from the United States were a must for the regime and the country to deal with subversive activities by Vietnamese Communists. Diem and his brothers, had a hard time, not only with their Communist foes, but also with their U.S. friends and rival nationalist groups.

French educated and children of an elitist Roman Catholic family, Diem and his brothers were very proud of their background and rather dogmatic, sectarian, uncompromising, and closed minded. It was, indeed, extremely difficult for them to get along well with Americans and to meet U.S. expectations of building a pluralistic democracy in South Vietnam to justify the increasing cost of military and economic assistance. The country could not be closed to the Western press and human rights organizations without cutting off its sources of foreign aid. More drastic control measures could not be used without provoking increasing criticism from the foreign press and further undermining the legitimacy of the regime.

The Strategic Hamlet program, for instance, aimed at concentrating the rural population in strategic areas to isolate them from Viet Cong infiltration, was implemented only halfway, due to U.S. refusal of support. Meanwhile, North Vietnam, excelling in the use of power to keep the population tightly within its grip, had the support of the entire Eastern bloc propaganda machinery in its attempt to destroy the legitimacy of the Diem regime. Communist cadres were sent to the South to engage in abrasive activities and occupy some strategic areas. Several attempts to assassinate or overthrow Diem were made, not only by the Viet Cong but also by some of the nationalist factions and armed forces units; it was suspected that the latter had encouragement from some U.S. quarters.

While Diem was unable to increase his power beyond a certain limit, the legitimacy of his regime was dealt the heaviest blow when his henchmen literally implemented his order to raid the Buddhist temples, carrying out the brutal and massive arrest of those bonzes who opposed the regime. This event led to Diem's overthrow by a group of generals whom he himself had used and promoted. The United States not only withdrew its support of the regime, but also played a leading role behind the scenes in the coup. Apparently convinced until the last minute that they were faithfully and sincerely serving a just and right cause, Diem and his brother Nhu proudly continued to behave as superior men in the presence of those who had arrested them. Rumor had it that Nhu insulted the plotters as betrayers in the pay of foreigners. The brothers were shot and killed in the armored personnel carrier that had brought them back from a church in Saigon Chinatown in which they had been hiding. In terms of legitimacy and power, the Diem era can be represented by figure 3.[2]

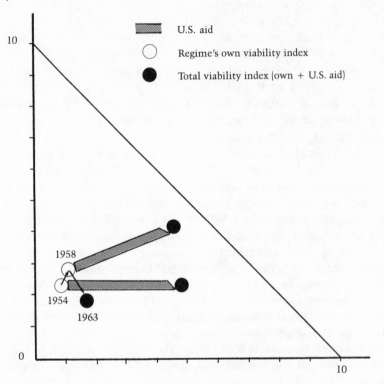

Figure 3. The Ngo Dinh Diem Regime, 1954–1963

(For further elaboration on conceptual framework, see Figure 1, Polity Viability Chart, and the section that precedes it in chapter 1.)

The Post Diem Regimes: 1963–1975

The overthrow of the Diem regime in November 1963 was a decisive setback for South Vietnam. What Diem had constructed in terms of legitimacy and power was completely destroyed by the coup. With the persecution of his followers and the destruction of the formal and informal power structures he had established, almost all the instruments of control and administration had to be rebuilt. With little legitimacy or power of their own, successive regimes led by Vietnamese generals relied almost exclusively on the power supplied by the United States. For all practical purposes, U.S. troops and military and civilian advisers ran the show. That outcome was precisely what Diem had wanted to avoid at all costs.

THE BIG MINH REGIME

The military junta that overthrew Diem was a loose coalition that had served successive governments, French, pro-French, and Diem. Nominally led by General Duong Van Minh, who was just an amiable individual, the junta was too divided and unprepared to provide a real source of power to compensate the new regime for its lack of legitimacy. The junta was overthrown by General Nguyen Khanh in late January 1964, less than three months from the day of the coup. Most of the junta generals were jailed by Khanh, but Minh was retained as a figurehead.

THE "STRONG MAN" NGUYEN KHANH ERA

As an opportunistic military officer who had served in the French army and quickly been promoted from the ranks for his support of Diem, Khanh suffered from a most serious lack of legitimacy. Ambitious but insecure, he attempted to emerge as the strong man to succeed Diem, but his effort to create a power base by seeking cooperation from several military and civilian factions failed miserably. Because his political competence was no match for his grandiose dream, his regime lasted only a little over a year during which he became a figure of ridicule. Deposed by a group of young Turk generals who had supported him in his coup against the first junta, Khanh went into exile as an ambassador at large in February 1965.

Under the pressure of strong opposition from Buddhist and Catholic groups, as well as several military factions, Khanh, in a desperate political move, had established a civilian government in late 1964, with Phan Khac Suu as head of state and Tran Van Huong as premier.

Thanks to the latters' records as honest and dedicated revolutionary patriots, the regime's legitimacy had been slightly enhanced. But the Huong government brought no power base to Khanh. In the face of strong Buddhist opposition, it collapsed in late January 1965.

Dr. Phan Huy Quat, a leader of the Dai Viet Mandarin faction who had served under several governments for Bao Dai, was appointed premier and asked to form a new government. He, too, had little power or legitimacy, nor did he get along well with Head of State Suu or the young Turk generals to whom the focus of power had shifted. Both Quat and Suu were removed in June 1965. They were replaced by Air Vice-Marshall Nguyen Cao Ky as premier, or chairman of the Central Executive Committee, and Major General Nguyen Van Thieu as head of state, or chairman of the National Leadership Committee. Both men were members of the young Turks who had supported Khanh in ousting the initial junta of older generals.

THE THIEU-KY ERA

Outspoken, straightforward, audacious, and more or less "cowboyish," Ky had established some power base as commander of the air force throughout this turbulent period. With the backing of air force officers, the commander of the marine corps, and a few other generals from his northern area, Ky managed to reestablish some order and stability by his bold attempts to keep opposition groups under control. This was no small achievement after twenty long months during which the country, crippled by coups and countercoups, had suffered from a leadership vacuum.

Despite some early misgivings, the United States was pleased with results and willing to give Ky its firm support. He was able to keep the situation under control for over two years until September 1967 when elections for a civilian government were to be held under a new constitution. During this period, Ky managed to eclipse Thieu, who remained a more or less powerless head of state.

Thieu, however, was determined to compete with Ky by running for the presidency of the republic under the new constitution. A shrewd and ambitious general who had been involved in almost every coup or countercoup without really siding with anyone, Thieu was ready to take advantage of the situation. Capitalizing on mistakes and abuses of Ky and his followers, Thieu rallied many generals from southern and central Vietnam whom Ky had alienated and succeeded in outmaneuvering Ky, persuading him to accept the merely ceremonial position of vice-president.

Having inherited a relatively stable situation from Ky, Thieu managed to keep things more or less under control until April 1975. Thieu was a more sophisticated manipulator of power than Ky; he used less direct oppression and more wealth to corrupt, buy off, or divide opposition groups, balance military groups, and remained on good terms with the United States.

It is to be noted that the regime's legitimacy was never high under Ky nor Thieu. Neither of these men had an outstanding past record to provide some legitimacy to the government both led through charisma. As professional soldiers catapulted to power as a consequence of their talent for petty infighting, both lacked the moral and political capacity to create government backing or a government capable of arousing enough enthusiasm to resist Communist aggression. The power base of each was also very restricted, being derived mainly, if not exclusively, from the armed forces.

As a matter of fact, the decisive source of power in the Ky and Thieu regimes came from the United States. As North Vietnam increased its covert and overt subversive activities, with ever-increasing support from the whole Communist bloc, the cost of this U.S. power supplement mounted in terms not only of material aid but also U.S. lives.

By mid-1965, two weeks after Ky took over as premier, President Johnson announced that 53,000 combat troops would be sent to South Vietnam. In the late 1960s, with about 600,000 U.S. military and a sizable number of civilian advisers and employees, Americans were seen in practically every city, town, village, and hamlet of that country. The gradual and ever-increasing U.S. presence in South Vietnam was a necessary response to the declining legitimacy and power of the local regime.

The U.S. presence, in turn, accelerated the downward spiral in several ways. The ubiquitous presence of foreign and Western troops in a former French colony just recently evacuated by French occupation forces significantly damaged the legitimacy of the South Vietnamese government. The abundance of Western material assets that accompanied that presence in a declining Confucian culture expanded opportunities for corruption, further reducing the legitimacy of the regime. At the same time, the U.S. military presence made South Vietnamese leaders less and less responsible for their country's destiny and more and more reliant on foreigners. The outcome was a further reduction in leadership capacity to use power effectively and positively to preserve national integrity.

As the war drifted on with no end in sight, the continuing and increasing cost of U.S. involvement became more and more difficult to justify to people in the United States. When this huge U.S. power supplement was decreased in 1973 with the Vietnamization of the war, the Thieu regime was shaken. And when this power source was finally withdrawn in 1975, while North Vietnam continued to receive Soviet and Chinese support, South Vietnam collapsed instantly.

Thieu resigned and fled overseas a week before the fall of Saigon. Power was transferred to Vice-President Tran Van Huong, who passed it to General Duong Van Minh. The latter occupied the Independence Palace for two days before surrendering to North Vietnamese troops on 30 April 1975. Figure 4 provides a summary sketch of post-Diem regimes' legitimacy and power.[3]

Cases of nonviable polity resulting from a lack of both legitimacy and power similar to that of South Vietnam abound in the non-Communist Third World. Readers familiar with other LDCs can draw their own charts for those countries' successive regimes.

COMMUNIST VIETNAM: 1945–1986

What happens in a developing country that has chosen the Communist model to build a viable polity is illustrated by the case of Communist Vietnam.

Some Legitimacy and Some Power

Taking advantage of the power vacuum created by the Japanese surrender at the end of World War II, the Vietnamese Communist party seized power in August 1945. Communist cadres taking over the government met with no significant resistance, for there was practically no government after the Japanese surrender. The French colonial government had been overthrown five months earlier. The local government established by the Japanese to succeed the French colonials had resigned after only a few months in office.

Of the revolutionary parties, the Communist party was by far the best prepared to seize the opportunity of the moment. Thanks to faithful and substantial support from Moscow, Vietnam Communists had built an elaborate underground network of cadres throughout the country. Nationalist parties that had sought help from the non-Communist world had been easily destroyed, divided, or otherwise weakened by the French, who made efficient use of diplomatic channels at their disposal. Moreover, the label that the Communist party was using at that time, Viet Nam Doc Lap Dong Minh Hoi (Union of Allied Parties for the Independence of Viet Nam), served its propaganda machine well, convincing the people that power was being seized in the

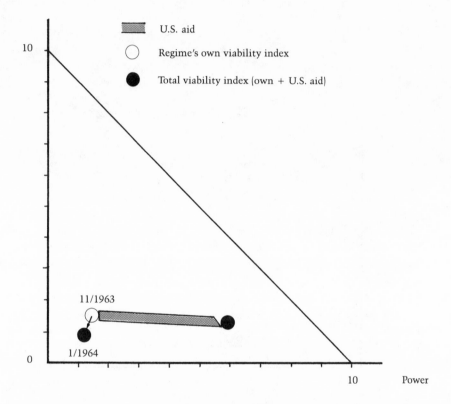

Legitimacy

U.S. aid

Regime's own viability index

Total viability index (own + U.S. aid)

10

11/1963

1/1964

0

10 Power

**Figure 4a. The Post-Diem Regimes: Big Minh Era
(November 1963–January 1964)**

(For further elaboration on conceptual framework, see Figure 1, Polity Viability
Chart, and the section that precedes it in chapter 1.)

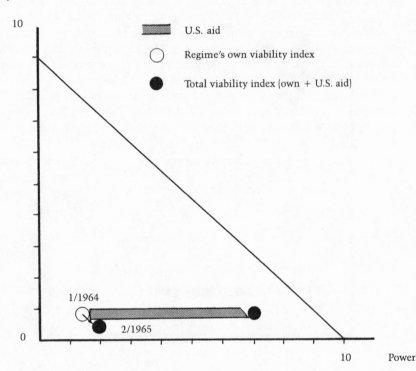

**Figure 4b. The Post-Diem Regimes: Nguyen Khanh Era
(January 1964–February 1965)**

(For further elaboration on conceptual framework, see Figure 1, Polity Viability
Chart, and the section that precedes it in chapter 1.)

Legitimacy

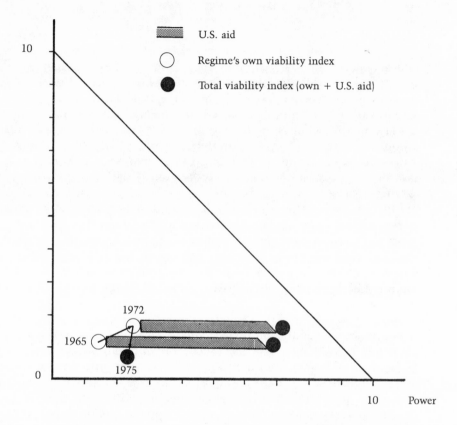

Figure 4c. The Post-Diem Regimes: Thieu-Ky Era (1965–1975)

(For further elaboration on conceptual framework, see Figure 1, Polity Viability Chart, and the section that precedes it in chapter 1.)

name of all revolutionary parties and with the support of the Allied powers.

The Determined Use of Power to Fill up the Legitimacy Gap

Shorty after the Japanese surrender, British troops occupied the south and Nationalist Chinese troops the north of Vietnam. With British help, the French reestablished control over practically all cities and towns south of the sixteenth parallel. French, Chinese, and the Ho Chi Minh governments then signed an agreement giving each of them a share in the benefits at the expense of the Vietnamese nationalist camp. By the terms of agreement, the Chinese repossessed from French rule some Chinese territories, and the French were able to replace withdrawing Chinese troops with French units. With the evacuation of Chinese troops, the Vietnamese Communist government was able to rid itself of nationalist parties led by the Vietnamese Kuomingtang or Viet Nam Quoc Dan Dang, whose occupancy of many strategic areas in North Vietnam constituted a serious threat to the Communist regime.

Building up Legitimacy by Resisting Foreign Conquerors

Having destroyed the nationalist forces, Communists turned against the French. With U.S. military and economic aid, the French then expanded control to include practically all remaining Vietnamese towns and cities. It is important to recognize that the policy of Western powers—the French colonial policy supported by Britain and the United States—made it impossible for Vietnamese nationalists to survive. Even the Chinese Kuomingtang was merely using its counterpart as a bargaining chip to extract bribes from Vietnamese Communists and territorial concessions from the French. Many Vietnamese nationalists had no choice but to join Communist ranks to fight against the French. Communists, benefiting from the legitimacy of the resistance movement and using their power with a heavy hand, resorted to the most inhuman means of terrorism to keep most of the countryside free of French control.

With the help of the whole Communist world, facilitated by the occupation of continental China by Chinese Communists, resistance troops succeeded in occupying many strategic areas and finally in defeating the French in 1954 at Dien Bien Phu.

The Persistent, Resolute, and Ruthless Use of Power with Unfailing Foreign Support

The Geneva Accord following the defeat of France partitioned Vietnam into North Vietnam under Ho Chi Minh and South Vietnam under Ngo Dinh Diem. Diem's charisma and success—with U.S. aid—in establishing the Republic of Vietnam, secure and independent of France, more developed economically and freer politically than North Vietnam, was a decisive turnaround for the nationalist cause and a heavy blow to the monopolistic Communist claim to legitimacy. For the first time, the nationalist camp had a viable government.

As previously described, the early success did not endure. The overthrow of the Diem regime, followed by successive coups and ineffectual governments and finally the withdrawal of U.S. support, enabled the Communist Vietnamese, with the determined and unfailing support of the unified Communist world, to succeed in defeating South Vietnam in 1975.

Since 1975, North Vietnam has tightened its grip and imposed its totalitarian government on the South. Most individual rights and liberties have been suppressed; millions of people have been jailed or sent to concentration camps without trial; and nearly the entire population has been impoverished by arbitrary economic measures. The National Liberation Front of South Vietnam, long promised by North Vietnam the authority to govern the South as an autonomous and federated state, has been reduced to powerlessness. In the same vein, ethnic minorities to whom government autonomy had been promised by Communists from the North found themselves only more closely controlled by Vietnamese Communist cadres.

Oppression, abuses, and corruption have reached a level unprecedented in the history of Vietnam. Braving all dangers, thousands of Vietnamese have tried to escape by boat or on foot every year—a migration unprecedented in Vietnamese tradition. Communist Vietnam has also tried to expand control over its neighbors, sending troops to occupy Cambodia and increasing its influence in Laos. The occupation of Cambodia starting in the late 1970s has seriously handicapped Vietnam's economic development, turned Red China from ally to most dangerous enemy, and strained relations with most non-Communist countries, thus considerably reducing the Communist regime's legitimacy and power. Nevertheless, as long as Communist Vietnam manages to expand its power sufficiently to maintain continuity and stability of leadership, as it has in the past forty years, and to receive a sufficient power supplement from Moscow, it will survive. The regime's status in terms of legitimacy and power is illustrated in figure 5.[4]

SOUTH KOREA: 1948–1986

Cases of viable polities in the non-Communist Third World, although rare, exist in a few countries, for example, South Korea and Singapore. While sharing with other LDCs the problems of deficient legitimacy and power, South Korean regimes, despite temporary setbacks, appear to have succeeded in the long term, especially since the early 1960s, in the firm and positive use of power.

Liberated from thirty years of Japanese colonial rule, the Korean people were in an exhilarated mood, eager to modernize the country in the aftermath of the Second World War. Under U.S. military government from 1945 to 1948, well over 300 political parties were formed. In 1948, a constituent national assembly created through popular elections agreed on a constitution and elected Syng Man Rhee president of the First Republic.

The Rhee Regime: First Republic

THE POSITIVE USE OF POWER THAT INCREASED LEGITIMACY

A veteran revolutionary patriot who had spent half a century overseas fighting for Korean independence, Rhee, with his image as a superpartisan "national father," brought additional legitimacy to the regime. Supported, however, by mainly a loose and drifting coalition of rightist political organizations, Rhee had to struggle to expand his power base. His regime succeeded in establishing a new and independent national government, upholding law and order, securing international recognition and support, putting into effect some urgent social programs (universal education, agrarian reform), and maintaining unity of purpose and national solidarity during the period of resistance against North Korea's massive armed aggression (1950–1953).

Accomplishing this nation-building task with considerable U.S. assistance during the first five years of the infant republic helped enhance the legitimacy of the regime. To assist the country's recovery from the war, the regime vigorously implemented a program of financial stabilization and industrial development during the period from 1953 to 1958. A series of institutional innovations for a long-range development plan also were put into effect. Given the magnitude of

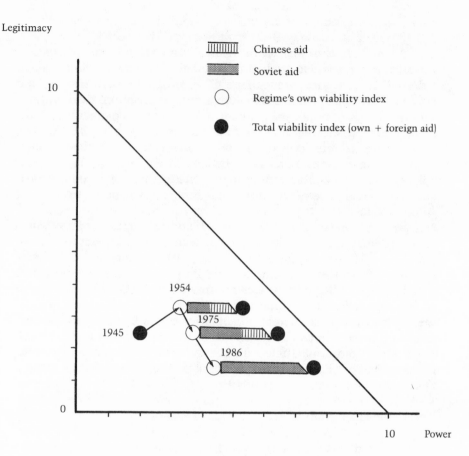

Legitimacy

10

Chinese aid

Soviet aid

○ Regime's own viability index

● Total viability index (own + foreign aid)

1954

1975

1945

1986

0

10   Power

Figure 5. Communist Vietnam Regime, 1945–1986

(For further elaboration on conceptual framework, see Figure 1, Polity Viability Chart, and the section that precedes it in chapter 1.)

war-related devastation, recovery tasks were relatively well performed and a credit to the regime, which should have enhanced its legitimacy.

Unfortunately, the effective recovery appeared to be offset by controversial measures Rhee used to consolidate and expand his personal power. A man of *yang ban* (upper class) origins with intensive and bitter experience of internal feuds among different political groups, Rhee was eager to retain sole control of political power and was jealous of anyone who showed promise as a likely successor. In creating his own party, Rhee abandoned his nonpartisan status and turned other parties against him. By treating his political lieutenants as either political rivals to be removed or mere instruments to be exploited, he failed to integrate different forces within his own party to serve a common cause.

After freely resorting to a series of political irregularities, Rhee ended up surrounding himself with obedient career bureaucrats turned politicians. These ambitious bureaucrats, who had served the Japanese colonial government, became an oligarchy within the Liberal party that dominated the political scene from 1957 to 1960. Power was more or less usurped by this group when President Rhee's energy and acumen declined as he entered his mideighties. The oligarchy's preoccupation with power control at the expense of economic development and its abusive exploitation, unchecked by moral scruples, led to the revolt of students and intellectuals that toppled Rhee's twelve-year regime and sent him into exile in April 1960.

The Democratic Administration: Second Republic

LEGITIMACY WITHOUT POWER

Emerging from an honest election organized by an interim administration consisting of respectable and politically neutral notables, the new government that opened the era of the Second Republic was led by the Democratic party that had opposed the Rhee regime. Having won a well-organized and clean election by a four-fifths majority, the Democratic administration started with a relatively high amount of legitimacy. The regime was, however, rather lacking in power. Indeed, despite its position as the sole organized political force in the aftermath of the April revolution and despite general support by the undifferentiated masses, the Democratic party had not originated the revolution that toppled its predecessor regime.

The Democratic party also suffered from a most serious lack of internal cohesion. As reported by Hahn Been Lee, the months following the election witnessed "the pathetic sight of a new ruling elite with an 80-percent majority in the National Assembly busily engaged in dangerous internal strife for hegemony with total disregard of the popular sense of urgency."[5] Factional strife paralyzed the party to the point of impotence at the threshold of power, created disenchantment, and aroused popular fury. These struggles destroyed whatever legitimacy or power the regime had and led to its demise after only nine months of existence, in May 1961.

The Park Chung Hee Era: Third and Fourth Republics

EFFECTIVE USE OF POWER TO ESTABLISH LEGITIMACY

The military administration that followed, taking over after a bloodless coup, suffered from an enduring handicap—its lack of legitimacy as a consequence of both its unconstitutional seizure of power and also a traditional cultural bias against the military. This lack of legitimacy was, however, effectively compensated by a positive use of power that the new administration possessed in rather substantial proportion, given the weakness of the civilian political sector and the support of military forces, which had been rapidly expanded and modernized following the war of 1950 to 1953. With the armed forces securing a basic framework of control for the regime, the military administration led by General Park Chung Hee integrated military and civilian managerial talents to prepare and put into effect the first Five-Year Economic Development Program.

BUILDING UP LEGITIMACY

Power was returned to a civilian government in December 1963 after two-and-one-half years of military rule. The strong man who emerged as president of the Third Republic was General Park himself. He had retired from the army to run for the presidency. With the legitimacy of his regime enhanced by the return to constitutional government and using the armed forces, the Korean Central Intelligence Agency, and the Democratic Republican party as power base, Park succeeded in transforming South Korea from a more or less traditional society into a modern industrialized one.

During Park's eighteen-year rule, the GNP grew at the remarkedly high annual rate of 10 percent from the early 1960s to the late 1970s. In the same period, per capita income rose from US $100 to $1,500, a highly respectable figure for an Asian country. To be sure, Park, in the interest of expanding his power base, took many measures that were controversial, especially in the eyes of many Western observers and groups opposing his rule. Examples are his amendment of the constitution of the Third Republic, and its later suspension and replacement by the *Yushin* (revitalization) constitution of the Fourth Republic, allowing him to continue in power; and the arbitrary methods used by his regime to deal with opposition groups.

Nevertheless, Park took great care to explain and justify these measures and submit them to the approval of public opinion through national referenda. More importantly, the outstanding results achieved thanks to his leadership, which, though highly authoritarian, was resolute, enlightened, and dedicated to the public good, appeared to more than offset the methods used.

While the whole nation can now be proud of these achievements and enjoy the fruit of Park's leadership, he and his wife paid for them with their lives. He was shot and killed by one of his close assistants, the director of the Korean CIA, on 26 October, 1979, apparently after a quarrel about the methods used to deal with the opposition. His wife had died five years earlier, victim of an assassination attempt carried out against him by a Communist terrorist. The way Park died presumably provided ultimate evidence of his quality as a Confucian superior man who chose as associates other gentlemen willing to serve a common and higher cause, but no small men (henchmen) whose primary concern is for their own selfish interests. As an oriental proverb goes, "While superior men disagree with each other but can live in harmony [because they are serving a higher cause], small men agree with each other but cannot live in harmony [because they are in conflict over the share of the pie in the long run]."[6]

The Fifth Republic: General Chun Doo Hwan

Perhaps thanks to this leadership oriented to the public good, after Park's abrupt death, South Korea appeared to remain in the hands of the positive forces that he had supported and left behind. To the observer, this legacy seemed to make the transition much smoother than it would otherwise have been. Following a transition period of less than a year, during which Premier Choi Kyu Hah served as acting president, General Chun Doo Hwan managed to be elected president in October 1980 by the National Conference for Unification in keeping with the provisions of the constitution of the Fourth Republic.

Early in 1981, a new constitution was proclaimed by Chun in an effort at reconciliation with the opposition, which had heavily criticized Park's *Yushin* constitution. Chun was elected president of the Fifth Republic in March 1981 under the new constitution, which provided for a seven-year term. He repeatedly vowed not to seek reelection.

Although the regime suffered a significant setback as a result of the sudden change in leadership, and especially due to the short period in which the Korean CIA was paralyzed, Korea has firmly continued its upward march toward modernization, joining the so called Gang of Four in the Pacific area who have performed economic miracles. The evaluation of the polity in terms of legitimacy and power, especially its upward movement since 1960, is summarized in figure 6.[7]

SINGAPORE: 1965–1986

Another regime that has admirably succeeded in building a viable polity is the People's Action party (PAP), led by Lee Kuan Yew in Singapore. A British Crown colony until 1963, Singapore enjoyed internal self-government beginning in 1959, became a semiautonomous state of Malaysia in 1963, and an independent republic on 8 September 1965. From that date, the people of Singapore have enjoyed continuing stability, prosperity, and progress under the enlightened leadership of Lee and his PAP.

Effective Use of Power to Create Legitimacy through Economic Development

Despite the many adverse factors confronting the republic at independence—the loss of economic hinterland and domestic market as a result of its separation from Malaysia and the reduction of its entrepôt trade due to conflict between Indonesia and Malaysia; the threat to its security and the loss of jobs resulting from the withdrawal of British troops—Singapore's economic growth, except for a short slowdown during the worldwide recession in the mid-1970s, has been remarkable throughout. With a GNP annual growth rate reaching 13 percent during some peak periods (1966–73) and per capita income reaching US $6,620 (1982), Singapore's standard of living is as high as Europe's.

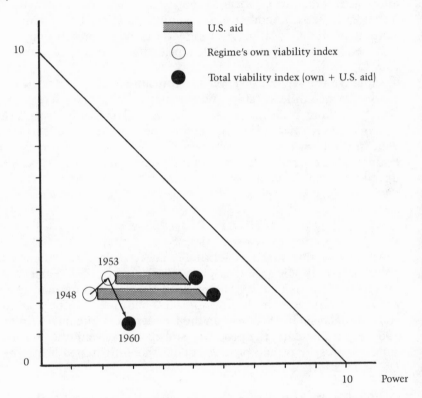

Figure 6a. South Korean Regimes: Syng Man Rhee Era (1948–1960)

(For further elaboration on conceptual framework, see Figure 1, Polity Viability Chart, and the section that precedes it in chapter 1.)

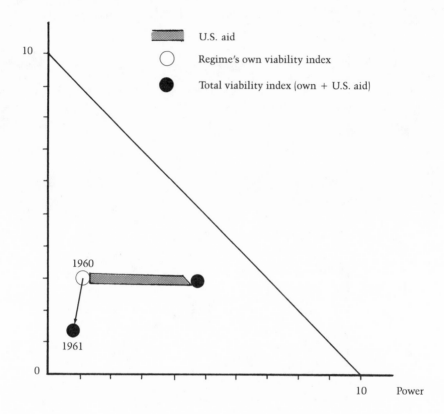

Figure 6b. South Korean Regimes: Second Republic Era (1960–1961)

(For further elaboration on conceptual framework, see Figure 1, Polity Viability Chart, and the section that precedes it in chapter 1.)

Legitimacy

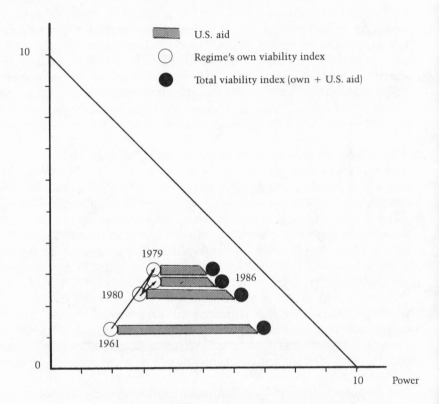

Figure 6c. South Korean Regimes:
Park Chung Hee (1961–1979) and Chun Doo Hwan (1980–1986)

(For further elaboration on conceptual framework, see Figure 1, Polity Viability Chart, and the section that precedes it in chapter 1.)

Credit for these achievements must go to policies soundly conceived by the leadership, which took fully into account the island republic's strengths and weaknesses, and to the effective implementation of these policies by a civil service reputed to be efficient and generally free of corruption.

CONSOLIDATION OF LEGITIMACY BY ESTABLISHING A MERITOCRACY

As in other LDCs, there is no real consensus on the political rules of the game among the people of Singapore. The parliamentary system borrowed from Great Britain may be familiar to a small minority of westernized members of the elite but is foreign to the majority of the Singaporeans, whose cultural origins are Chinese, Malaysian, or East Indian. Moreover, this elite's appreciation of the British system is academic rather than derived from real-life participative experience. In such a situation, application of the foreign model cannot by itself constitute a source of legitimacy for the government.

Premier Lee and his party have had to extend their power base to make up for insufficient legitimacy. By using power effectively and for the public good, they also have increased the legitimacy of their regime. Indeed, the labels commonly used by foreign observers to describe Singapore have been authoritarianism, stability, and efficiency. By adopting skills, performance, and dedication as criteria for status in the power hierarchy, the PAP has been able to supply parliament, cabinet, the higher civil service, citizen's groups, and community organizations with competent and dedicated cadres.

LEGITIMACY AND THE ROUTINIZATION OF CHARISMATIC LEADERSHIP

Achieving this meritocracy in employment, housing, education, multiracial harmony, and economic prosperity has made it progressively difficult for opposition parties to demonstrate a show of strength, offer significant alternative, or undermine popular confidence in Lee's leadership. Given Prime Minister Lee's dominance of the political scene for the last twenty or thirty years (thirty if the preindependence period is included), one may wonder about the succession problem, for Lee is now in his midsixties.

The answer may lie in the power structure of the PAP, which is likely to promote an orderly succession. Using merit as a basis for status in the party hierarchy, PAP has established an inner core of power that is notably cohesive and stable. Most members of the party's highest policy-making body also hold cabinet and parliamentary posts and were comrades in arms during the preindependence period. Lee's charismatic personality has been dominant in helping establish and consolidate a new and independent government; nevertheless, he remains a sort of primus inter pares, but not an autocrat.

The new system, moreover, seems to have reached a certain level of routinization or institutionalization that will allow an orderly search for Lee's successor and permit the latter to work with the support of the system. There are thus valid reasons to believe that the polity will be able, with or without Lee, to continue its steady improvement in legitimacy and its economic growth in the future. Figure 7 illustrates the viability index of Singapore under the Lee Kuan Yew regime (1965–86).[8]

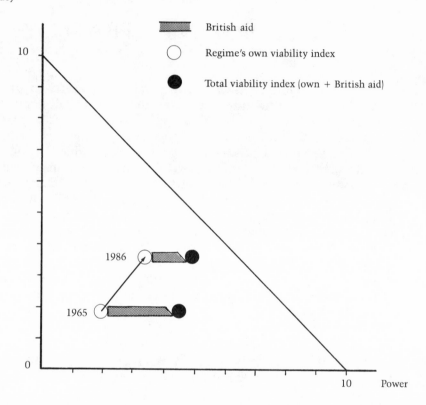

Legitimacy

British aid

Regime's own viability index

Total viability index (own + British aid)

10

1986

1965

0

10   Power

Figure 7. Singapore: Lee Kuan Yew/PAP Regime (1965–1986)

(For further elaboration on conceptual framework, see Figure 1, Polity Viability Chart, and the section that precedes it in chapter 1.)

4

DEVELOPMENT STRATEGY

THESE CASES OF SUCCESS AND FAILURE SUMMARILY REVIEWED DEMON-
strate the overriding importance of the political dimension of
development: The success or failure of development efforts made at
the micro level ultimately depends on success or failure at the macro
level, which in turn depends on whether the political leadership of an
LDC succeeds or fails in building a viable polity. The strategy proposed
as an alternative to the Communist model, with its characteristic
disregard of human rights, involves non-Communist LDC leadership
using power in a positive way to increase legitimacy of the regime, that
is, the willing self-compliance by the ruled (or consent of the governed,
in Western parlance). This, in turn, will permit a gradual decrease in
the use of power, that is, compliance through external constraints by
rulers. Here are the basic elements of the strategy: cultural renewal,
positive leadership, polity institution-building, and resolution of the
basic constraints.

CULTURAL RENEWAL AS A WAY OF ENHANCING A
SYSTEM'S LEGITIMACY

No society can survive without a moral foundation. As earlier discussion evinces, LDC culture has deteriorated to its lowest point after
centuries of contact with a dominating Western culture. This deterioration has made it extremely difficult for LDC leadership to use power
positively to increase the legitimacy of an LDC regime. The exercise of
power, which can hardly escape being taken advantage of by prevailing
negative forces, has rather undermined legitimacy and led to a vicious
cycle. Thus, an absolute need exists for cultural revival or depending
on the case, culture renewal, that is, a restoration of culture ideals that
creates favorable conditions for positive forces to triumph over negative ones and to make a positive use of power. Cultural renewal can be
achieved by integrating positive facets of both the home-grown and

imported values. If Japan, and to a certain extent, Singapore, and South Korea have been able to accomplish this, there is the possibility that other LDCs can do the same.[1]

A cultural revolution along these lines creates among the people a pride in their country, an essential element for building a nationalist ideology as an antidote for alien ideologies, for example, communism. It is imperative for people in the developing world to deny vehemently and eloquently that all negative features identified with their countries by Western and Eastern literature—oppression, abuses, corruption, authoritarianism, paternalism—*are* their cultural *values*.

Indeed, these social ills are behavioral realities reflecting the violation of LDC values rather than the values themselves. This is an extremely important qualification because the westernized elite, influenced by the overwhelming body of extant literature, often tends to believe that its national culture must be despised and rejected and replaced by a new culture imported from the West. An LDC elite who accepts this negation of his or her national culture is alienated from his or her own people.[2] Westerners who don't make that distinction between values and behavior tend to become cynical, disillusioned, or desperate after deploying futile efforts to change by imposing their own values.

Positive and Negative Interpretation of Cultures

All cultures that have enabled a community or society to survive the ups and downs of its history must contain many positive elements. The more fully people sharing a culture live up to its ideal elements, the better off the community or society; if the cultural ideals are violated, the community or society is diminished.[3]

The LDC societies are now in a period when violations of the ideal have become so prevalent that they are general rules rather than exceptions. But this is not necessarily an indictment of their cultures; to illustrate: What is labeled authoritarianism/paternalism reflects a violation of the oriental Confucian ethic but not the ethic itself. Hierarchy, an ideal feature of Confucianism for establishing societal order, assumes that superordinates possess more rights but also greater *responsibilities* than subordinates.

Superiors become authoritarian only when they pay more attention to their rights and privileges than their responsibilities; when they send subordinates' children to battle but their own overseas for graduate study; when they penalize subordinates but not their relatives for criminal behavior.

If superiors fail to do their duty and fulfill their obligations, if superiors commit abuses, subordinates cheat or revolt. Societal order is then disrupted. But whenever superiors are more conscious of responsibilities than their rights, subordinates follow their example, from either respect or fear, and societal order is maintained and enhanced. Rewards and punishments induce people to contribute to social order and progress if people perceive them to be fair and just.

In a deteriorating culture, old values continue to exercise a pull on some members of the society. The final month of South Vietnam's struggle against North Vietnam illustrates the pull of old values as well as the deterioration of the social order due to South Vietnam's crises in values previously described. Rather early in the last month before the fall of Saigon, many Vietnamese generals left their troops, fleeing overseas. But at least some generals chose to stay with their men and committed suicide because in their view they had failed to fullfil their responsibilities.[4] Similar instances can be found in the tug exerted by, and the resistance displayed to, nepotism, favoritism, and corruption in the deteriorating culture of some modern LDCs.

Nepotism is a negative form of the extended-family ideal. In keeping with the Confucian ethic, the family is the "technical prop" that helps realize the value of mutual solidarity. This social value has been promoted in the Orient as a way for society to deal with an unstable environment created by the vagaries inherent in rice cultivation. Family members in distress can expect to receive help from relatives. The best way for oriental individuals to achieve status is to give more help than they receive. This can best be achieved by entering the officialdom after studying hard and passing a difficult examination, given the high honor and economic income provided by the officialdom. Indeed, as confirmed by popular wisdom, "whenever a family member becomes a mandarin, the whole extended family benefits from it."

The negative side of helping one's family consists in granting illegal favors to relatives or engaging in corruption and fraud in order to be in a better financial position to provide for them. The positive side consists in fulfilling official duties with competence, dedication, and integrity so that the whole family can share one's good reputation, and of course in living frugally in order to be able to help a poor but bright cousin pursue his or her studies, to come to the rescue of an uncle whose crop has been destroyed by a long drought or a poor aunt who has been suffering from a long illness. Those who receive help are in turn expected to return it in some way when their situation allows them to do so or to provide help to their benefactors or the latters' offspring whose situation may decline or worsen at some later time.[5]

A case study illustrates how a mandarin lived up to this family ideal in ancient times: The emperor awarded a mandarin an invaluable and rarely found peach as recognition of the latter's integrity and dedication. The mandarin, who remained uncorrupted and poor, convened all members of his clan to share the emperor's award. The way the clan decided to share the honor was to boil the peach in a big pot of water so that each clan member could drink a small cup.[6]

Living under this ethic, Vietnamese also remind one another that "the law does not favor relatives."[7] A gentleman would say to his loved one who asks a favor, "I love you, darling, and put this love in my heart; as far as my official duties are concerned, I have to abide by the rules."[8] To her husband who feels saddened by the prospect of separation as he is about to join the armed forces to fight against foreign invasion, a lady would say that "public interest should take precedence over our private concern."[9]

The Need to Use Power to Restore and Reinforce a Culture's Positive Substance

This Confucian ideal can best be realized when those at the top who bear greater responsibility provide an example for those below. Emperors who put the interests of the country and people above that of their families' and their own have increased and strengthened the legitimacy of their rule to the extent that little force was needed.[10] There have also been emperors who did not hesitate to deal with the destructive forces of cultural decay by a heavy-handed use of power: capital punishments, such as having criminals eaten by tigers or thrown in boiling oil; cutting off a robber's hands. Provided that these drastic penalties were justified by the situation and directed to the public good, they contributed to the restoration of law and order and helped increase the legitimacy of the dynasty and decrease the necessity of relying on power in the long run.[11]

It can be assumed that like Confucianism, any culture has both its positive and negative sides. The usually dark picture of LDC cultures painted by most Western scholars appears to reflect mainly the negative. The bright picture of these same cultures provided by a few others seems to be based mainly on the positive. Presumably, the ideal and positive aspects of all cultures tend to converge around some universal values serving as a base for human values. The revival of Third-World cultural values may thus greatly facilitate the cross-cultural transfer of modern technology to serve development.[12]

Cultural Revival and Articulation with World Environment

Thus, many positive elements are already available in the LDC's culture, in the conscious and subconscious of LDC leaders and people. There is no need to turn to the "progressive" values of either the West or the East. The LDC has only to make a thorough study of its own culture, revive its ideal spirit, and create an environment encouraging and if need be, compelling, its people to live up to this spirit. Since every culture must adapt to, and evolve with, the modern national and international environment, cultural renewal does not mean reviving traditional formalities—rituals, ceremonies, costumes—that may be antiquated or traditional penalties based on the law of retaliation that may destroy the legitimacy of the new system. As demonstrated by Japan, most if not all modern technology, techniques, or processes and institutions can be adopted or adapted within the framework of this cultural renewal. But what does not work, what is futile, is borrowing indiscriminately from the West or from the East.[13]

POSITIVE LEADERSHIP

Cultural renewal cannot be achieved by reviving traditional institutions or creating modern institutions, such as a Department of Culture funded by foreign aid. The traditional institutions may not respond to modern needs; the new ones have been corrupted. Cultural renewal has to start with those sharing the culture returning to the positive aspects of the culture. This is no small or easy job given the duration and predominance of negative forces.

Qualities of Leadership

The role of top political leadership in this endeavor is therefore of prime importance. Only the power wielders have the means of accomplishing the objective. The success of such an effort by the leaders depends on several conditions. First, the top leaders themselves have to be able to live up to the cultural ideal, to provide the supreme example. It would be best if they were capable of establishing a record like that of Mahatma Gandhi, who succeeded in achieving a cultural renewal in India through his charismatic leadership. While it is unrealistic to expect charismatic leaders like Gandhi to emerge overnight in all or many LDCs, it should be noted that leadership charisma can be developed over time through outstanding achievements—recall Singapore's Lee and Korea's Park.

Second, LDC leadership should have the moral and physical courage to engage in such an endeavor, to take risks in dealing with negative forces that are ready to challenge them. Third, LDC leaders must have the intellectual capacity to devise a strategy to implement this renewal. While space does not permit discussing further such strategy, it suffices to say here that it would of necessity vary with each specific situation, taking into account the leader's power base and relative strengths and weaknesses of the negative and the positive forces.

Breaking the Vicious Cycle

Overall, the strategy consists in surrounding top leaders with other positive leaders who in turn provide the leverage and momentum for extending positive leaders down the line, ultimately giving the positive forces control over the environment.

Factors favoring this strategy are: (1) The negative forces, by their nature, are divided or can easily be divided to be defeated; (2) the effort has legitimacy; and (3) there is readiness on the part of the majority who have thus far violated cultural norms to return to positive behavior once the environment encourages them to do so.

The unfavorable factor is the difficulty of finding enough positive elements in the environment at the outset to support top leadership in this endeavor. If, however, top leaders have sufficient charisma, they should have the following to support them in their task. This is the route by which to break the vicious cycle confronting most LDC regimes, thus enhancing the legitimacy of the government, facilitating the positive exercise of power, and creating an atmosphere favorable to the resolution of other problems confronting the polity.[14]

POLITY INSTITUTION-BUILDING

Positive leadership behavior that exemplifies the ideal spirit of cultural values and contributes to the legitimacy of the system can hardly be sustained without an institutional framework that supports that behavior. To be sure, the confidence and respect inspired by a dedicated and enlightened or charismatic leadership are a badly needed major source of legitimacy during a transitional period when neither the out-of-fashion old institutions nor the newly imported legal-rational institutions can provide a firm basis of legitimacy for the polity.[15]

Legitimacy based on human charisma can nevertheless be easily eroded by human frailties and fallibilities in the absence of positive institutional norms to guide behavior and facilitate performance. Indeed, exemplary conduct can hardly be sustained and little can be accomplished in a bureaucratic system if civil service salaries do not permit employees to survive at even the minimum subsistence level let alone fulfill their legitimate obligations toward relatives. Under those conditions, no police chief can effectively enforce price control policies, especially when, for example, the price set has nothing to do with realities and makes it impossible for producers to survive. Nor can positive behavior be exemplified by applying cruel corporal penalties required by a legal system based on traditional religious law, such as severing limbs of convicted criminals. These devices, which served their purpose for a time, ought to be changed and replaced by new methods that are more appropriate to today's world.[16]

As a result of the vicious cycle discussed earlier, current institutions in most LDCs tend to be the product of a gradual accumulation of negative aspects of both ancient and modern institutions. With the support of culture renewal and positive leadership, the situation is now favorable for institutional regeneration through a happy integration of the positive sides of both. With regeneration, conditions can be created for effective organizations and effective people to mutually support the common effort to break the vicious cycle and sustain positive development. If served by competent and dedicated people, new institutions will be tested, adjusted, and adapted to changing circumstances. As these mature and become routinized with time, their values and norms will be accepted and internalized by the culture. When the new system reaches such a high degree of routinization that it is taken for granted, or becomes a way of life, it will be the main basis of legitimacy for the polity. Such is the case with the democratic system of government in Western countries like the United States or Great Britain.[17]

It is important to note that it takes generations or even centuries for a polity to reach that level of consensus about the basic rules of the game. What LDCs can hope for at this stage is to set the basis, the conditions, and directions for the process to start. The role of leadership in creating and supporting the new institutions remains dominant, as demonstrated by the Singapore and South Korean cases cited earlier. The appropriate institutional framework should vary with each country's specific situation. Some general guidelines can nevertheless be proposed here for consideration.

The Polity

Given the predominance of capitalism and communism in today's world, the choice available to LDCs tends in the final analysis to be quite restricted. There are two basic polity models to choose from: the Western democratic model or the Communist model.

THE COMMUNIST MODEL

Experience has demonstrated that successful adoption of this model requires conditions that are not easily obtained. One is the willingness to abide by discipline imposed by the monolithic Communist bloc headed by one big boss, which means, for all practical purposes, surrendering forever a country's independence. The second condition is readiness to adopt the Communist ideology as interpreted and reinterpreted by the Kremlin, an ideology that may be completely alien to the LDC culture. The third condition is the ability to create an elaborate and monopolistic party apparatus to implement this totalitarian ideology by intensive and extensive use of power that disregards all human rights.

Without accepting the first condition, which trades national independence for unfailing support from the Soviet Union, the successful application of the second and third conditions proves extremely difficult, if not impossible, given pressures exerted by the free world. Moreover, once having fallen into the Soviet orbit, the country can hardly hope to leave it. The bitter loss of Yugoslavia and China has made the USSR more determined than ever not to let any satellite escape its control again, as has been demonstrated by the cases of Hungary, Czechoslovakia, Poland, and Afghanistan.

Without national independence, any regime would find it very difficult to increase or even maintain its legitimacy. A shortage of legitimacy requires an ever-increasing use of force for the sake of survival. Since a regime's own ability to resort to power is limited, additional power must come from the USSR to help the regime survive. Increasing dependency on a foreign master further undermines a regime's legitimacy, which in turn necessitates further power supplements from, and further dependency on, a foreign master. The difficulty is further compounded by the latter's firm determination to keep the satellite in its tight grips. Poland appears to be struggling desperately to find a way out of this dilemma. It behooves LDC leaderships to think twice, therefore, before deciding to commit their countries to this venture.[18]

THE WESTERN MODEL

Although it is in no way perfect, the Western model of democratic government appears to be the only alternative for non-Communist LDCs that want to survive and grow in today's world.

Familiarity of the Model. The Western model has indeed become a norm for LDCs, especially if they must depend on the West for aid. Not only is Western-styled democracy taken for granted by Western countries' taxpayers, whose ultimate agreement is necessary for the continuation of foreign aid, it also permeates the values, attitudes, and behaviors of most non-Communist donor institutions and their staffs. The westernized Third-World intelligentsia tends to see some form of this model as a must for their countries, too. As a result of pressures from all these quarters, most, if not all, non-Communist LDC regimes have had to adopt some version of the Western model or have at least promised to do so within a certain time frame. In short, a democratic form of government is needed to provide some basis of legitimacy for the regime, especially vis-à-vis the external world and the local elite. This legitimacy in turn facilitates the acquisition and exercise of power by the regime to enhance its legitimacy further.[19]

Adaptability of the Model. Fortunately, the Western model is broad and flexible enough to lend itself to meaningful adaptation by each LDC, taking into account specific situations. The model allows for retention of a monarch who can serve as supreme representative of the state, symbol of national unity, and mediator between competing groups. It can accommodate a dominant party, two-party, or multiparty system. The Western model can take the presidential form, the parliamentary form, or a mixture of both, and it can fit into a unitary state or a federation of states. It allows for a wide variety of centralization and decentralization or separation and integration of authority. The model provides the regime with legal and technical devices to deal with all kinds of emergencies. The LDC leadership can carefully study different variations of the model or their combination and experiment with those that best fit the country's situation.

Confluence of the Democratic Spirit in All Cultures. With cultural renewal and positive leadership, a meaningful democratic base can be established, the more so since all cultures, in ideal terms, contain some basic elements of democracy from which to build a democratic form of government. A study of Confucian cultures, for example, is quite revealing in this respect. According to Confucianism, the emperor, or heaven's son, is mandated to rule by executing heaven's will. But heaven's will has been interpreted explicitly by some Confucian schools as nothing else than the people's will; thus, to follow the people's will is to follow heaven's will. The modern rational-legal concept or "the right person for the right job" is also expressed in such teachings as "one must use people just like using wood" or "the king must behave as king, the mandarin as mandarin, the father as father, and the son as son" (in accordance with the rights and duties befitting each position in the hierarchy). A monarch who does not fulfill his or her responsibilities does not deserve the title anymore because "to eliminate a tyrant is no different than to eliminate any dangerous criminal."[20]

A great effort has also been made to improve the rationality of the system of selecting office holders. In order to prevent royal successors of ill repute from harming the dynasty and the nation, the rule of automatic succession by male primogeniture was often replaced by more flexible rules permitting the king, in his will, to designate among his children the one he thought best qualified to succeed him or charging a group of senior mandarins to do so. The change sometimes went so far as to abolish the rule of hereditary succession altogether and replace it with the rule of "succession by merit" according to which a council of senior mandarins selects as the deceased king's successor that mandarin who most deserved to succeed him. In the same vein, the feudal system of selecting mandarins through hereditary succession was replaced for good long ago by a democratic system of recruitment by examinations in which any qualified individual among the common people could participate.[21]

Government structures and processes were also established by impersonal and general rules to encourage positive behavior and discourage negative behavior. The king was supposed to make decision to enhance public interest in consultation with the council of ministers. It was his duty to serve the country and care for his people as his own children. The control mechanisms usually established as checks on his behavior were: (1) limits on his authority set by tradition, on which senior mandarins were supposed to advise him; (2) the historian-mandarin, who was required to record faithfully what the king did, whether good or bad. The historian's writings could not be influenced by anybody and were to be kept in public archives as national history. (3) Imperial censors whose job was to advise the sovereign against any wrongdoing; some of these mandarins, in showing their fidelity to the regime, went as far as to commit suicide in front of the sovereign as the ultimate attempt to convince him to act correctly. To prevent corruption, abuses, and oppressions in the officialdom, such objective rules as reward and penalty in accordance with fair and impartial rules were instituted. Offices too powerful to be checked on, such as that of the queen, heir apparent, or prime minister were sometimes abolished altogether.[22]

Integration of Home-grown and Imported Elements. The preceding examples show the possibility of reviving ideal institutional elements that already exist in an LDC culture and integrating them with newly imported institutions to create a viable polity based on the Western democratic model as an antidote to the Communist model. Yet, little research has been done to this effect. To be sure, many discrete features of the Western polity model have already been applied in non-Communist LDCs. Used and misused, however, as mere power instruments by successive regimes preoccupied with short-run political expediencies, modern institutions borrowed from the West have become corrupted, perverted, and dysfunctional.[23] Short-run considerations at the micro level have apparently led to a failure to consider basic conditions at the macro level that help the model to work. These conditions appear to be (1) symbiotic relationships between the political party and government system; (2) symbiotic relationships between public and private sectors; and (3) the legal system that defines these relationships as well as the function and operational procedures of institutions in each system and sector.

The Party and the Government

THE PARTY AS AN INTEGRATING INSTITUTION

The modern institution that serves as the unifying element of the nation-state is the political party. This is the mechanism, par excellence, that looks at society as a whole and provides integration of its various parts by linking people and government, different interest groups, and by relating different branches, sectors, and levels of government and society to one another.[24] The political party is by far the most important institution in Communist countries. Indeed, training leadership cadres in ideology, organization, strategies, and tactics to integrate different means of achieving the proletarian revolution has been heavily emphasized by Moscow.[25]

On the free world's side, the effort to build political parties as integrating institutions appears to be grossly inadequate if not completely neglected. Thanks to the fight for independence, many former colonies managed to create outstanding revolutionary nationalist parties. But once independence was regained, the latter lost their fervor and become divided, corrupt, and ineffectual as instruments of government. Besides, the fact that good—that is, dedicated, effective, successful—revolutionaries do not necessarily make good politicians and administrators, the main reason for this incapacity appears to be loss of common denominators that unified party cadres and shielded them from corruption: the cause of independence and the common enemy.[26]

IDEOLOGY AS AN INSTRUMENT TO UNIFY AND ACTIVATE THE PEOPLE

There is no dearth of common denominators that LDC leadership can tap to sustain or restore the momentum: modernizing the country, establishing social justice, improving the standard of living, preserving national sovereignty. These higher national causes would not become slogans to be contradicted by daily realities if the leadership were to show dedication and competence in achieving them. Backed by a movement of cultural renewal and exemplary leadership, these causes can provide a strong moral incentive for people and groups to join and use the party as a forum to aggregate, articulate, and adjudicate divergent interests. Such an atmosphere would facilitate the integration of parochial interests, making them mutually consistent and supportive and contributive to national interest.[27]

THE PARTY AS AN INSTRUMENT TO FACILITATE EFFECTIVE EXERCISE OF GOVERNMENTAL POWER

A party that can effectively integrate positive forces to serve the public good constitutes a strong power base for the government. It supports the government by providing leadership cadres and mobilizing the people to help implement governmental programs. It also helps maintain stability and order and prevent abuses, fraud, and corruption. The government, in turn, provides the means for the party to realize its purpose, train its cadres, and develop its membership. Since this symbiotic relationship between party and government leads to prosperity and progress for the nation, the legitimacy of the regime will increase. Singapore provides a good illustration of effective cooperation between both institutions within the framework of a parliamentary form of government adapted from Great Britain. As observed earlier, both party and government use the same criteria for merit—dedication and performance—to recruit and allocate human resources in the service of the country. Further study of this experience would be of great help to other LDCs.[28]

Public and Private Sectors

Another fundamental consideration at the macro level that would allow for successful institution-building at the micro level is the symbiotic relationship between public and private sectors. Without the private sector as an economic base, the public sector can hardly support itself. On the other hand, without a public sector that provides internal and external security, and a basic infrastructure, the private sector can hardly develop.

LIBERATION AND DEVELOPMENT OF THE PRIVATE SECTOR AS A MEANS OF ENHANCING LEGITIMACY AND FACILITATING EFFECTIVE USE OF POWER

For a variety of reasons, many non-Communist LDCs have strongly emphasized the role of the public sector in development. As time goes on, the neglected and impoverished private sector becomes unable to support the ever-increasing cost of public sector operations through taxes or public service fees. The day comes when the overextended public sector finally succumbs to its own weight.[29]

It is thanks to resources provided by a developed private sector that governments can afford to pay public servants a decent salary and provide them with the necessary means for doing their jobs. A strong private sector, conscious of its rights and responsibilities, can also serve as a check on bureaucratic abuses and corruption. Again, the Singapore experience deserves to be cited. With a rational allocation of resources according to merit, backed by strong disciplinary measures and a generous compensation system made possible by a developed private sector, this country has been able to keep the prestige and morale of public employees high and to maintain a public service that is effective and generally free from corruption.[30]

PUBLIC SECTOR TO SUPPORT BUT NOT SUBSTITUTE FOR THE PRIVATE SECTOR

For the public-private symbiosis to work, the public sector must extend its role only to the extent necessary to facilitate development of the private sector. What the government should do first, and do well, is fulfill the classical role of the so-called "gendarme" state in providing security, justice, basic education, public health and welfare, and the physical infrastructure. In the field of economic development, the government should confine its role to creating a favorable environment that encourages the private sector to operate.

Instead of overextending its role and finally becoming bogged down with thousands of projects run by bureaucratic units or parastatals, the government should concentrate its effort on developing an economic and financial infrastructure that favors development of the local private sector and attracts the foreign business sector. Most LDCs already possess many comparative advantages on which foreign enterprises want to capitalize, such as cheap labor, abundant raw materials, and unexploited mineral resources.[31] To these advantages, governments can add an atmosphere in which the free enterprise system can operate and flourish: guarantees that there will be no arbitrary nationalization, liberal exchange rates, appropriate tax incentives, reasonable regulation and control, a fair and effective judicial system, reliable communication and transportation structures, and attractive profit remittance rates.

EFFECTIVE USE AND CONTROL OF FOREIGN CAPITAL INVESTMENT

The public sector can facilitate and encourage joint ventures between local and foreign private sectors. If the local private sector is too weak to engage in such ventures, the government can create mixed enterprises with government participation to start with and increase participation of the local private sector over time. To preserve the country's sovereignty and independence, the government should involve business firms from many countries, so that no single country exercises too heavy an influence on the local economy. The government should also maintain an effective control mechanism to make sure it receives its fair share of taxes and to prevent fraud and corruption.[32] The more the private sector develops, the more resources can be shared by the public sector to improve and expand public service in support of the expanding private sector. Economic and technological development require more and more intervention on the part of the government, and effective intervention requires more resources, which have to be supplied by the private sector. It is necessary to maintain this balance between the public and private sectors in order to avoid the vicious cycle now entrapping so many LDCs.

REALIZING SOCIAL JUSTICE IN ORDER TO ENHANCE LEGITIMACY

Adopting the free enterprise system does not prevent LDCs from realizing their social policies in a way congruent with their cultures. Many technical devices have been used effectively in Western countries to correct deficiencies of the market economy without doing too much harm to its successful operation. These are, for example, the progressive income tax system and the mechanism of income transfer through various welfare policies that allow the state to take care of the poor, old, handicapped, and underpriviledged. Unless a developed private sector provides a larger pie, there is not much to share, nor is there much with which to build an effective public service capable of developing and enforcing appropriate social policies.[33]

In short, maintaining a dynamic equilibrium between the public and private sectors by fostering their symbiotic relationships is a necessary condition for making both sectors effective, responsible, and respectable. This in turn will facilitate the regime's positive exercise of power to improve economic productivity and production and achieve equal justice. These achievements will help increase the legitimacy of the polity, thus augmenting the upward spiral.

THE LEGAL SYSTEM

Government by law but not by people is one of the most basic features of the Western model of democracy.[34] All institutions must operate within the framework of law. The law, that instrument with which individuals and groups achieve societal goals, is closely related to the legitimacy and power of public institutions, in particular, and of the whole polity, in general. To the extent that a law is accepted as legitimate, institutions will share that legitimacy and have an easy job implementing it. Otherwise, they have to use power, that is, legal action in this case, to enforce it.

The Pervasive Problem of Noncompliance in LDCs

In Western countries, self-compliance is usually the norm and forced compliance the exception. This is the way social stability, order, and progress are sustained at a manageable cost to the whole society. In most non-Communist LDCs, laws and regulations tend to remain merely on paper due to the lack of both self-compliance and forced compliance. This low level of legal compliance has already led to a more or less anarchic situation in many countries in the Third World.[35] Thus, an urgent need exists to improve the legitimacy of the law as well as the power to enforce it in order to increase the level of legal compliance.

Leadership and Legal Compliance

The legitimacy of the law and its enforcement through self-compliance can be greatly improved if the law is followed first and foremost by the leadership itself, starting with the very top. Leadership's law-abiding behavior serves as an example for others to follow. This condition does not appear to be too difficult to obtain in an atmosphere of cultural renewal backed by positive leadership already discussed.[36]

Legitimacy of the Law

Law-abiding behavior, nevertheless, can be self-induced only to the extent that the law itself is perceived as legitimate. A great deal of effort should be made to improve the quality of the legal framework, especially by dropping arbitrary, unjust, absurd, or unenforceable rules that result from successive piecemeal measures taken to deal with short-run political issues. An improved political climate made possible by cultural renewal and positive leadership, as well as a gradual return to, or progress toward, a market economy, will facilitate any efforts to enhance the legitimacy of the law.[37]

Law Enforcement

Making good laws it not enough if they cannot be enforced. An effective use of legal power to force compliance is necessary not only to achieve social goals of order, stability, and progress, but also to increase the legitimacy of the legal system itself and thus to increase self-compliance. Abuse or misuse of legal power will lead to reverse results, which may be called the legal vicious cycle.[38]

Improvement in the law enforcement capability of the public sector is thus an absolute need. Modern techniques of legal self-compliance that are applied firmly and fairly with due respect for human rights will enhance the credibility of the legal institutions, in particular, and of the polity, in general.

The legitimacy of the law can be increased even more rapidly if the enforcement effort is directed, first and foremost, at the strongest negative forces in the society, the manifestly illegal vested interests acquired during the long period of cultural decline, the large fortunes amassed through abuses, corruption, and frauds. South Korea, for instance, has confiscated substantial illegally accumulated private assets to be used by the government to develop the country. One politician has offered to turn over his private fortune of $36 million to the state and stay out of politics as a price for his freedom.[39] Concentrating law enforcement efforts on the largest targets first can help persuade smaller ones to give up their resistance, making them much easier to deal with. On the other hand, attacking small, weak, and easy targets while sparing the strongest ones because they are difficult to handle, undermines the legitimacy of the system and increases resistance, making it much more difficult and costly to complete the task.[40]

THE RESOLUTION OF BASIC CONSTRAINTS

A review of the formidable list of constraints currently confronting most LDCs at the macro level calls attention to (1) a heavy foreign debt on which the interest alone can hardly be serviced without creating political turmoil and hampering further development efforts; (2) a gradual but steady deterioration of the construction, equipment, and materials left by foreign aid; (3) an ineffectual, inert, underpaid, and overextended public sector; (4) an unproductive parapublic sector ever relying on foreign funding for survival; (5) a backward private sector; (6) an apathetic rural mass devastated by misery and famine as well as deforestation and soil erosion on an unprecedented scale; and (7) an alienated urban population frustrated by unemployment and inflation and ready to revolt against any attempt to reduce or abolish its vested interests, such as food price subsidies.[41]

Together, this situation constitutes a vicious cycle that defies all uncoordinated solutions. Its resolution requires a dramatic improvement in the polity's performance. The strategy previously proposed offers a basic framework for a comprehensive, long-term national policy to achieve this objective. Charismatic leadership, cultural revival, and institutional renewal join forces to ensure societal compliance in dealing with these problems.

Cooperative Atmosphere Created by Consensus on Rules of the Game

Cultural revival helps leadership restore mutual respect and confidence in society. In this atmosphere, which encourages well-mannered behavior, friends and foes can sort out disagreements and come to a consensus on the highest law of the land and on the basic rules of the game and then faithfully implement them. This is the atmosphere in which democratic forms of government integrating the best sides of the home-grown and imported cultures can be meaningfully developed. A polity built on this basis can lend itself to long-term legitimization both internally and externally.

Mutual Support between Politics and Administration

The symbiotic relationship between party and government, as defined by an effective legal framework and nurtured by committed law-abiding leaders will allow for a harmonious coexistence of politicization and professionalization within the public sector work force. There is little harm if the party member is at the same time a professionally competent bureaucrat. If he or she is a dedicated law-abiding individual, the combination of both roles might even permit the party member to serve better public interests. If both professional and political competence cannot be combined in the same person, politicians and career officials can complement each other effectively in an atmosphere of mutual respect to serve higher institutional interests. Putting the right person in the right place is one of the basic conditions for boosting the morale and competence of the personnel and thus enhancing the legitimacy and authority of public employees and institutions. This is a necessary condition for administrative or technical development programs to succeed at the micro level, whether in manpower training or institution building.

Privatizing and Improving Public Sector Performance

A gradual process of privatizing public enterprises and liberalizing the private sector economy to allow free enterprise will relieve the public sector of many unnecessary burdens. Expanding the market economy will provide a firm basis for the symbiotic relationship between the public and private sectors. This will permit removal of two basic constraints that have stood in the way of reforms to improve the performance of the public sector: (1) the gross and absurd inequalities in compensation between the civil service sector funded essentially by local resources and the parastatal sector funded by foreign aid; (2) the often too-low salary level for civil servants. Eliminating inequities and restoring public sector compensation to a decent level as compared with salaries/wages in other societal sectors is also a necessary condition for improving the morale of the public sector work force, for reducing corruption and abuses, and enhancing institutional performance in the public sector.

Performance Improvement as a Result of Professionalization of the Public Work Force

Professionalization as the moral incentive and compensation as the material incentive are required elements for improving performance capacity in all sectors and institutions. They can hardly be obtained without drastic and painful policy changes at the macro level, as proposed in the preceding strategy. Since they involve fundamental and long-term decisions on allocating national resources, such changes create a viable framework for development projects at the micro level. These projects can then contribute meaningfully to the improved performance of institutions in various sectors and areas. An overall improvement in performance will help resolve other difficulties.

The Upward Spiral

Strong and effective public and private sectors will restore domestic and international confidence, allowing for easier borrowing to further economic development and reimburse foreign debt; to operate and maintain enterprises begun with foreign aid; and to deal with such obstacles to rural development as soil erosion and deforestation. If nothing succeeds like success, the upward spiral will feed itself to sustain the momentum. As the political and economic situation spirals upward, there is considerable hope that local capital deposited abroad and local human resources residing overseas will return to contribute to the development of the home country.

5

PROPOSED CHANGES IN
DEVELOPMENT ASSISTANCE
POLICY

IT IS HIGH TIME FOR THE FOREIGN AID COMMUNITY TO TAKE A HARD look at costs and benefits of its work in general systems terms. How much has been spent and how much has been gained in overall results? How much have taxpayers in advanced countries contributed, and to what benefit, to those who live in poverty in the Third and Fourth worlds? Development organizations would be well advised to undertake self-evaluations to determine (1) to what extent they have helped the developing world; (2) to what extent they have caused or contributed to Third-World problems: and (3) who in the final analysis has benefited the most from the total amount of aid—the poor or the privileged of the Third World; Western commercial firms; or development bureaucrats, experts, and specialists? After such soul searching, after rethinking its overall approach at this strategic level, the development community will find it necessary to broaden its outlook, to abandon its predilection for piecemeal or blueprint solutions and solely professional/technical terms of reference, and to undertake a hard quest for ways to tackle the political dimension.

VICIOUS CYCLE FOR FOREIGN AID

Western foreign aid thus far provided to nonviable LDC polities has created a real dilemma. Among the problems to which there have been no satisfactory solutions, one can cite the following.

Intervention versus Nonintervention, Security versus Economic-Social Humanitarian Aid

The long-extended debate between those who want to intervene and those who do not and between those who emphasize economic/social/

humanitarian aid and those who advocate military aid appears to miss the mark, leading nowhere. Nonintervention in LDCs where regimes possess neither legitimacy nor power would seem to precipitate their fall into the Communist orbit.[1] International communism with overt or covert parties everywhere is more than ever ready to take advantage of chaotic situations. Impotent regimes lacking both legitimacy and power cannot but become an easy prey to national chapters of an extensive and sophisticated international revolutionary network directed by a superpower that has been preparing to dominate the world since the Soviet Revolution of 1917. With an ideology appealing to the poor, weak, and oppressed and a propaganda machinery capitalizing on injustices and excesses created by capitalism, imperialism, colonialism, and neocolonialism accepted by revolutionaries ready to live or die for a cause and trained by Moscow in the technique of *agitprop* (agitation and propaganda), it is relatively easy for Communist parties to seize power and establish some rudiment of legitimacy. Their advantage is greater because other parties in the disintegrated society, lacking support of such a monolithic international network, can hardly compete.

In any event, the local Communist shortage of legitimacy, however serious it may be, can be fully compensated for by whatever amount of power is needed. It is a well-known fact that Communist regimes have excelled in using power to establish a new order by destroying all opposition parties and eliminating all vested interests. In this endeavor, they have a ready model to follow and the strongest international network to support them. And more importantly, this network has seldom failed to be a faithful ally offering continuing support until it achieves its ends.

Western intervention, either military or economic, may prolong an impotent regime's survival. Ultimately, either strategy ends in disaster because it is impossible to continue increasing amounts of aid forever.[2] Guns and butter can, of course, help a "soft" regime survive by increasing its power. Misuse of these means for the sake of a regime's survival in an environment dominated by negative forces, however, decreases that regime's legitimacy, as discussed earlier. If such a regime is to survive, increasing power and thus increasing foreign aid are required to make up for decreasing legitimacy. And the vicious cycle sets in until foreign aid ceases. Then the regime falls. Other non-Communist regimes may take over, repeating the same cycle until a vacuum for a Communist take-over is created. Once Communists are in control, the situation becomes irreversible.

If the effect of foreign aid is viewed in such long and general terms, incremental correctional measures, such as investigations to check whether aid monies or materials have been diverted to questionable purposes, do not make sense. In the long run, such measures become a joke and cannot but reflect the donors' naïveté. Such ineffective controls not only create tension between donor and recipient governments but may also damage whatever scarce legitimacy the aid-receiving regime has at a time when its survival requires the injection of more power, which, in the final analysis, must come from additional aid.

Publicized scandals about Western corporations resorting to unethical means, such as bribes, kickbacks, and influence peddling to do business with LDC government officials, undermine a regime's legitimacy and can erode confidence in the free enterprise system. Moreover, the stricter Western governments are in applying negative sanctions against nationals' corrupt dealings, the more difficulties they create for their business firms competing in the Third World with other international corporations. Indeed, in such an LDC business environment, companies failing to participate in corruption lose out to competition. Firms wishing to preserve their integrity have no recourse but to withdraw their business altogether from the LDCs, leaving the latter in the hands of unscrupulous competitors. Is such withdrawal congruent with national interest?

More importantly, withdrawing help from a friendly country in a distressing situation during its fight against communism is something a donor country can hardly afford to do or cannot do without losing the confidence and respect of other allied countries.[3] It is well for Western country leaders to realize that an open debate over continuing or withdrawing aid, not necessarily actual withdrawal, constitutes, in the eyes of the recipient country's leaders, nothing less than a kangaroo court in which their very lives are at stake and can be a sort of self-fulfilling prophecy. Doubts about their fate urge such leaders to prepare for their eventual fall from the tiger's back and the preparation will precipitate the fall.[4]

Bureaucratized and Self-Serving Donor Institutions

Since World War II, donor institutions that, in principle, were created to put themselves out of work have instead prospered and expanded with the increasing number of grants, loans, and accumulated debts of LDCs.[5] Despite half a century of effort, almost everything seems to remain at the experimentation stage:[6] A variety of approaches combining physical and social sciences, involving all kinds of experts and specialists appear to have been futile in resolving the problems of underdevelopment. What has emerged clearly from this long and persevering effort of experimentation, surveys, implementation, appraisal, and evaluation is a proliferation of bureaucracies in all sectors—public, private, nonprofit—with their vested interests in development assistance. With this bureaucratization, experts in many specializations have acquired life-time tenure. Despite numerous reforms undergone by these bureaucratic institutions, no real way for them to work effectively for the development of LDCs has emerged.

Indeed, there is little that Western donor institutions and experts can offer nonviable LDC polities. The reason is obvious. While the former work under the assumption of the Western democratic model, the latter have followed no model at all. What these LDC regimes have done thus far has been dictated by short-run political considerations, a patchwork of inconsistencies and contradictions resulting in a labyrinth defying all the Western model solutions that have conditioned Western donor institutions and experts. In fact, there is little the Western and westernized professional development community can hope to contribute in situations requiring political rather than administrative or technical answers.

It is easy under these circumstances for organizations to become self-serving bureaucracies sheltering themselves under more and more complex rules and procedures whose observance becomes an end in itself and a way for employees to justify their existence rather than a means of accomplishing results.[7] Since few conscientious professionals want to continue after repeated unsuccessful trials, those who remain within the bureaucracies may be motivated more by perks of the office than a desire to help LDCs. The dilemma confronting the aid community seems to be well summarized by Hilary Ng'Weno, a columnist for *Newsweek International* and editor-in-chief of the *Weekly Review* in Nairobi, Kenya. Having declared African leaders responsible for the misfortunes suffered by their peoples, he refers to foreign aid in these terms:

> Now there is much less awe in Africa about the foreign expert who flits from one capital to another discussing economic cures from his briefcase. Back in their home countries many of these people would probably not be allowed to tinker with a small-scale firm, let alone an entire nation.[8]

Given the dismal overall results of Third-World development attempts, something seems basically wrong with using an expert at an average annual cost of about $150,000 to extend help to a farmer whose annual income may be less than $50. The cost is all the more difficult to justify when it is included in the loan to be reimbursed later by the farmer and his offspring.

The Dependency Cycle

Aid would work to the benefit of both giving and receiving countries if imported equipment and materials could be used to generate more capital, thereby providing recipient countries with operation and maintenance funding and facilitating the importation of new equipment and materials for further development. Instead of being used to expand international trade, aid has created an ever deeper cycle of LDC dependency on advanced countries, generating needs for more and more grants and loans to import more equipment, materials, and commodities. Commercial firms in industrialized countries may benefit from this cycle in the short run at the expense of taxpayers in both developed and developing countries. However, this cycle cannot be prolonged beyond a certain limit without creating a general bankruptcy when LDCs can no longer afford to service their debts. In order to avoid a state of affairs that disrupts the world economic order, more grants and loans will be required repeatedly and forever. Can the economic situation in industrialized countries permit such a game to continue indefinitely? Can an aid system that by 1985 had led to an annual net flow of capital from LDCs to developed countries be maintained or tolerated any longer? The answer has to be no.[9]

Refugees from LDCs

While Western countries may benefit from the LDCs' brain drain, large numbers of refugees from Third-World countries have already created insoluble problems. Yet no light can be seen at the other end of the tunnel. The political, security, and economic situation in many LDCs tends to encourage more and more nationals to leave by whatever means regardless of the dangers. The illegal inflow of Latin Americans to the United States of America is common knowledge, and Europe is expected to be submerged by Afro-Asians and Latin Americans by the end of the century. According to a French government estimate, for example, more than half of France's population under twenty-five will be of foreign origin by the year 2,000. In quite a few countries, negative reactions against foreigners from the Third World have been accumulating. With the massive number longing for resettlement and the deteriorating situation in LDCs pushing out more and more people, no end appears to be in sight.[10]

GENERAL AID POLICY IMPLICATIONS

All these problems appear to require a common political solution: the development of viable polities, polities capable of enlisting societal compliance in the service of public good through a positive use of power to increase their legitimacy. Thus, a pressing need exists for Western donor institutions to redirect their efforts, to tackle the political dimension of development. This may mean helping to establish Third-World polities capable of beating the West at its own game by successfully adopting the Western democratic free enterprise model of development. In this way, groundwork will be established for symbiotic relationships between LDCs and Western democracies as equal partners working for the long-term benefit of both sides.

The West's Interest Lies in LDC Independence

Paradoxically enough, it is in the West's interest to create independent Third-World polities that are able to compete with the West. During colonial times, the dependent relationship between mother country and its colonies worked because the latter, while not independent, were viable polities. Colonies, with some notorious exceptions, were well governed and administered. Even though the legitimacy of colonial governments could not be high for obvious reasons, power was in most cases freely and effectively used to ensure security, stability, and progress. When LDCs were nominally independent, their dependent economic relationships with dominant trade centers tended to make them informal colonies. The unequal relationships, which benefited metropoles more than peripheries, nevertheless conformed with a world order agreed on among international forces at the times.

With the access of former colonies to political independence, many Western powers have attempted to maintain previous economic relationships between them and their former colonies.[11] What is missing in this relationship, however, is a viable polity in the independent LDC, a polity capable of replacing the former colonial government in creating favorable conditions for shaping and maintaining this relationship. In many LDCs, so-called liaison elites have been induced to serve short-run interests of privileged minorities at the expense of the LDC masses. In this role, these elites can hardly earn enough respect to establish and increase their regimes' legitimacy. Trained to depend on foreign masters, to make a good life the easy way, and emphasize perks more than responsibility, the elites often do not dare to use power to span the legitimacy gap. When they do, they must think of protecting their own interests, of the day when they fall off the tiger's back.

Consequently their use of power is indecisive, clumsy, and damages the regime's legitimacy. If these elites are determined to make full use of power, their effort is diverted by negative forces to serve selfish interests, which in turn require ever-increasing power beyond the limit acceptable to world opinion. In short, the LDC petite bourgeoisie serving as an instrument for the neocolonial policy adopted by the West is no match for Communist forces trained and nurtured by Moscow for a revolutionary cause in behalf of the masses.

It behooves the West, for the sake of its long-term interest, to rethink its basic policy toward the Third World. Western countries must support LDCs' genuine national independence as an antidote to communism as well as the only way of avoiding the dependency-bankruptcy dilemma just described. This means that anti-Communist, anti-colonialist, and nationalist revolutionary movements must be supported to establish viable polities in the LDCs. Within these movements, one can hope to find uncorruptible and dedicated elements enjoying enough popular confidence to provide the regime with some initial legitimacy; to lead positive forces in achieving a cultural renaissance; and to use power to master negative forces and enhance the regime's legitimacy. These elements alone have indispensable insights into, and sensitivity to, LDC environmental and cultural factors to avoid the vicious cycle discussed earlier and realize the upward spiral. Moved by a nationalist cause, these patriotic elements that have fought against Western colonialism and imperialism, remain the only ones ready to live and die in their native land with their compatriots and to make the necessary sacrifices to better their country. They are also the only elements possessing enough moral integrity and compassion to better the lot of the poor and weak in the Third World and thus to compete successfully with Communists and to prevent the latter from preempting and taking advantage of the nationalist cause. The West is thus well advised not to corrupt such elements, not to sow discord among them in order to divide and conquer and leave them no alternative but the Soviet Union. It is also important for Western powers to realize that in their competition for influence over the Third World support provided to different groups that are congenial to the interest of each specific donor can cause further dissensions among the local elites and thus be self-defeating for the free world as a whole. In the long run, this competition for short-term economic interests is beneficial only to the Soviet bloc.

By adopting such a policy reversal, Western countries will gain the confidence and trust of positive forces in Third-World nations, rid themselves of the ugly colonial or neocolonial image, and establish a sound basis for long-term cooperation through increased trade between equal partners. Time has come to transfer to LDCs the capacity to increase productivity and thereby create wealth through trade instead of transferring wealth as a form of welfare.

As a matter of fact, prosperity and progress of both the West and LDC nations can only be achieved effectively when LDCs are capable of increasing exports to advanced countries, which in turn permits them to increase imports from the latter. Non-Communist industrialized powers have indeed benefited more from trade relations with the Gang of Four (South Korea, Taiwan, HongKong, and Singapore) than from aid to LDCs. While these countries of the Pacific rim have steadily increased their exports to, and their imports from, advanced countries and effectively handled their debt services, many Third-World countries have run into trouble and sought more grants and loans to avert bankruptcy. It is thus in the West's interest to help expand the ranks of the Gang of Four; this is also the most effective way of dealing with the threat of Communist expansion. It is well for the West to remember that South Korea and Taiwan really began to fare better only after they redirected their nations' efforts toward export industries, that is, economic independence through trade, not aid.[12]

The current development policy change advocated by some Western circles, which confines itself to economic reforms aimed at liberalizing the private sector and developing free enterprise in the Third World, can only force both the West and LDCs deeper into the vicious cycle. By neglecting political reform, such a policy—for example, the Baker debt initiative, which calls for more lending or the Bradley plan, which advocates writing off part of the debt and cutting interest rates—is likely to generate greater dependency, more liaison elites, corruption, bureaucratization of development agencies, and waste of taxpayers' money, and, in the final analysis, to precipitate a collapse of the present order, which can only encourage the Communist world to fill the vacuum.[13] Indeed, in nonviable polities, economic development through the private sector, not unlike economic development through the public sector, has also led to the same disastrous results as in the case of pre-Castro Cuba, Somoza's Nicaragua, South Vietnam, Shah Pahlavi's Iran, Marcos's Philippines, and Duvalier's Haiti.

The drastic change of policy needed to concentrate the free world's efforts on establishing viable polities must be led by political establishments of Western powers, not by professional development establishments. Here again, intellectual vision and moral courage on the part of Western leaders are needed to overcome short-term pressures and the here and now of their limited terms of office to engage in a basic and radical policy change that can provide a sound basis for the future of the world. If these leaders can agree on such a common policy vis-à-vis the Third World, the probability of its success will be higher.

Such an overall policy change would reverse the order of priorities established by current aid policies as follows.

Developing Political Leadership Cadres

Moscow has for over half a century put its heaviest emphasis on training well-rounded generalist political cadres. These tend to be hard-core revolutionaries determined to spend their entire lives fighting for an ideology. They are versed in capturing, organizing, leading, and controlling the masses. Committed to a dogmatic cause, they have learned and become more and more sophisticated and experienced over time in the methodology of using agitation and propaganda to destroy the legitimacy and power of established regimes and to rally the people, especially those at the grass-roots level, to their cause. To the Communists, politics, that is, seizing and then monopolizing power to achieve a purpose, overrides all else.[14]

In contrast, Western countries have concentrated their efforts on training specialists from LDCs for Third-World *economic* development—specialists who end up being of little use because their home countries lack dedicated and experienced statesmen capable of integrating them into the political scene. Lacking a cause and positive political direction, a number of professionals have become involved in politics in secondary and subservient roles to share in the spoils. While a few have been burned, many have managed to amass fortunes. Others shy away from politics and seek lucrative jobs in foreign firms or public enterprises. Some prefer to remain in the West to work for multinational corporations or international organizations. The majority have thus become the liaison elite, ultimately serving nobody's interest but their own. All envy and emulate the standard of living of the upper class, foreign experts, and people in the West. No time nor energy is left to consider the lot of the poor. A minority who struggle hard to preserve their integrity find their hands tied; they remain powerless and barely survive.

The obvious shortage of committed and well-trained political leaders in the non-Communist Third World can be traced to former colonial powers' policies of persecuting patriot revolutionaries and reserving all top-level and most middle-level government positions for expatriates.[15] After such a long period of neglected development of leadership cadres, the politics of developing areas has practically become the preserve of political amateurs, opportunists, and adventurers whose power base rests ultimately on the use of the armed forces and whose outlook and policies have been biased by their professional experience and background and selfish interests.[16]

To fill this dangerous gap, it is necessary to develop a critical mass of top-level policy-making cadres capable of relating many different disciplines—political, military, legal, economic, scientific, humanities—to achieve national objectives. This involves developing a process of selecting candidates for training among those committed to pursuing a moral purpose and a nationalistic cause. Such a critical mass of polity builders expected to wield power in LDCs may change the picture of Third-World politics.

Perhaps some existing international organization, such as the UN university may be assigned this development mandate, or donor agencies might consider supporting in-country institutions, such as national staff colleges and development institutes to organize forums, seminars, and workshops in leadership training. The exchange of information and viewpoints on critical national issues integrating interdisciplinary and intersectoral dimensions can hopefully provide parochial, sectarian, and narrow-minded officials with a common interest and language that can elicit and facilitate cooperation to achieve national goals. Candid discussions and debates on development models, dimensions, and experiences behind closed doors, in an atmosphere that encourages freedom of expression and mutual respect among participants may lay the groundwork for policy making at the highest government level. Involving leaders of different interest and pressure groups in such training programs may help create an atmosphere of mutual trust and confidence that facilitates the integration of opposing individuals and groups in the service of common higher causes. Leadership development is a crucial effort to which Western donors can and should contribute. Even though the issue is politically sensitive, controversial, and difficult to handle, it deserves, nevertheless, to be given serious consideration and ways can be found to tackle it.

A Synthesized and Strategic View of Development

The organization of foreign aid has been fragmented among fields of specialization and donor countries with little coordination among aid-giving institutions. The different and sometimes contradictory policies, procedures, biases, and interests, as well as the varied machinery, equipment, and materials provided have further added to the disintegration of recipient countries. More importantly, such a division of labor has not allowed an organization, unit, nor individual to acquire a comprehensive view of development nor be in a position to meet the needs peculiar to a specific recipient country.[17]

If it is true that well-chosen, well-designed individual technical projects do not make sense in an environment of inadequate, inappropriate, overly constrained general policies, there is a pressing need to improve this environment. The LDC leadership development effort, which has been proposed to this effect, should be paralleled by a similar endeavor on the part of foreign aid. Perhaps some leading aid institution should start looking at development as an integrated whole in order to provide coordination among various aid efforts.

For that purpose, a unit should be established that is staffed by broad-gauged generalists capable of relating different aspects of development—political, social, cultural, and economic—in recipient countries and of advising their leadership on different development policy alternatives. These generalists should possess both knowledge of, and experience with, LDCs' problems, issues, constraints, advantages and opportunities, development models or strategies that have or have not worked, their positive and negative consequences; setting development direction, purpose, and goals; and shaping broad categories of programs to achieve development objectives in terms of stage and sequence, rate and synchronization. The generalists should be able to analyze the overall situation of a specific country, its assets and liabilities, its comparative advantages in the world environment, and the inherent possibilities that can be exploited and come up with policy options. The generalists should also be able to empathize with the political difficulties confronting LDC power wielders, and they should have enough prestige and stature to engage in some candid and meaningful dialogue with them and to help them find some workable long-term development policy as well as strategies and tactics for its implementation.

Macro Research Studies

This generalist capacity, which is rather weak due to the compartmentalization of knowledge, can be acquired over time by concentrating foreign aid research effort on macro policy studies. Information about each recipient country should be collected, updated, and organized, as a basis for policy analyses and development alternatives. Individual country studies can serve as a basis for comparative studies for identifying crucial variables and formulating hypotheses to test successes and failures. In particular, such success or relative success as the Gang of Four in the Pacific area should be thoroughly studied. In this way, idiosyncratic and monothetic studies can complement each other to provide relevant and useful information for LDC and foreign aid top-level policymakers.

Research studies should aim particularly at finding strategic elements that may help develop symbiotic relationships between the West and developing countries. To that effect, development institutions are well advised to make a thorough evaluation of past research trends and experiences in order to find research results that foster the development of these healthy relationships. The following cursory review of the literature provides a preliminary attempt in that direction.[18]

THE LIBERAL DEVELOPMENT MODEL

It should be noted that research orientations advocating Western liberal democracy as a model of development, which have been strongly criticized as ethnocentric, culture bound, and inapplicable to the Third World, do not appear to be completely ruled out by empirical facts. At least a small minority of LDCs—the Gang of Four—have to a major extent followed the Western path of economic development with spectacular success. Although these developing countries on the Pacific rim, like Japan, are dubbed by Western scholars as democracies with one party-and-a-half, they have performed economic miracles and vastly improved their people's standard of living. They appear to have passed Rostow's take-off stage and stage of sustained growth and are now entering the stage of maturity. If democracy is understood more in terms of substance—respect for human rights, polity legitimacy—than form, it seems fair to say that in that respect these countries score much higher than all Communist countries and most non-Communist LDCs. After all, why should they possess all the formal features that exist in the West? The main challenge confronting the Gang of Four now is to steadily increase their polity's legitimacy and institutionalize the succession of top-political leadership, which takes time and long-term effort. As Lucian Pye has observed, "In time, however, a variety of modernized Asian states will emerge. Then, as now, Asian success should not be measured against parochial Western standards, but against more universal models that will overarch the enduring gulfs between the world's great civilizations."[19]

THE HISTORICIST APPROACH

The historically oriented social scientists have made a positive contribution by offering several qualifications of early Western liberal theory; in particular, development does not necessarily follow a unilinear path exactly replicating the Western democratic model; modernity can lend itself to a variety of combinations of economic foundations, government structures, value systems, and social institutions but is not necessarily confined to a rigid whole like the *gesellschaft* or urban, universal, secular ideal; and traditional LDC cultures do not necessarily constitute a barrier to development. With these qualifications, the applicability of the general Western model advocated by Western scholars has been vindicated by experience of nations on the Pacific rim.

THE MANAGERIAL APPROACH

Successful application of the model by western-educated leaders of these Asian nations is, however, too haphazard to overcome the general spirit of pessimism generated by failures elsewhere in the Third World. Hence, another research orientation emphasizing the managerial approach has turned its focus away from abstract deductive models and toward practical issues of management, problem solving, and policy evaluation. While political scientists study the performance and capacity of political systems and strategies and sequences for realizing changes, public administration-oriented scholars turn their attention to institution building and program/project administration.

It is to be noted that policy recommendations from these studies have proved inadequate for improving the situation in most of the Third World not because they are necessarily inherently wrong, but because of failure to give priority to developing viable polities. In the absence of the latter, attempts to apply these recommendations, which for obvious reasons were confined to technical, nonpolitical levels, have been distorted and swept away by political vicissitudes already described. Indeed, as long as an LDC is not under the control of positive forces, there is little hope of any development model working. Many of these policy recommendations and managerial processes and techniques underlying democratic values have been adapted and put to successful use in nations on the Pacific rim but not in many others. This is because moral courage and intellectual vision of Pacific rim nations' political leadership have succeeded in overcoming negative forces in culture and solved the problem of compliance through a balanced use of power and legitimacy, internally and externally. To this effect, these nations have turned their cultural heritage to advantage by reviving the Confucian democratic tradition of humanist government by virtuous, meritorious, superior people, and the "sage" whom any one can aspire to become through his or her own efforts, regardless of social or ethnic origin.

THE NEO-MARXIST APPROACH

Disenchanted with the futility of the preceding approaches, various neo-Marxist groups or dependency theorists for the last decade have attempted to attribute underdevelopment to the impact of international forces. In the view of these intellectuals, many of them from the Third World, LDCs are victims of colonial and neocolonial policies of Western industrialized countries. Their studies do not focus on the forces of local tradition and hostility to change on which conventional Western writing on modernization have concentrated, but on unequal relationships between developed countries as metropoles or cores and LDCs as peripheries. This unequal relationship inherited from colonial times leads to the development of underdevelopment or creates the dependency condition of LDCs with all the social evils and structural defects of the peripheral economies documented by the conventional Western modernization theory school.

With documentation of the effect of this historically unequal division of labor in which the industrialized country always gains and the LDC receives the shorter end of the stick, the Third World appears to have its revenge, polarizing development writings between liberals led by scholars of donor and lending countries of the West and the radicals led by scholars of aid-receiving and borrowing countries. The Western thesis is now confronted by the LDC antithesis, both well documented and both true, but only partially. The challenge to development students now appears to be not simply formulating a synthesis but a search for reasonable alternatives based on facts ignored by past analysts.

Proposed Research Direction: The Search for Reasonable Alternatives

The present study is an attempt in this direction. It agrees with the early modernization school that internal deficiencies of Third-World societies are true and do constitute definite obstacles to development. It does not agree, however, that these barriers can be attributed to LDC cultural values. It agrees with the historicist school that there are alternative paths to development depending on each country's situation and that traditional cultures and values can contribute positively to national development. This study argues, however, that it is a losing game to take the dreadful behavioral realities in some LDCs as cultural values themselves and to find ingenious ways of justifying and defending them. Flattering as this may be to LDC leadership, this game is self-defeating in the long run: It tends to encourage the perpetuation of negative forces in the Third World.

STRATEGIES OF CULTURAL RENEWAL

The need exists, therefore, for researchers to distinguish between ideal values and daily negative behavior encouraged or compelled by environmental forces and to help discover ways of inducing people in each culture to live up to its positive values. This is a missing research link that social scientists, especially anthropologists, must fill.

This study also agrees with the dependency theorists that international forces have a lot to do with the current deplorable situation in many LDCs. To be fair to the West, however, it also includes in international forces those of the Communist world for a more comprehensive and balanced view. Moreover, this theory attributes the situation not merely to policies of industrialized countries but also to policies of LDCs themselves.

At the very least, the latter are responsible for letting themselves be conquered and dominated; for remaining weak, poor, and dependent; for failing to react positively to these forces by capitalizing on possibilities in the environment—conflict between East and West and among Western powers themselves—to preserve independence and dignity. To be sure, the impact of international forces has been overwhelming for LDCs, but to explain underdevelopment and dependency merely in terms of exogenous factors while completely ignoring the reactions of endogenous forces is at the least one sided, deterministic, and contemptuous of LDC peoples.

Like dependency theorists, this author believes that some kind of cultural revolution is needed to provide a new, positive basis for LDCs to start with; he does not concur with the idea that a socialist revolution is the only way out of underdevelopment. As argued earlier, a socialist revolution along the Communist ready-made model and with the support of the Communist bloc can only help an LDC escape one state of dependency for another that is even worse and irreversible. This new dependency may help restore stability and order, but not necessarily foster development, and at great cost in human sacrifices.

On the other hand, a non-Communist socialist revolution, given the state of noncompliance in the Third World, negative pressures from both free and Communist worlds, and the half-measures taken as a consequence, has proven futile. The revolution advocated in this study, which consists of reviving and rejuvenating LDC culture, is more humane and acceptable to world opinion and congruent with national aspirations of LDC people, yet it can help the LDC adapt positively and contribute to world progress and prosperity. Research aimed at developing strategies of cultural renewal will benefit not only LDCs but also

non-Communist industrialized countries by establishing a more harmonious and productive world order.

COUNTRY STUDIES

Since cultures vary in configuration, racial composition, political,
economic, social, and sociopsychological factors and thus differ in
reaction to exogenous forces as well as in approaches to determining
and shaping specific development strategies, one important line of
research that the development community should encourage is more
penetrating analyses of specific LDCs. Given the significant role of
leadership in cultural renovation, studies of specific LDC national
elites, in particular, identifying uncorruptible and dedicated elements
capable of breaking the vicious cycle that entraps society, should be
conducted thoroughly. Also important is research on different power
groups in society as well as various strategies for turning them into
positive forces that can support the top political leadership in achieving the cultural revolution.[20] Along the same line, research is needed
on charismatic political leaders throughout the history of a nation;
how they regenerated national values and institutions; and how these
later were ingrained in the society. Findings from such studies should
be most useful for policy-making purposes.

VALUE SYSTEMS

Another line of research that can contribute significantly to a rap-
prochement of the West and the Third World is the study of the value
system of each LDC, focusing on positive aspects that can serve as a
foundation for building a viable democratic polity. This study can be
supported by research on world cultures, including the major religions
and philosophies that influence them, their impact on specific countries or groups of countries, and their democratic values. Cross-
cultural transfer of institutions, technology, processes and techniques—in particular, what can be assimilated by the LDC concerned,
including political features—should also be explored.

COMPARATIVE ADVANTAGE

To help developed and developing countries harmonize with one
another, research on how the economic theory of comparative advantage could and should operate on a worldwide scale for the benefit of
participating economies is badly needed. Some economists advocate,
for example, that capital-abundant economies export capital-intensive

products and import labor-intensive ones, while labor-abundant economies export labor-intensive goods in exchange for capital-intensive
imports. Such a division of labor appears to have existed between a
group of industrialized and developing nations for the last two decades.
As the cost of labor increases and employers compete for labor as a
result of economic growth, firms in high-growth centers in Western
countries and Japan, are forced to specialize in producing high-tech,
capital-intensive goods and to leave to LDCs where labor costs are low,
the manufacture of such labor-intensive products as textiles, toys,
apparel, footwear, plastic, and rubber commodities.

By importing foreign capital and technology from Western countries
and Japan, then exporting these goods to industrialized countries,
labor-abundant countries of the Pacific Basin area have achieved unprecedented economic prosperity and become secondary centers of
production. As the cost of labor increases in these Pacific Basin area
economies, their firms in turn must produce commodities requiring
more capital-intensive technology and leave more labor-intensive production to other LDCs, for example, Malaysia, Sri Lanka, and
Thailand, where labor is less expensive. The latter in their turn will
repeat the process, taking up more and more capital-intensive industries and leaving more labor-intensive industries to areas where labor
is more abundant and cheaper.

This is, in oversimplified terms, the way the theory of comparative
advantage has been applied in real-life situations. Economic prosperity
is thus transferred from the primary to the secondary then to the
tertiary centers of production through world trade and multinational
corporations, gradually and steadily raising the cost of labor and thus
the standard of living of people in countries participating in this system.[21]

If one adds other economic factors, such as the cost of raw materials,
transportation, and a country's natural resources, a country's ability to
capitalize on its economic advantages are limited by only its nationals'
imagination and its resources. However, considerations other than the
purely economic—political, social, national security, and defense—
would also modify application of the theory in practice. Research
studies on a worldwide basis can, nevertheless, help each LDC discover
its own comparative advantages vis-à-vis the whole world and formu-
late its economic development strategy accordingly, taking into account other noneconomic factors.

CAPITALIZING ON THE MULTINATIONALS

The role of multinational corporations in linking these economic
zones of prosperity is crucial. Since the comparative advantage in

creating wealth lies in the private sector and the comparative advantage in transferring it lies in the public sector, international development organizations are well advised to support mutinationals in their effort to help increase wealth in developing economies rather than disparaging and replacing them. This support can be achieved through research aimed at developing international legal systems and institutions, such as contracts, agreements for joint ventures defending and protecting the legitimate rights of both sides and fostering cooperation beneficial to both parties. Experiences of such countries as Singapore and South Korea that have succeeded in capitalizing on the participation of multinationals while preserving independence and sovereignty should be thoroughly studied and the findings diffused. The image and effectiveness of multinationals can be improved not only through their increased awareness of their social responsibility, but also through increased ability of the LDC public sector to take advantage of multinationals and to curb their excesses.[22]

CONDITIONS FOR SELF-HELP

Along the same line, strategies should be developed for turning asymmetrical relationships between former colonies and colonial powers into mutually beneficial cooperation between equal and interdependent partners, a form of cooperation that minimizes the LDC's dependency and maximizes self-help. Meaningful roles that weak LDCs can play in interdependent and many-layered international environments, and the regional socioeconomic structures that provide adequate bases for various development programs should be explored.[23]

LEGITIMATION

Last but not least, research on a polity's ability to induce self-compliance (legitimacy) and compliance by external means (power) along the lines suggested by this study is most needed to help develop viable polities. Tools should be designed and indicators identified to measure the capacities of LDC regimes and to monitor progress made or setbacks suffered through time. This would help a regime know where it stands at a given time in terms of legitimacy and power and permit it to take actions required to improve its status. Later measurements can test the effectiveness of these actions and change and improve them accordingly. In this way, measurement tools and techniques as well as actions to maintain the balance between legitimacy and power can be refined and improved as the regime proceeds through its course. This technique of policy analysis can also be used for institutions at the lower levels—provinces, districts, villages, departments, agencies. These are, of course, sensitive materials and may have to be kept confidential, especially at the national polity level.

Note that the proposed research studies are intended to guide development policies and actions. Ways should therefore be found of closing both the usual time gap between research findings and their dissemination and the loop between research and operational applications.

Back to Law-and-Order-Oriented Administration

Considerably greater resources should be devoted to supporting the development of legislative and law enforcement abilities in LDC polities. Unanticipated negative consequences resulting from attempts to strengthen the LDC civilian and military bureaucracies appear to have led foreign aid to concentrate its efforts on the so-called development sector—the economy, finance, agriculture, public works, creating innumerable autonomous public agencies. Little attention has been given to traditional public sector institutions responsible for law and order—the legislature, judiciary, foreign service, security forces. An effective and humane law enforcement system enhances the legitimacy and power of the polity and facilitates development efforts in all other areas. Economic growth can hardly be sustained or equitably distributed in an atmosphere of anarchy, insecurity, or uncertainty about the future.[24]

Support to the LDC public sector should be restricted to strengthening its capacity to assure law and order and provide an economic infrastructure and environment that can attract, encourage, support, and control local and foreign private sector investments and growth.[25] Paradoxically enough, the ultimate success or failure of intergovernmental assistance through bilateral and multilateral institutions to non-Communist LDCs should be evaluated in terms of how much it has finally contributed to development of the private sector.

One of the yardsticks that can be used for this evaluation is the increase or decrease in private local and foreign capital investment. The latter may also be used as one of the criteria for measuring the credit worthiness of a borrowing country. Again, the example of South Korea is illustrative. Despite a debt service that required about $5 billions per year from 1981 to 1985, there has been not only a willingness but also an eagerness on the part of foreign private banks to make new loans to South Korean firms.[26] The West has been conditioned by this model of development for so long that this part of the world can excel in expanding this model of free enterprise. Western donors have little to offer LDC public sectors that want to substitute for the private sector by engaging directly in economic production and to dictate the operations of the economy through control measures that completely disregard the law of the market.

One of the basic policy changes required of many LDCs now is phasing out foreign funding to public enterprises and their gradual privatization with the involvement of the foreign private sector. Economic enterprises should be left in the hands of private businessmen whose survival is linked with the success or failure of the enterprise. Recipient government and donor agency officials are well advised to recognize that they can excel in transferring but not producing wealth, which must be left to the private sector.

The participation of private foreign capital is crucial for the future of non-Communist LDCs. This will facilitate the transfer of technology that can be used to produce exports. In this way, foreign exchange can be earned for capital imports, which in turn helps increase exports.

Integrating the LDC economy into the international market place through participation in world trade creates conditions for real economic development, self-sufficiency, independence, and thus for national pride and dignity. It is perhaps for this reason that the late president of South Korea, Park Chung Hee, over strong objections from almost all quarters, made a great effort to normalize relations with Korea's former colonial master and archenemy, Japan, and to welcome Japanese private sector investment. In fact, foreign private capital, especially from the United States and Japan, has played a significant role in the Korean economic miracle. It is worth repeating that such rapid growth could not have been possible without the support of a Korean public sector capable of providing law and order and an environment favorable for free enterprise to operate.[27]

Division of Labor, Redefinition of Missions, and Reallocation of Resources among Aid Institutions

The structure of development assistance has been heavily skewed toward governmental and intergovernmental institutions at the expense of nongovernmental organizations. Moreover, international institutions concerned with economic development have overshadowed those responsible for other sectors.

STRENGTHENING GOVERNMENTAL SUPPORT TO PRIVATE INVESTMENTS AND VOLUNTARY HELP IN THE THIRD WORLD

Considerably more resources should go to institutions responsible for encouraging private investment overseas through such measures as guarantees against arbitrary nationalization, capital participation, supplying information on investment conditions, and facilitating negotiations between foreign and local business firms and governments. People to people assistance through nongovernment organizations (NGOs) should be given a lot more emphasis. These groups possess several advantages over bureaucratic agencies: They are not entangled in bureaucratization and cost much less; they rely on their own resources and are staffed mostly by volunteers, motivated by the desire to serve the underdogs and ready to mix with them long enough to understand their problems and help improve their lot. Volunteers imbued with such moral incentives can contribute a great deal to local culture renewal and improve the image of Western countries and the West-LDC relationships. Volunteers' modest material lifestyle as well as their moral dedication are likely to inspire self-respect and self-help on the part of local people. Cooperation between public development assistance institutions and voluntary groups should therefore be heavily strengthened through such formulas as fund matching.

MULTILATERAL AID INSTITUTION FOR SENSITIVE AREAS

A multilateral institution should be established to provide assistance to the political and security sector, or existing international organizations should be much more involved therein. This sensitive area has been left entirely in the hands of bilateral institutions, especially the superpowers. Concerned for their sovereignty and legitimacy, LDCs are more likely to seek aid for this sector from an international organization than a single country. An alternative and/or supplemental solution consists in having Scandinavian countries concentrate efforts on military and police assistance. With a neutral foreign policy and without a colonial past, they can enlist more confidence on the part of Third-World countries.

MORE RESOURCES TO NONECONOMIC ASPECTS OF DEVELOPMENT

There should be a more even distribution of resources among international development institutions. Those concerned with improving the public sector's performance as a whole, need more resources to fulfill their mission. The world development scene has been dominated by the two economic giants—the World Bank and the International Monetary Fund (IMF). Bankers, economists, and financiers predominate in these two agencies, which appear to have created more and more work for each other and ended up monopolizing resources at the expense of other institutions concerned with noneconomic aspects of development.

The bank's approach to development lending, which concentrates on supporting tangible, quantifiable economic projects at the micro level that are run by the public sector, can hardly escape the vicissitudes of Third-World politics. Thus, this approach contributes to the saturation of the economic environment and the deterioration of the so-ciopolitical situation in many LDCs. The IMF has to come to the latter's rescue with package loans for financial stabilization, which helps LDCs in some way to honor debt service commitments through rescheduling, postponing, and extending payment while putting some order in the country's finances. But financial stabilization hampering further economic development makes it more difficult to service the accumulated debts. The bank, therefore, must step in with more lend-ing to save ongoing development projects from collapsing or to fund new projects.

Furthermore, since 1980 the bank has departed from its traditional emphasis on project-based lending and has resorted increasingly to policy-based lending in the form of structural adjustment loans that can be used by the borrowing country to finance temporary structural imbalances resulting from macroeconomic policy changes or balance-of-payments shortfalls and foreign exchange shortages. With this new source of credit that can be used for practically any purpose, and reinforced as needed by another kind of lending, called sectoral adjust-ment loan, the bank hopes the debtor country will be able to achieve economic reforms that permit it to grow while continuing to honor its debt obligations. In giving loans tied to changes in economic policy in the borrowing countries rather than to specific development projects, the bank makes its role little different than that of the IMF. It can be argued that while the fund is concerned with short-term adjustment, the bank as a development-lending agency is responsible for long-term adjustment. Since balance-of-payments deficits, which are the IMF's concern, have become a chronic problem for most LDCs, the boundary between long-term and short-term adjustments appears blurred, in-deed.

Such a division of labor makes both institutions continually need more resources to fulfill their missions. More and more financial contributions are needed from rich industrial countries in terms of members' increased paid-in and callable capital or funds replenished to aid the International Development Association, the bank's "soft-loan window" that provides concessionary loans to the poorest LDCs. Be-cause the necessity of preventing a collapse of the world's economic and financial order is always of paramount importance, whatever re-sources advanced member countries can afford should go first to these two institutions. While the two economic giants continue to prosper and flourish in proportion to the worsening situation in the Third World, there is little left to support institutions concerned with other aspects of development.

SCALING DOWN THE TWO ECONOMIC GIANTS

As has been observed earlier in connection with the Baker plan, economic solutions encouraged or imposed by bilateral or multilateral donor institutions can hardly change the basic picture in many Third-World countries. At best such solutions postpone the financial crisis for some time but in no way solve it. Moreover, putting off the crisis by injecting more and more loans, the major part of which is used for servicing debt amortizations and interest, will make it worse in the future. Indeed, the higher the total amount of debt, the more drastic would be the shock suffered by the world's financial and trade systems in case of progressive and generalized default.

As argued in previous chapters, unless the LDC political leadership is determined *and* able to break the vicious cycle confronting the polity by carrying through a cultural revolution to keep negative forces in check, there is little hope of improving the macroeconomic environment in many LDCs. Indeed, the IMF's stand-by agreements and the bank's policy strings attached to such "untied" (not project-based) credits as reconstruction loans, sector loans, or local cost financing (precursors of the new structural adjustment loan) are not innovations but have been used for decades with scant success by the IMF and the bank to influence borrowing countries' economic policy. Besides, the need to stave off outright default or debt repudiation especially on the part of the most heavily indebted countries in order to avert a generalized financial crisis must take precedence over long-term economic reform.

The pressure is strong for the IMF and the bank to use these policy-based loans first as a means of averting bankruptcy and a catalyst for private capital flows. Thus, the risk is great that loan funds will be disbursed to fulfill this overriding need regardless of whether intended policy changes actually take place or not. Moreover, economic reform cannot go so far as to endanger the regime's survival. The IMF has already been accused of encroaching too much on the sovereignty of borrowing countries. Where the IMF, which is endowed with the traditional staff expertise to compel economic policy reform, has often failed, it will be more difficult for the World Bank, whose staff expertise has thus far been concentrated on project lending, to succeed. Finally, the well-known low level of societal compliance with government rules and regulations in the Third World makes it very difficult, if not impossible, for borrowing countries to comply with conditions attached to loans. There are numerous ways for people to circumvent and take advantage of the law.

All these costly efforts to improve the economic environment may actually end up as either cosmetic reforms or half-way measures adopted by debtor countries in order to obtain the next loan disbursement portion. In case economic policy changes are directed at promoting free enterprise as usually required by loan arrangements, some form of "crony" capitalism may result that benefits greedy ruling elites and unscrupulous international corporations at the expense of the masses. This may in no way solve the debt problem but actually create more favorable conditions for a socialist/Communist revolution to succeed. In short, the bank's policy of adjustment with growth may work in some rare cases where the LDC political leadership is able and determined to improve the sociopolitical environment. As a rule, however, it is apt to become another victim of Third-World politics and to remain merely a fad added to the development agencies' list of officially approved clichés, such as "growth with equity," "New Style," and "Basic Human Needs."

Economic solutions have often failed not because they are unsound but because they lack complementary assistance efforts to improve the LDC's sociopolitical conditions. Resources should be redirected toward this assistance, which must come from political establishments of donor countries. A coordinated development assistance program must resort to both direct and indirect, formal and informal means. It would be difficult for the bank and the IMF to succeed without complementary efforts on the part of the political establishments to help improve Third-World politics.

Within the framework of this multipronged approach, the need exists for the two leading institutions to confine their roles to what they can do best; that is, to redirect resources for improving the LDC governmental capacity to support development of the private sector but not to substitute for the latter. As discussed earlier, this consists of helping strengthen the capacity of institutions responsible for the formulation and implementation of economic policies and the improvement of the economic infrastructure, as well as serving as catalysts for joint ventures between private foreign and domestic capital. Since the supply of foreign capital is to be handled by the private sector, especially the multinationals, the bank will need little capital for that purpose.

To avoid imbalances and waste created by the current cart-before-the-horse economics, social overhead and capital improvement must go hand-in-hand with the rate of growth rather than preceding it; that is, support the construction of new structures—highway, bridge, dam—only when they have some chance of being productively used and the recipient government becomes capable of maintaining them through an increase in revenues resulting from economic growth. This also means that the bank's need of capital for concessional loans will be reduced.

Less and less capital will be needed as debtor countries' economies improve through participation in world trade, making it possible for them to repay their debts on time and to rely more and more on lending commercial sources. With balanced economic growth, imbalances in balance of payments and foreign exchange shortages will be much less frequent, thus reducing capital needed by the IMF. In addition, consideration should be given of having the World Bank return to its original purpose of supplementing private capital by serving as an insurance or reinsurance agency for private investment projects in the Third World. The bank appears to be moving, albeit slowly and unwillingly, in that direction through the International Finance Corporation, its arm devoted to private sector development.[28]

The two international economic giants can thus be scaled down, leaving resources for upgrading other institutions concerned with political and administrative improvements, so that a more balanced approach to development can be achieved. After all, aid should lead to economic independence through trade, not to more dependency and more aid and more aid agencies at the expense of the taxpayers. A foundation must be laid to permit aid agencies to put themselves out of work and the sooner the better.

AID FOR DEVELOPING THE POLITY

There are thus far, at least in the formal sense, no international nor national institutions concerned with political development, or more exactly, development of the LDC polity as a whole. This is quite understandable, given the need, at least on the surface, to respect national sovereignty and independence.

All development organizations—multilateral or bilateral—have been assigned professional, technical, or administrative functions, with the assumption that discrete and separate improvements in these fields will lead to overall development, including political. As demonstrated in this study, realities have proven otherwise. In the absence of formal agencies responsible for this sensitive area, the job has fallen on a host of disparate institutions (office of the president or prime minister, legislative houses, department of foreign affairs, department of national defense, and intelligence agencies). Not only is coordination among these institutions lacking, but also conflicts among them over basic policies as well as processes and procedures are the order of the day. Furthermore, LDC affairs constitute only a small fraction of each of these institutions' missions; they are often assigned to administrative divisions or lost at lower levels, making policy coordination all the more difficult and complex.

In the final analysis, the effectiveness of policy leadership and coordination in dealing with Third-World problems depends, to a great extent, on the chief executive's personality and power base. A strong and forceful president or premier may achieve consistent policy during his or her term of office and be replaced by a weak one who wavers and zigzags under contradictory pressures of the moment. Unpredictable electoral politics influenced more by domestic issues than those relating to the LDCs has, indeed, made it difficult for Western countries to have a long-range and consistent policy vis-à-vis the Third World. All this, as said earlier, has made it necessary for LDC leaders to find ways of protecting themselves by carefully preparing their departure.

Although these problems appear to defy solution, some remedies can neverthelelss be used to alleviate them. First, top-political leaders of Western powers can seek an agreement on basic policy toward the Third World: support genuine LDC national sovereignty and independence as a way of preventing a LDC from falling into the Soviet orbit; support patriotic, anti-Communist, nationalist leaders in mastering negative forces and achieving a cultural renewal to establish viable polities; divide zones of influence among Western powers so that each concentrates its forces on a limited number of LDCs or aid functions as a primary sponsor with the support of others as secondary sponsors; agree on supporting an international agency to focus on LDC political development. Agreements of this type, reached on an incremental, step-by-step basis by Western governments, can go far to insulating development assistance from the vagaries and discontinuities that now characterize Western aid for genuine, sustainable LDC development.

Second, agreement should also be sought among key in-country policymakers—party leaders, legislative committee chairs and minority leaders, chief executive and executive department heads—on basic long-term policy regarding the Third World. Third, offices and divisions within the foreign service concerned with the Third World, especially the country's sections and embassies, should be provided with more resources to fulfill their mission toward each specific LDC. Finally, covert agencies—the U.S. CIA, the British Secret Service, the French Deuxième Bureau, or Direction Générale de la Sécurité Extérieure (DGSE), or whatever—can join forces to improve the viability of non-Communist LDC polities.

Thus far, covert agencies have been well known for their success in helping overthrow oppressive and corrupt LDC regimes. In contrast, their success in helping establish viable polities, if any, has been negligible, as non-Communist LDCs in general demonstrate. In bringing down corrupt regimes without developing good and viable regimes to succeed them, covert agencies have helped the West win successive dramatic battles that have ironically led to loss of the war in the end.

While it is difficult to document approaches adopted by covert agencies, it appears that the main incentives used thus far in LDCs are economic and material. Although this dollar approach has helped achieve short-run purposes, it has added further to the disintegration and corruption of the LDC society in the long-run, thus deepening the vicious cycle. A challenge lies ahead for covert agencies to think hard about more positive ways of helping without corrupting and destroying, of bringing positive forces together to break the vicious cycle and lay a sound basis for a viable polity.

Once this task has been successfully completed, the job of overt-development agencies in improving nonpolitical areas will have a lot more chance of succeeding. With a viable political system, an LDC can stand on its own feet, establish its development policy, and coordinate its development programs and projects. The job of development assistance will become much more meaningful, rewarding, and effective.

CONCLUSION

THIS STUDY STARTS WITH THE PREMISE THAT THE INABILITY OF MOST LDCs to establish and maintain viable polities has been the cause of failure of past development efforts. A great many LDC regimes have taken turns succumbing to the vicious cycle generated by their inability to cope with the crisis of legitimacy. As little compliance exists through internal or external controls, foreign aid as well as local resources end up falling into the hands of negative forces that have taken root in Third-World cultures decaying after centuries of contact with a dominating Western capitalistic civilization. The study has demonstrated how the imbalance between *legitimacy*, which generates self-compliance, and *power*, which induces compliance by external means, has made it so difficult for LDC regimes to develop viable polities. Preceding discussion has shown that this imbalance has distorted and ultimately destroyed most development programs and projects. Case studies of LDC regimes that have failed or succeeded in dealing with this issue of delegitimation have been provided. A strategy that may help overcome the crisis of legitimacy and establish viable polities supporting rather than hampering development efforts has been proposed. Consequent changes in foreign assistance policy aimed at implementing this strategy for the long-term benefit of developed and developing worlds have also been suggested.

NO MORE BEATING AROUND THE BUSH: ATTACK CAUSES, NOT SYMPTOMS

It is hoped that the message conveyed by the study is by now clear enough. What basically went wrong with development assistance is not what has been advanced and vividly debated thus far: that foreign aid has overemphasized project assistance at the expense of program assistance or vice versa; or that it has put too much stress on security assistance at the expense of economic assistance or vice versa; or that it has focused on developing the public sector at the expense of the private sector or vice versa; or that it has concentrated too much of its effort on bilateral instead of multilateral aid; or that it has adopted a trickle-down approach and neglected to provide for the basic needs of the poor; or that aid projects did not last long enough to allow for systems institutionalization, or they failed to provide for sustainability; or that aid encouraged the development of industry at the expense of agriculture; or that there has not been enough decentralization, debureaucratization, local participation, and "empowerment."

While these issues may have their own merits at the micro level, they are merely symptoms of a systemic defect. Attempts to tinker with symptoms will lead nowhere as long as the fundamental issue, the viability of the polity, remains unsolved. In fact, all these solutions and approaches have been tried here and there, back and forth, off and on, for over four decades now. Not only have they produced little improvement, they have also created more and more insoluble problems. To focus on solutions to these symptoms while shying away from the fundamental issue is to "beat around the bush." This can only result in an increasing waste of taxpayers' monies that could have been put to better use than filling the pockets of negative forces. Continuing current policies will further deepen the debt crisis and vicious cycle, entrapping both the aid-giving and receiving sides and eventually lead to a collapse of the non-Communist world order.

A SOUL SEARCH FOR LDC TOP LEADERSHIP

The ultimate survival of the free world requires every participant in the game to make a soul search to find out whether his or her work has contributed to improving or destroying this world. Let the LDC leadership have second thoughts about its interminable appeals for help, more aid, grants, concessional loans, (to see whether these appeals for charity echoed from one meeting to another reflect any pride or dignity on the part of the nations they represent.) LDC leaders are well advised to remember that, as a Vietnamese proverb goes, "Help can only be given to people in distress, but not in poverty" (*Giup ngat, khong ai giup ngheo*). National independence should at least mean making an effort to live within one's means and trying to help oneself. In concentrating their energy on restoring their people's and their own pride and dignity in being independent rather than continuing to seek foreign aid, LDC leaders will create an atmosphere more receptive to self-help. Pride and dignity will urge them to try their best to make full use of what they have first; of their professionals and technicians trained and left unused because of mismanagement or political reasons; of their own educated nationals who work and settle abroad instead of

participating in the development of the native land; and of their countrymen's assets deposited in foreign banks or invested in Western
countries rather than at home. Dignity and pride will urge them to
resolve to make the necessary sacrifices and set examples for their
compatriots to follow. Once negative forces have been subdued, legitimacy established and strengthened, and confidence restored, national
reconstruction and development through self-help will be much easier,
respect from foreign countries forthcoming, and a sound foundation
laid for future growth.

In accepting to ride the tiger, LDC leadership must also accept the
risk of being overthrown and consumed by that tiger. Although the risk
is high, the leaders should not fear the tiger once they have accepted
the task of subduing and taming it. They should be equipped with the
weapons of sincerity, integrity, and dedication in carrying out this
noble mission. As only "real gold is not afraid of playing with fire," this
weapon will help them earn, if not love at first, at least fear and then
respect from the tiger. With this moral weapon in hand, leaders should
be firmly convinced that even if fate turns against them, they will be
able to say to their conscience that they have tried their best to do what
they believe should be done for their country. They must realize that
this is the lot that may befall LDC leadership that considers as its duty
the sacred mission of leading its people out of decadence, dependency,
misery, and poverty toward pride, independence, and self-help. After
foreseeing and appreciating the danger, if the leadership does not think
it possesses the superior moral courage and intellectual ability required to do the job, it had better leave the task to others or better yet
prepare the ground for and support those to whom the job should be
entrusted. The leadership can be sure that history will not fail to
record the good as well as the bad things done for the country and that
dedication and sacrifices will never be forgotten.

A SOUL SEARCH FOR WESTERN POLITICAL LEADERS

It thus behooves Western country political leaders to empathize
with their LDC counterparts' difficult situation and to try to make life
easier for the latter. The West must realize that it is in the long-term
interest of the West and the world to support LDCs' efforts to establish
viable polities as a prerequisite for development. The issue confronting
both the Third and Western worlds is first and foremost a moral one:
the legitimacy of the LDC polities, which depend on their capacity to
work as proud, independent, and equal partners with the West.

After World War II, British leaders took the lead in dramatically changing their policy vis-à-vis some colonies, recognizing in good faith aspirations for independence and negotiating with, as well as supporting, the very nationalist movements and patriot revolutionaries who fought against British rule. France was rather late in changing the rules of the game. After a bitter experience in Vietnam as well as a long, costly, and unsuccessful struggle against the Algerian nationalist movement for independence, France has begun to adopt more liberal policies toward her colonies. This dramatic change has not been easy, however. A great deal of moral courage and intellectual vision on the part of a leader of such stature as De Gaulle was needed to brave French colonial forces and return independence to Algeria, thus reversing traditional French policy of keeping colonies under the metropole's grip.

These steps, although significant, are not enough if unequal economic relationships between the former metropole and the newly independent colony remain practically the same as before. This state of economic dependency maintained through liaison elites supported by the former mother country makes political independence merely nominal. Viable polities can hardly be established as long as LDC leaders are perceived by their people to serve the interest of foreign masters instead of their own country. Polity legitimacy can hardly be earned and maintained as long as Third-World leaders continue to prepare for a future in Western countries, not in their homeland. No amount of military or economic aid can deal with this issue. Western leaders must avoid the easy solution of installing puppet regimes and learn to accommodate and support LDC leaders who put the people's interest above their own; who are determined to preserve their country's pride and independence. These leaders are more difficult to work with, but they are the necessary condition for LDCs to contribute to world prosperity and progress by participating in international trade.

Western country leaders' part in helping LDCs become independent and equal partners is thus no less difficult than that confronting Third-World leaders. It requires an agreement among Western powers to adopt policies permitting LDCs to become independent non-Communist polities maintaining relationships with all countries as dictated by national interests. Aid policy of Western countries should not be aimed at achieving short-term economic or foreign policy objectives, such as exporting surplus goods and services, solving unemployment at home, keeping the former colony away from other competing powers, or buying LDC votes at international meetings. This radical policy change requires intellectual vision to look beyond one's term of office to set a new direction for the future; a moral courage to resist pressures coming from establishments with vested interests in continuing the current aid policy; and the political acumen to convince different interest groups to sacrifice short-term interests for the sake of long-term national and international benefits.

A SOUL SEARCH FOR DEVELOPMENT ASSISTANCE PROFESSIONALS

Western and international development experts/specialists are reminded that helping LDCs involves more noble elements than an ordinary profession. It is rather a special kind of international public service that requires a great deal of dedication to, and sacrifice for, underprivileged people of the world. Professional performance can hardly be measured in terms of demonstrated effort, but of results achieved that benefit the target people. Professionals should thus think more of the result of their work in behalf of the Third World than of profits made by their organizations; material perquisites attached to their jobs in terms of tax breaks, per diem, expatriate allocations; or the applause of peers from journal articles or conferences. If professionals decide that the sociopolitical environment of a recipient country does not allow professional and technical solutions to work, they should have the professional probity to speak out, to advise against enterprises, and ultimately to resign and look for other jobs. Wherever high-level political answers are clearly required before professional solutions can be attempted, specialists in technical fields are well advised to avoid and leave to others the job of improving the environment rather than trying to stick to their jobs by advocating the impossible. All kinds of precepts and jargon—"adapt, not adopt," "appropriate technology," "intermediate technology," "to work oneself out of a job," "to be socially oriented rather than merely technically oriented," "new direction," "basic needs"—have become but mere slogans if not jokes when confronted with Third-World realities. Are they, in the final analysis, a means for the development community to perpetuate and expand itself at the expense of both donor and recipient countries?

A SOUL SEARCH FOR THIRD-WORLD PROFESSIONALS

As for LDC specialists and experts serving their own countries, they must remember that professional freedom, dignity, integrity, and probity are not readily given but must be earned and fought for. These professionals must participate in the political struggle to revive positive elements in country's culture, to actively seek out and support political leaders in this endeavor. Only then can professionalism develop and flourish. It does not make sense for Third-World professionals to compare their situation with that of expatriate experts; the comparison should instead be with their own countrymen, especially the poor and weak whose lot needs to be improved and whose involvement in the development effort must be preempted from Communist forces.

DEVELOPMENT AS A MORAL ISSUE

In short, Third-World development is first and foremost a moral issue involving political leadership and the professional development community in both developed and developing countries. Let every participant in the game ponder over the legitimacy of his or her role and try hard to develop an integrated effort to solve the difficult and complex problems confronting the Third World. In raising the issue, this study may not please anyone who has participated in the game. But if it succeeds in provoking a dialogue among participants and in directing their attention to this key issue, it will have fulfilled its purpose.

NOTES

INTRODUCTION

1. Literature on Third-World development abounds. Overall, assessments of the accomplishments of foreign aid over the last four decades have been more pessimistic than optimistic. Despite some disagreements over evaluation methodologies and criteria as well as measurement techniques, there is general agreement that the picture is rather dismal. A wide gap exists between expectations and achievements.

a. For a comprehensive summary of management and institutional issues confronting Third-World countries, see World Bank, *World Development Report 1983* (New York: Oxford University Press, 1983). Given the bank's politically sensitive position as an international lending institution, it is to be praised for tackling, in the words of its president, "a difficult and important subject not previously broached so directly by the Bank" (foreword, p. iii). Interestingly, this staff report, which strives to observe strict neutrality, nonetheless tends to attribute responsibility for development success or failure solely to recipient countries. Indeed, the overall impression created by the report is that the bank does not have much to do with these results despite its leading role in funding, designing, and implementing development projects. The bank's recommendation that all LDCs try to maximize exports and minimize imports appears to be unworkable on a global basis. Understandably, even though political commitment, political backing, political leadership's "integrity, vision, and concern for the public welfare" or commitment to "high standards of performance and integrity" are stressed here and there as a condition crucial to successful development efforts, no solution involving these concerns are proposed.

b. For an overall assessment of the administrative capacity of LDCs, see Dennis A. Rondinelli, *Development Projects as Policy Experiments: An Adaptive Approach to Development Administration* (London and New York: Methuen, 1983). See also the literature cited in n. 11 of chap. 1.

c. The slow-growing and declining PCIs of LDCs are reported in World Bank *Report 1983* and reports for following years. (See especially the updated world development indicators.) The bank's general comment in its 1983 report is that "in relation to expectations and potential, . . . progress in many countries has been unsatisfactory" (p. 41). See also Charles L. Taylor and David A. Jodice, *World Handbook of Political and Social Indicators*, 3d ed., vol. 1, *Cross National Attributes and Rates of Change* (New Haven and London: Yale University Press, 1983), pp. 110–13; Hartmut Sangmeister, "The Economic and Social Situation of the Least Developed Countries (LLDCs)" *Economics* (Tubingen) 30 (1984): 129–41; Hartmut Sangmeister, "World Development Indicators," *Development and Cooperation* 1 (1983); Herbert Sperber, "The

Efficiency-Reducing Effects of Official Development Aid," *Intereconomics* (March/April 1983): 84–89. Sperber points out that, despite considerable disbursement of official development aid (US $250 billion) from 1960 to 1980, the average per capita income in LDCs increased only US $125 over the past thirty years as contrasted with a US $2,950 increase in Western industrialized countries. The prosperity gap increased from a ratio of 10 : 1 in 1950 to 12 : 1 to 13 : 1 by 1980 if corrected for systematic estimation errors. In many cases, the least development progress was recorded in those countries receiving the most support in proportion to their national income, whereas substantial improvements were found in countries receiving hardly any assistance at all; Jacques Lou, *Can the Third World Survive?* (Baltimore: Johns Hopkins University Press, 1983; originally published in France, 1980). This book by a World Bank economist provides a comprehensive review of the social and economic changes in LDCs over the last three decades. Although from 1950 to 1980 the per capita income more than doubled on an average, many countries experienced very limited growth. Development in agriculture was particularly weak, especially in the poorest countries, and living conditions did not improve for the most destitute people. The book points to the remarkable achievements of the socalled Gang of Four and the disappointing failures, particularly in Sub-Saharan Africa and South Asia where conditions remain very poor. *Compact for African Development, Report of the Committee on African Development Strategies,* Lawrence S. Eagleburger and Donald F. McHenry, cochairmen, a joint project of the Council on Foreign Relations and the Overseas Development Council, December 1985, points out that "the most optimistic current projection from the World Bank is that per capita income in Africa will decline slightly in the next ten years. But if interest rates are high and the industrial countries undergo another recession, African income will slip by at least another 5 percent" (p. 6).

d. The debt burdens of LDCs and their capacity to service their debts are widely discussed currently. The total external debt and the number of LDCs in default are increasing daily. See daily newspaper reports, for example, *Washington Post* or the *New York Times,* and publications from official sources, as indicated by the World Bank's *World Development Report 1985* (New York: Oxford University Press, 1985), pp. 22–23, box 2.2, such as *World Debt Tables,* published annually by the World Bank; *International Financial Statistics, Supplement on Balance of Payments,* published annually by the IMF; *Development Co-operation* and *External Debts of Developing Countries,* both published annually by the Organisation for Economic Cooperation and Development; *International Banking Developments* and *Maturity Distribution of International Banking Lending,* published quarterly and semiannually, respectively, by the Bank for International Settlements; and *International Financial Statistics,* published monthly by the IMF. Some selected information follows.

World Bank, *Debt and the Developing World: Current Trends and Prospects; an Abridged Version of World Debt Tables.* 1983–84 edition (Washington, D.C.: World Bank, 1984), reports the total amount of debt disbursed and outstanding for 1983 for the 102 countries reporting under the Debtor Reporting System was US $575 billion; the debt service, $96 billion (principal: $50 billion, interest: $46 billion). The total net transfer was negative: – $11 billion. For major borrowers, who owed $360 billion, the net transfer was: – $21 billion. This means that the amount borrowed was not enough to service the debt for this year. See also, for updated information, the World Bank's *World Development Report 1985*, chap. 2, especially pp. 20, 23, 24, 26.

See also, "The Two Faces of Third-World Debt: A Fragile Financial Environment and Debt Enslavement," *Monthly Review* 35, no. 8 (January 1984): 1–10. This leftist-oriented journal article demonstrates the vicious cycle created by U.S. bank loans to Latin America and concludes that the problem is insoluble and can only be postponed until the imperialist system collapses. Nationalizing U.S. banks is advocated as a solution; Henry F. Jackson, "The African Crisis: Drought and Debt," *Foreign Affairs* 63, no. 5 (Summer 1985): 1082–94. After reviewing the debt status of African countries, the author argues that rescheduling debts is not enough and advocates a moratorium and/or conversion of loans into grants; *Compact for African Development* points out that "by the end of 1986, the payments required to cover the interest on Africa's debts will be equal to two-thirds of all the money the continent receives in aid, leaving very little for new development efforts (p. 7). According to U.S. Treasury Secretary James A. Baker III, the Third World's external debt is expected to reach $1 trillion by the end of 1986 ("Third World's Economic Outlook Hopeful," *Washington Post*, 10 April 1986, p. E1). For updated information on country-by-country, external public debt and debt service ratios, terms of public borrowing, and official development assistance from OECD and OPEC members, see World Bank, *Report 1985*, pp. 204–9; also see chap. 2 for an analysis of the general debt situation.

e. For a summary review of the current debate over the failure of U.S. aid programs to Africa, in particular, and to the Third World, in general, see David B. Ottaway, "Frustrated by Failure to Avert Famine, U.S. Seeks a Better Way to Aid Africa," *Washington Post*, 18 January 1986, pp. A4 and A5.

For an overall summary appraisal of development assistance efforts in Africa, see *Compact for African Development*, pp. 6–10. On U.S. aid to Latin America, see Lawrence E. Harrison, "We Don't Cause Latin America's Troubles: Latin Culture Does," *Washington Post*, 29 June 1986, p. C1f; and his book, *Underdevelopment Is a State of Mind: The Latin American Case* (Lanham, Md.: Center for International Affairs, Harvard University and University Press of America, 1985). For a summary review of Third-World development performance, see Coralie Bryant and Louise G. White, *Managing Development in the Third World* (Boulder, Colo.: Westview Press, 1982), chap. 1. For a qualified defense of official development assistance (ODA), see World Bank, *Report 1985*, chap. 7.

For an evaluation of different aspects of foreign assistance, see Aart van de Laar, *The World Bank and the Poor* (Boston: Martinus Nijhoff, 1980); Karl Borgin and Kathleen Corbet, *The Destruction of a Continent: Africa and International Aid* (San Diego, Calif.: Harcourt Brace Jovanovich, 1982); Tony Jackson and Deborah Eade, *Against the Grain: The Dilemma of Project Food Aid* (Oxford, U.K.: OXFAM, 1982); John Cathie, *The Political Economy of Food Aid* (New York: St. Martin's, 1982); and William Loehr and John P. Powelson, *Threat to Development: Pitfalls of the NIEO* (Boulder, Colo.: Westview Press, 1983).

CHAPTER 1. THE ROOT CAUSE OF DEVELOPMENT FAILURE: POLITICS

1. For a conceptualization of the polity as the leading subsystem, see David Easton, *The Political System* (New York: Knopf, 1953); "An Approach to the

Analysis of Political Systems," *World Politics* 9 (1957): 383–400; *A Framework for Political Analysis* (Englewood Cliffs, N.J.: Prentice-Hall, 1965).

2. Based on the author's personal observation and experience. The avoidance of politics by the professional community can be inferred from its efforts, so far futile, to isolate development work from the mainstream of the regular government bureaucracy by creating autonomous project units and parastatals, by emphasizing cooperation with local communities or organizations, and by relying heavily on expatriates.

3. See, for example, World Bank, *Report 1983* and George Honadle and Jerry VanSant, *Implementing for Sustainability; Lessons from Integrated Rural Development* (West Hartford, Conn.: Kumarian Press, 1985).

4. See the extensive literature on development politics, development economics, and development administration. For a critical review of development politics, see Irene L. Gendzier, *Managing Political Change: Social Scientists and the Third World* (Boulder, Colo., and London: Westview Press, 1985). For a review of the literature on development administration, see Dwight Waldo, ed., "A Symposium—Comparative and Development Administration: Retrospect and Prospect," *Public Administration Review* (November/December 1976): 615–54. The symposium includes articles by six political scientists—Brian Loveman, Lee Sigelman, Jonathan Bendor, Jorge I. Tapia-Videla, J. Fred Springer, and Jong S. Jun—and an answer by Fred W. Riggs, leader of the Comparative Administration Group; "From the Professional Stream: Currents and Sounding," *Public Administration Review* 40, no. 5 (September/October 1980): 407–33, which includes a series of articles evaluating U.S. technical assistance in public administration in light of the Iranian experience by John L. Seitz, Frank P. Sherwood, William J. Siffin, John D. Montgomery, Milton J. Esman, and John L. Seitz; Marcus D. Ingle, "Implementing Development Programs: A State-of-the-Art Review," final report prepared for the Office of Rural Development and Development Administration, Develpoment Support Bureau, U.S. Agency for International Development, under contract AID/ta/147-612, January 1979, mimeographed; and Dennis A. Rondinelli, "Development Management in AID: A Baseline Review of Project and Program Management Assistance in the U.S. Agency for International Development" (Washington, D.C.: Technical Cooperation Project, National Association of Schools of Public Affairs and Administration, 1984), mimeographed. For a summary review of economic approaches to development, see Bryant and White, *Managing Development*, pp. 5–13. For a critical review of development economics, see Deepak Lal, *The Poverty of "Development Economics"* (Cambridge: Harvard University Press, 1985). For an evaluation of development theories, see Elbaki Hermassi, *The Third World Reassessed* (Berkeley: University of California Press, 1980), chap. 2.

5. Although there is an abundance of literature on the macro environment in LDCs and on project design and implementation at the micro level, attempts to link these two seem to be missing or at least very underdeveloped. One book known to this author, which provides a framework for the development manager to use in dealing with the political environment accepted as given is Marc Lindenberg and Benjamin Crosby, *Managing Development: The Political Dimension* (West Hartford, Conn.: Kumarian Press, 1981). Some measures are proposed to alleviate political and other constraints by Jerry VanSant and Paul R. Crawford, "Coping with Political, Economic, Environmental, and Institutional Constraints," in Elliott R. Morss and David D. Gow, eds., *Implementing Rural Development Projects: Lessons from AID and World Bank*

Experiences (Boulder, Colo.: Westview Press, 1985), pp. 1–32. And some attempts have been made to develop a managerial infrastructure based on a country's past history and culture, including political and legal systems; see Kenneth L. Murrell, "The Managerial Infrastructure in Economic Development: Its Importance and How to Analyze It" *SICA Occasional Papers Series*, 2d ser., no. 12 (Austin: Institute for Latin American Studies, The University of Texas at Austin and the Section on International and Comparative Administration, 1986).

6. The concepts of legitimacy, authority, and power as used here are similar to those in Amitai Etzioni, *Modern Organizations* (Englewood Cliffs, N.J.: Prentice-Hall, 1964), pp. 50–57; and by Lucian W. Pye in *Asian Power and Politics: The Cultural Dimension of Authority* (Cambridge, Mass.: Belknap Press, 1985), pp. 18–19, 283–84 (for a definition from the cultural viewpoint).

For a discussion of the concepts of political authority and legitimacy, see Carl Joachim Friedrich, *Man and His Government* (New York: McGraw-Hill, 1963), chaps. 12 and 13. On the Weberian bases and types of legitimacy and authority, see H. H. Gerth and C. Wright Mills, eds., *From Max Weber: Essays in Sociology* (New York: Oxford University Press, 1946), chaps. 8–10, pp. 294–300, and passim. For a summary and interpretation of Weber's concept of authority with a focus on charisma as a source, see Ann Ruth Willner, *The Spellbinders: Charismatic Political Leadership* (New Haven: Yale University Press, 1984), chap. 1.

Legitimacy of governments was discussed by Guy J. Pauker, *Sources of Instability in Developing Countries* (Santa Monica, Calif.: Rand Corporation, 1973); and W. Howard Wriggins, *The Ruler's Imperative: Strategies for Political Survival in Asia and Africa* (New York: Columbia University Press, 1969), pp. 38–41 and passim.

For a comparative study of the relationship between legitimacy of political leadership and societal structure using Max Weber's typology of traditional, charismatic, and rational-legal legitimacy and Fred W. Riggs's model of prismatic society, see Paul R. Dettman, "Leaders and Structures in Third-World Politics: Contrasting Approaches to Legitimacy," in Norman W. Provizer, ed., *Analyzing the Third World: Essays from Comparative Politics* (Cambridge, Mass.: Schenkman Publishing Company, 1978), pp. 408–32.

For an operational definition of the concept of legitimacy in quantitative terms, see Peter A. Busch, *Legitimacy and Ethnicity: A Case Study of Singapore* (Lexington, Mass.: Lexington Books, D. C. Heath and Company, 1974).

Interestingly enough, legitimacy, authority, and power are also central concepts in oriental political thought and practices. Indeed, they constituted the main topic of debate for over two thousand years between the humanist and legalist schools in China. The former advocated a humane government based on internalized control induced by moral examples from virtuous men; the latter a government by law based on externalized control through the use of law, techniques, and naked power (punishments, coercion, force). See Wing-Tsit Chan, "The Path to Wisdom: Chinese Philosophy and Religion," in Arnold Toynbee, ed., *Half the World: The History and Culture of China and Japan* (New York: Holt, Rinehart, and Winston, 1973), pp. 116, 118, 119, and passim. For an analysis of the traditional Vietnamese philosophy of government, which reconciles humanist and legalist schools, see Nghiem Dang, *Vietnam: Politics and Public Administration* (Honolulu: East-West Center Press, 1966), pp. 51–59.

7. The concept of conflict between old and new values and norms in LDCs has been developed and applied by Fred W. Riggs in many of his publications. See, for example, *Administration in Developing Countries: The Theory of Prismatic Society* (Boston: Houghton Mufflin, 1964); and *Thailand: The Modernization of a Bureaucratic Polity* (Honolulu: East West Center Press, 1966). See also Pauker, *Sources of Instability.* For an analysis of the legitimacy issue confronting Arab polities, see Hermassi, *The Third World*, chap. 5.

For an analysis of relationships between social conflict, legitimacy, and democracy, see Seymour Martin Lipset, *Political Man: The Social Bases of Politics* (Garden City, N.Y.: Anchor Books, Doubleday & Company, 1959), chap. 3; quoting Alexis de Tocqueville, Lipset describes the loss of legitimacy from aristocratic monarchies to democratic republics:

"epochs sometimes occur in the life of a nation when the old customs of a people are changed, public morality is destroyed, religious belief shaken, and the spell of tradition broken." The citizens then have "neither the instinctive patriotism of a monarchy nor the reflective patriotism of a republic; . . . they have stopped between the two in the midst of confusion and distress." (p. 65)

On how the United States confronted this crisis of legitimacy at the early period of her history, see Seymour Martin Lipset, *The First New Nation: The United States in Historical and Comparative Perspective* (New York: Basic Books, 1963), part 1.

8. On the issue of irreversibility of totalitarian, Communist regimes, see Charles Krauthammer, "What Has Happened to Totalitarianism?" *Time Magazine*, 10 November 1986, p. 114.

For an analysis of how ruling elites in the Soviet Union and Eastern Europe attempt to gain popular acceptance through sources of legitimacy, such as goal rationality (versus formal-legal rationality of the West), charisma, paternalism (security versus freedom), and familiarity, see T. H. Rigby and Ferenc Feher, eds., *Political Legitimation in Communist States* (New York: St. Martin's Press, 1982). Interestingly, Chinese Communist leadership has openly questioned the Marxist doctrine. The general secretary of the Chinese Communist party, Hu Yao-bang, in a 1984 interview with the Italian Communist daily *L'Unita* pointed out the fundamental problems in these terms: "Since the October Revolution (of 1917, which enthroned Soviet Marxism), more than 60 years have passed. How is it that many socialist countries have not been able to overtake capitalist ones in terms of development? What was it that did not work?" (See "China Deng Xiaoping Leads a Far-Reaching, Audacious but Risky Second Revolution," *Time Magazine*, 6 January 1986, pp. 24ff, p. 28 for quotation.)

The only Communist regime that has been overthrown by external invasion from the non-Communist world was Maurice Bishop's regime in Grenada following a bloody internal power struggle with a rival Communist faction and an invasion by U.S. troops late in 1983. The only Communist regime that has been overthrown thus far by anti-Communist internal forces (with the help of external forces) was Salvador Allende's Chile. Allende, a Marxist revolutionary candidate, became president through a free and orderly election in September 1970 and was overthrown by the Chilean armed forces after about two years in power. This case may not, however, be considered as an exception, since the

Chilean Community party was but one element in a left-wing coalition and thus not yet in full control of the country at the time.

On how Soviets have demonstrated a superior will and ability to defend Communist Third-World regimes from actual or planned coups, see Steven R. David, *Defending Third-World Regimes from Coups d'Etat* (Lanham, Md.: University Press of America and the Center for International Affairs, Harvard University, 1985), pp. 78–80.

9. See Wriggins, *The Ruler's Imperative:*

If it were possible to measure the attention a ruler gives to different problems, it could probably be shown that he devotes more time and effort to aggregating around himself and his government sufficient political power to permit him to stay on top than to any other single purpose. (p. 11)

10. See, for example, Ali Shaukat, *Nation Building Development and Administration: A Third-World Perspective* (Urdu Bazar, Lahore, Pakistan: S. Aziz Shah Bukhari, Aziz Publishers, 1979), especially chaps. 6 and 7; Frank Tannenbaum, "The Influence of Social Conditions," in Martin Kriesberg, ed., *Public Administration in Developing Countries* (Washington, D.C.: Brookings Institution, 1965), pp. 33–42; Riggs, *Thailand;* Hahn Been Lee, *Korea: Time, Change, and Administration* (Honolulu: East West Center Press, 1968), especially chaps. 5 and 7; Ferrel Heady, *Public Administration: A Comparative Perspective,* 3d ed. (New York and Basel: Marcel Dekker, 1984), pp. 293–437; Wriggins, *The Ruler's Imperative,* especially chap. 4.

On wealth as a means of maintaining power and preparing for the fall from power, see literature and media reports on coups, *pronunciamiento,* or revolutions. On the business ventures of Nicaragua's Somoza, for example, see Bernard Diederich, *Somoza—and the Legacy of U.S. Involvement in Central America* (New York: E. P. Dutton, 1981), pp. 73, 91–92, 100, 115, 131–132, 143, 174, 327. Somoza's fortune was estimated in 1961 at 10 percent of Nicaragua's GNP. On the Philippines' Marcos, see press reports after his fall, for example *Washington Post,* "Marcos Documents Discovered," 1 March 1986, front page f; "Associates of Marcos Resurfacing," 27 February 1986, p. A28; "Tax Returns, Receipts Document Marcos' Spending, Investing," 26 February 1986, p. A12; "Palace Papers Hint at Marcoses' Wealth," 2 March 1986, front page f; "Sources of Markos' Fortune Documented," 6 March 1986, front page f (his fortune was estimated at US $5 to $10 billion); "The Philippines: Anatomy of a Looting," 30 March 1986, front page f; and "Real Estate Agents Tell of Marcos Buys," 10 April 1986, front page f. On Haiti's Duvalier, see *Washington Post,* "Haiti Seeks to Tie Losses to Duvalier," 12 May 1986, front page f (Duvalier's overall worth was estimated at $900 million, with $367 million in banks in Switzerland); and "Haiti Says Duvalier Removed $33 Million," 30 May 1986, p. A27.

11. On bureaucratic pathologies in LDCs, see World Bank, *Report 1983,* pp. 41–127 passim; Heady, *Public Administration,* pp. 252–92 passim; Jon Moris, "The Transferability of Western Management Concepts and Programs: An East African Perspective," in Joseph E. Black, James S. Coleman, and Lawrence D. Stifel, eds., *Education and Training for Public Sector Management in Developing Countries* (New York: Rockefeller Foundation, March 1977), pp. 73–83; Rondinelli, *Development Projects as Policy Experiments;* U.S. General Accounting Office, *Financial Management Problems in Developing Countries Reduce the Impact of Assistance,* report to the administrator, Agency for

International Development, GAO/NSIAD -85-19, 5 November 1984, pp. 6–19; Jamil Jreisat, "Building Administrative Capacity for Action: The Arab States" *SICA Occasional Papers Series,* 2d ser., no. 8 (Austin: Institute of Latin American Studies, University of Texas at Austin and the Section on International and Comparative Administration, 1985); Dele Olowu, "Bureaucratic Performance in Developed and Developing Countries: A Review of Recent Literature and Developments," *Public Administration Review* 44, no. 5 (September/October 1984): 453–58; Jack Koteen, "Key Problems in Development Administration," in Kenneth J. Rothwell, ed., *Administrative Issues in Developing Economies* (Lexington, Mass.: Lexington Books, 1972), pp. 47–67; Harold Ross and Jan Bouwmeesters, *Management in the Developing Countries: A Field Survey* (Geneva: United Nations Research Institute for Social Development, 1972); Bryant and White, *Managing Development,* pp. 23–26, 51–53, and passim; Kempe Ronald Hope, "Politics, Bureaucratic Corruption, and Maladministration in the Third World," *International Review of Administrative Sciences* 51, no. 1 (1985): 1–6; and the following articles on same topic by Dele Oluwu on Nigeria, (pp. 7–12); Ledivina V. Carino on the Philippines (pp. 13–18); and Edwin Jones on the Commonwealth Carribbean countries (pp. 19–23); and O. P. Dwivedi, "Ethics and Values of Public Responsibility and Accountability," *International Review of Administrative Sciences* 51, no. 1 (1985): 61–66.

12. On capitalism's negative impact on LDC cultures, see Robert E. Gamer, *The Developing Nations: A Comparative Perspective* (Boston: Allyn and Bacon, 1976); Chinweizu, *The West and the Rest of Us: White Predators, Black Slavers, and the African Elite* (New York: Vintage Books, 1975), especially parts 1 and 2; Chinweizu, "Africa in the Eighties," *Africa* 125 (January 1982): 54–55; Colin M. Turnbull, *The Lonely African* (Garden City, N.Y.: Anchor Books, 1963); also "The Lonely African," in Stanley M. Davis, ed.,*Comparative Management: Organizational and Cultural Perspectives* (Englewood Cliffs, N.J.: Prentice-Hall, 1971), pp. 32–40; Albert Memmi, *Portrait du colonisé précédé du portrait du colonisateur* (Paris: Payot, 1973); Frantz Fanon, *The Wretched of the Earth* (New York: Grove Press, 1966); Frantz Fanon, "The Pitfalls of National Consciousness," in Stanley M. Davis, *Comparative Management: Organizational and Cultural Perspectives* (Englewood Cliffs, N.J.: Prentice-Hall, 1971), pp. 40–70; Andre Gunder Frank, *Capitalism and Underdevelopment in Latin America* (New York and London: Monthly Review Press, 1969); Andre Gunder Frank, *Latin America: Underdevelopment or Revolution* (New York and London: Monthly Review Press, 1969); Harrison, *Underdevelopment Is a State of Mind;* and Hermassi, *The Third World,* chap. 7.

For an insightful analysis of the negative impact of French colonial policy on Vietnam's political traditions, see John T. McAlister, Jr., and Paul Mus, *The Vietnamese and Their Revolution* (New York: Harper and Row, 1970), pp. 29–43. The negative portrait of LDC people can be compared to that of a South Vietnamese night club girl whose behavior is guided by a kind of amoral materialism resulting from the corruptive impact of colonialist cynicism and the destructive influence of naïve U.S. good will, as described by Graham Greene in *The Quiet American* (New York: Modern Library, 1955).

13. For an analysis of the moral foundation of capitalism, see Max Weber and Kemper Fullerton, "The Protestant Ethic and the Spirit of Capitalism," in Ross Weber, ed., *Culture and Management* (Homewood, Ill.: Richard D. Irvin, 1969), pp. 91–112; Max Weber, *The Protestant Ethic and the Spirit of Cap-*

italism, Talcott Parsons, trans. (New York: Scribner's, 1958); and Gerth and Mills, eds., *From Max Weber,* pp. 302–23. On the U.S. value system, see Tri Q. Nguyen, "Culture and Technical Assistance in Public Administration: A Study of What Can Be Transferred from the United States to Vietnam" (Ph.D. diss., University of Southern California, January 1970), pp. 95–140 (for the value of material well being, see pp.123–28. It is to be noted that Greek, Roman, and other constitutional concepts are probably as strong in U.S. culture as the puritan ethic described here according to the cultural anthropology school of thoughts cited in Nguyen's dissertation.

14. See Nguyen, "Culture and Technical Assistance in Public Administration," pp. 410–13.

On corruption, see Ronald Wraith and Edgar Simpkins, *Corruption in Developing Countries* (New York: W. W. Norton and Company, 1964); David J. Gould, *Bureaucratic Corruption and Underdevelopment in the Third World: The Case of Zaire* (New York: Pergamon, 1980); *Time Magazine,* 16 January 1984, special issue on "Africa's Woes: A Continent Gone Wrong"; *Compact for African Development,* p. 9; Bryant and White, *Managing Development,* pp. 30, 51–53, 66; Hope, "Politics, Bureaucratic Corruption, and Maladministration" and articles following Hope's cited in n. 11.

15. See Gabriel A. Almond and James S. Coleman, *The Politics of the Developing Areas* (Princeton: Princeton University Press, 1960); Arthur Bank and Robert Textor, *A Cross-Polity Survey* (Cambridge: M.I.T. Press, 1963); Christopher Chapman, *Third-World Politics: An Introduction* (Madison: University of Wisconsin Press, 1985); Robert H. Jackson and Carl G. Rosberg, *Personal Rules in Black Africa: Prince, Autocrat, Prophet, Tyrant* (Berkeley: University of California Press, 1982); and Hermassi, *The Third World,* chap. 6. See also the literature on specific countries, for example, Riggs, *Thailand;* and Gregory Henderson, *Korea: The Politics of the Vortex* (Cambridge: Harvard University Press, 1968); Oluwu, "Bureaucratic Corruption and Public Accountability in Nigeria: pp. 7–12; Ledivina V. Carino, "The Politicization of the Philippine Bureaucracy: Corruption or Commitment?" *International Review of Administrative Sciences* 51, no. 1 (1985): 13–18; and Edwin Jones, "Politics, Bureaucratic Corruption, and Maladministration in the Third World: Some Commonwealth Caribbean Considerations," *International Review of Administrative Sciences* 51, no. 1 (1985): 19–23.

16. David J. Gould's observation appears to apply to the situation in many LDCs:

> The chain of tolerance of corruption is such that everybody is corrupt and corrupting. Potentially honest individuals are caged, willy nilly, into a bureaucratic system which one knowledgeable observer characterized as institutionalizing "hydra-headed dishonesty". . . . "the malady . . . reveals a profound crisis," leading to a situation in which "the individual has no choice left but to seek a solution in active corruption in order to defend his rights." (*Bureaucratic Corruption and Underdevelopment,* p. xiv)

Along the same line, in a review of some recent books on bureaucratic performance in LDCs, Dele Oluwu pointed out the problems of corruption in these terms:

The problem confronting the Third World is what one of the authors has aptly described as "systemic" or "institutionalized corruption." This situation is referred to as one in which

"the administrative system tolerates wrongdoing and actually penalises propriety and integrity. Its symptoms are that (Public servants) set themselves above and beyond the law and moral convention. They believe they can do anything and get away with it. They behave arrogantly and treat everybody also with contempt." ("Bureaucratic Performance in Developed and Developing Countries," p.456)

The LDC people appear to be familiar with the following practice described by Nigerian writer Chinua Achebe:

"A structure that costs us, say, $200 million carries a huge hidden element of kickbacks and commissions to Nigerian middlemen. . . . It carries inflated prices of materials caused largely by corruption; theft and inefficiency on the site fostered by more corruption; contract variation, corruptly arranged midstream in execution. . . . When all these factors are added to others which our corrupt ingenuity constantly invents, you will be lucky if on completion our structure is worth as much as $80 million." (Quoted by Blaine Harden, "Price Drop Threatens Nigerian Economy," Washington Post, 25 January 1986, p. A14).

Also see literature on other LDCs. On the contribution of corruption to the fall of South Vietnam, see Guenter Lewy, America in Vietnam (New York: Oxford University Press, 1978), pp. 90–95, 169, 201, 217–220, and 280. On corruption in Korea, see Henderson, Korea, passim (see index, corruption).

17. For background on non-Communist LDC elites, see Vincent A. Mahler, Dependency Approaches to International Political Economy: A Cross-National Study (New York: Columbia University Press, 1980), especially pp. 47–68, which reviews dependency theory literature on the role of the so-called "bridge head elite," "internationalized bourgeoisie," "comprador bourgeoisie," "managerial bourgeoisie," or "technocratic elitism" in LDCs; Gamer, The Developing Nations, pp. 101–68; Charles Wagley, "The Dilemma of the Latin American Middle Class," in Stanley M. Davis, ed., Comparative Management: Organizational and Culture Perspectives (Englewood Cliffs, N.J.: Prentice-Hall, 1971), pp. 144–50; Stanley M. Davis, "Politics and Organizational Underdevelopment in Chile," in Davis, Comparative Management, pp. 188–209; Frank, Capitalism and Underdevelopment; Frank, Latin America, especially chap. 4 passim; Harrison, Underdevelopment Is a State of Mind; Hermassi, The Third World, pp. 91–92; Gould, Bureaucratic Corruption and Underdevelopment, pp. 9–19, 34–56; and Chinweizu, The West and the Rest of Us, especially part 4.

18. On the "pariah" entrepreneurs, see Riggs, Administration in Developing Countries, pp. 116, 163, 173, 188–193; and Thailand, pp. 249–54.

19. For a general view of political instability in LDCs, see Taylor and Jodice, World Handbook, vol. 2. On political instability in Latin America, see Bradley Graham, "Move to Democracy Is Uneasy Balance—Latin Civilians Debate Role of Military," Washington Post, 12 November 1986, pp. A21 f.

For an analysis of the fall of the Shah of Iran stressing the legitimacy issue, see Melvin Gurtow and Ray Maghroori, Roots of Failure: United States Policy in the Third World (Westport, Conn.: Greenwood Press, 1984), chap. 2. The authors maintain that "without legitimacy, even the 'impressive economic gains' of Iran under the Shah could not invest his regime with stability (not to mention the fact that those economic gains were enjoyed by only a select minority)" (p. 93).

For an analysis of non-Communist LDC leaders' strategies for aggregating power, see Wriggins, *The Ruler's Imperative*, part 3.

For an analysis of the relationship between legitimacy and effectiveness (power), see Lipset, *Political Man*, pp. 64–70.

20. On competition among world powers over LDCs, see the literature on international relations. The conflict between Communist and Western powers is obvious and well known; that among Western powers has been covert and latent. Rivalry between France and the United States over Vietnam, for example, was successfully exploited by Communists and contributed to the loss of Vietnam to the Soviet orbit. The United States supported France militarily, economically, and politically to reconquer her former colony as a price for France's partnership in NATO and containment of Communist expansion in that part of the free world. The U.S. refusal to increase support as time went on and especially at the decisive battle of Dien Bien Phu led to the loss of half of Vietnam. The French still hoped to retain control over the other half, but the United States helped Diem drive them out of South Vietnam. France, in turn, supported Laos and Cambodia, which, under the label of neutrality, let their territory be used as sanctuaries from which North Vietnamese troops attacked South Vietnam. Cambodia, under Sihanouk, even went as far as to allow the Soviet Union and China to use the Sihanoukville facilities to supply armaments to the Vietnamese Communists in South Vietnam. The final results have been seen: the sovietization of the whole of former French Indochina, including Vietnam, Cambodia (Kampuchia), and Laos. On some negative aspects of French-U.S. relations over Vietnam, see Bernard B. Fall, *The Two Vietnams: A Political and Military Analysis*, 2d rev. ed. (New York: Praeger, 1967), pp. 68–71, 255, 269, 322; and Marianna P. Sullivan, *France's Vietnam Policy: A Study in French-American Relations* (Westport, Conn.: Greenwood Press, 1978). On the involvement of, and competition among, advanced countries in LDCs' politics, see Steven R. David, *Third-World Coups d'Etat and International Security* (Baltimore: Johns Hopkins University Press, 1987).

CHAPTER 2. NEGATIVE IMPACT OF THE CRISIS OF LEGITIMACY ON INTERNATIONAL DEVELOPMENT ASSISTANCE

1. On the magnitudes of development assistance, see Elliott R. Morss and Victoria A. Morss, *U.S. Foreign Aid: An Assessment of New and Traditional Development Strategies* (Boulder, Colo.: Westview Press, 1982), chap. 1; World Bank, *Report 1985*, pp. 94–97. On the evaluation of foreign aid effectiveness, see introduction, n. 1.

2. On political instability, see Taylor and Jodice, *World Handbook*, vol. 2. Concerning economic growth rates, see *Ibid.*, vol. 1, especially pp. 130–41.

3. The evolution of foreign aid away from the general, program approach toward a tighter and tighter project approach, which is discussed later in this chapter, can be seen as a reflection of this increasing emphasis on control and an example of the Catch-22 situation of donor agencies.

4. Poor operation and maintenance of enterprises left by foreign aid is a current hot issue. See citations in n. 20.

5. On the flight of capital, see World Bank, *Report 1985*, pp. 64–65; "An Exodus of Capital Is Sapping the LDC Economies: It Has Also Created a Tremendous Distortion of Global Money Flows," *Business Week*, 3 October 1983, pp. 132–34:

> Thousands of individuals, small businesses and multinational corporations . . . shipped more than $120 billion out of the developing countries from 1973 to 1983 to make investments ranging from Miami condominiums to deposits in numbered Swiss bank accounts. In the last three years alone, a staggering $71 billion has been spirited out of seven of the world's biggest debtors, even while those countries' foreign debt ballooned by $120 billion. (p. 132)

See also James S. Henry, "Where the Money Went," *New Republic*, 14 April 1986, pp. 20–23.

Capital flight has also been deplored by World Bank, IMF, and Western officials responsible for foreign aid (see, for example, *Washington Post*, 28 April 1985, p. K8; and 8 October 1985, p. A22). According to Henry ("Where the Money Went," p.21), a member of the Federal Reserve Board recently said that "the problem is not that Latin Americans don't have assets. They do. The problem is, they're all in Miami."

On capital flight from the Philippines, for example, see Dale Russakoff, "The Philippines: Anatomy of a Looting," *Washington Post*, 30 March 1986, front page f.: "Philippine officials estimate that as much as $30 billion left the country in the Marcos era, about the amount of the gross national product—this, in a country where unauthorized export of foreign exchange is illegal."

For an account of how the first ladies in LDCs spent money overseas, especially in Western countries, see "Dragon Ladies under Siege," *People*, 3 March 1986, pp. 28f.

6. On Western expatriates' share in developing funding, see World Bank, *Report 1983*, p. 12. Over half of donors' expenditures on technical assistance goes to finance expatriate staff; and the cost of an expert can go up to $15,000 or $16,000 per month.

Whether these expatriates are worth the money spent can be inferred from the report's observation that host governments often accept expatriates as a way of getting aid without being convinced of needing their services; recipients may not be consulted on the expertise needed; donors' salary and lifestyle can cause resentment; experts' qualities, valued in donor countries, may be unsuitable in the host country; and expatriates' technical skills may be irrelevant for training local counterparts rather than doing the job itself. These observations appear to be congruent with the following comment:

"The criticism of TA (technical assistance) . . . is currently widespread within donor agencies and recipient governments. This criticism results from dissatisfaction with the quality of TA personnel, confusion about the appropriate functions of TA, and disagreement over the role that TA personnel should play" (George H. Honadle, Jerry M. Silverman, and Donald R. Mickelwait, "Technical Assistance Shortcomings," in Elliott R. Morss and David D. Gow, eds., *Implementing Rural Development Projects—Lessons from AID and World Bank Experiences* [Boulder, Colo.: Westview Press, 1985], pp. 83–84).

7. On the brain drain, see World Bank, *Report 1983*, pp. 103–6; UNCTAD

Secretariat, *The Reverse Transfer of Technology, Its Dimensions, Economic Effects, and Policy Implications: A Study* (New York: United Nations, 1975); and Andre Payenne, "Plugging the Brain Drain—A Third-World Call for Western Reparations," *World Press Review* (August 1985): 33–34.

8. Some evidence of convergence of interests among developed and developing countries' organizations and individuals can be found in the following:

a. As pointed out by Evan Thomas, "The U.N. Mid-Life Crisis," *Time Magazine*, 28 October 1985, p. 40:

> The money from U.N. welfare and development agencies . . . does not always reach its intended beneficiaries. Some African nations draw up "shopping lists" under the guise of program proposals, confident that U.N. officials will not probe deeply enough to find out that much of the aid for the rural populace is being siphoned off by the urban elite. In Third World countries, well-paid U.N. staffers tend to hole up in expatriate ghettos and rely on overly optimistic government status reports on their projects.

b. According to Morss, donor staff are well aware of the repeated failures of recipient governments to honor commitments to deliver local counterparts and take care of recurrent expenditures for project operation. But the staff cannot afford to act as if it expects these failures to occur because "they are paid to plan and disburse monies through development projects; [and] they could not get their projects through their own agency's approval process if they made realistic estimates of the recipient countries' abilities to make resource commitments to projects." As a result, no capacity building can occur while "the hypocritical cycle repeats itself" (Elliott R.Morss, "Institutional Destruction Resulting from Donor and Project Proliferation in Sub-Saharan Countries," *World Development*, 12, no. 4 [1984]: 467).

c. In the words of VanSant and Crawford,

> The . . . option—abandoning the project—is even more rarely chosen. The decision to proceed is often made before the design team is in the field. If not, the design team itself may have a vested interest in later implementation, however serious the recognized constraints may be. All too often, the result is a project doomed to fail before it begins. ("Coping with Political, Economic, Environmental, and Institutional Constraints," p. 17)

d. According to Borgin and Corbet,

> Africans themselves are fully aware that national and international aid organizations and the various organizations belonging to the UN are staffed with useless, ignorant—ignorant about Africa, that is—and incompetent bureaucrats. What Africans, especially the intellectual Africans, say among themselves and to the few Europeans they take into their confidence is entirely different from what they say in speeches about the generous help from overseas without which agriculture and industry cannot be developed. In one way they could not care who these international bureaucrats are as long as the millions keep on coming in from overseas taxpayers. (*The Destruction of a Continent*, p. 30)

In the opinon of these same authors, development assistance officials, for their part, "will probably remain utopians forever," because if they were realistic and honest, they would have to declare that there is little they can do for the developing world with the present development system. They could not afford to do that simply because "If they did, they would be without the best-paid and most secure jobs in the world" (*Ibid.*, p. 44–45).

e. The preceding observations seem to be in line with the critical comment by the Council on Foreign Relations and the Overseas Development Council that "Most donors, including international institutions, have jumped from one fad to another to justify development expenditures" (*Compact for African Development*, p. 10).

f. On a more general plane, this confluence or collusion of interests can be seen within the framework of dependency relationships between international forces and Western-oriented LDC elites, as maintained by the dependency theorists. For a review of dependency theory, see works cited in chap. 5, n. 9 and 11.

9. My former school, the University of Southern California and its faculty and consultants, as well as several former presidents of the American Society for Public Administration (ASPA), who had been involved in some development projects in Iran, were so accused after the fall of the Shah. See assessment of advisory role by four ASPA past presidents in 15 May 1979 *Public Administration Times*, pp. 1, 4, 5, 7; by former ASPA president, Donald C. Stone in the 1 June 1979 issue, pp. 3 and 7; letter to the editor by Ali Fazadmand in 1 July 1979 issue, pp. 2 and 10; and letter to the editor by Frederick C. Thayer in 1 August 1979 issue of the same newspaper. See also a series of articles by John L. Seitz, Frank P. Sherwood, William J. Siffin, John D. Montgomery, Milton J. Esman, and John L. Seitz on the Iranian experience in "From the Professional Stream: Currents and Sounding," *Public Administration Review* 40, no. 5 (September/October 1980): 407–33. The general issue has been pointed out by Gendzier, *Managing Political Change*, p. 2, in these terms:

"US policy makers extol Development in terms of democracy, yet they support authoritarian regimes that manipulate social and political change.

For many, terms like Development and Modernization have lost their meaning. They have become code words. They refer to policies pursued by governments and international agencies that enrich ruling elites and technocrats, while the masses are told to await the benefits of the "trickle down" effect. . . . And for many, *social scientists who have rationalized the interests of governments committed to such policies are accomplices in deception.* (emphasis added)

10. For an appraisal of the capital transfer approach and other approaches to foreign aid, see Milton J. Esman, "Foreign Aid: Not by Bread Alone," *Public Administration Review* 31 (January/February 1971): 92–100; Milton J. Esman and John D. Montgomery, "Systems Approaches to Technical Cooperation: The Role of "Development Administration," *Public Administration Review* 29 (September/October 1969): 507–39; and Morss and Morss, *U.S. Foreign Aid.*

11. On the reverse transfer of capital from developing to developed countries, see n. 5. For an argument that the shortage of capital in LDCs is not real but imposed by former colonial powers to create a need for foreign investments in order to dominate the LDC economies, see Chinweizu, *The West and the Rest of Us*, pp. 270–82.

12. See Esman and Montgomery, "Systems Approaches to Technical Cooperation."

13. The reader is referred to the literature on appropriate technology. For background, see, for example, Pradip K. Ghosh, ed., *Appropriate Technology in Third-World Development* (Westport, Conn.: Greenwood Press, 1984). For a review of appropriate technology as a development strategy, see Morss and Morss, *U.S. Foreign Aid*, pp. 35–37, 65. For a negative view of appropriate technology, see Borgin and Corbet, *The Destruction of a Continent*, pp. 118–25 and passim; and Lal, *The Poverty of "Development Economics,"* pp. 59–60, 79, 95–96, 99–100. For a refutation of the Brandt report's accusation that multinational corporations transfer inappropriate technology to LDCs, see Melvyn B. Krauss, *Development without Aid—Growth, Poverty, and Government* (New York: McGraw-Hill, 1983), pp. 134–38.

For an analysis of Japanese management, which is permeated by values quite different from, if not opposed to, U.S. values but equally if not more effective, see Gabino A. Mendoza, "The Transferability of Western Management Concepts and Programs: an Asian Perspective," in Joseph E. Black, James S. Coleman, and Lawrence D. Stifel, eds., *Education and Training for Public Sector Management in Developing Countries* (New York: Rockefeller Foundation, March 1977), pp. 61–71. For the transfer of Japanese management techniques and processes to the United States, the reader is referred to the literature, especially on "quality circle."

China, ranked among lower income economies together with such countries as Guinea, Haiti, and Sri Lanka (World Bank, *Report 1983*, p. 148), managed to stage its first nuclear test in 1964 and to produce nuclear weapons since then, apparently without adopting Western management techniques nor values nor following precepts of the appropriate or intermediate technology school. See Frederica M. Bunge and Rinn-Sup-Shinn, eds., *China: A Country Study* (Washington, D.C.: Foreign Area Studies, American University, 1981), pp. 35, 464, 467, 469, 476–77; and Gilbert Rozman, ed., *The Modernization of China* (New York: Free Press, 1981), pp. 247–48, 434–35, 464). South Korea's emphasis on heavy industry during the 1970s did not seem to adhere to technological stages or appropriate technology either. The country developed its own defense industry, and in 1978 heavy industry (petrochemical, steel, shipbuilding) accounted for 51 percent of all industrial output and one-fourth of all exports. See Frederica M. Bunge, ed., *South Korea: A Country Study*, 3d ed. (Washington, D.C.: Foreign Area Studies, American University, 1982), pp. 112–14.

14. For a review of cultural anthropology literature on culture, value, and behavior, see Nguyen, "Culture and Technical Assistance in Public Administration," chap. 1; and Geert Hofstede, *Culture's Consequences: International Differences in Work-Related Values* (Beverly Hill, Calif.: Sage Publications, 1980), pp. 44–50.

15. On adviser-counterpart relationships, see Irving J. Spitzberg, Jr., ed., *Exchange of Expertise: The Counterpart System in the New International Order* (Boulder, Colo.: Westview Press, 1978); refer also to articles concerning advisers and counterparts published in Focus in the *International Development Review*, as indicated by Spitzberg. A summary discussion of the management of expatriates is presented in World Bank, *Report 1983*, pp. 112–13. See also Denise Harari, *The Role of the Technical Assistance Expert: An Inquiry into the Expert's Identity Motivations and Attitudes* (Paris: Development Centre, Organization for Economic Cooperation and Development, 1974). Ac-

cording to the latter, the French expert's motivation for wanting to go overseas was ranked as follows from highest to lowest: to avoid service in the armed forces, curiosity, professional experience, interest in Third World, financial advantage, more responsibility, to leave home country, humanitarian consideration (pp. 125–27). The reader will realize the extent of the dilemma from two recent articles discussing personnel problems facing recipient governments and the technical assistance problems facing donor agencies, respectively, Elliott R. Morss, Paul R. Crawford, and Gene M. Owens, "Personnel Constraints," in Elliott R. Morss and David D. Gow, eds., *Implementing Rural Development Projects—Lessons from AID and World Bank Experiences* (Boulder, Colo.: Westview Press, 1985), pp. 65–81; and Honadle, Silverman, and Mickelwait, "Technical Assistance Shortcomings," in Morss and Gow, *Implementing Rural Development Projects*, pp. 83–106. For a discussion of the incentive structure that makes it difficult for foreign experts to transfer skills to LDC nationals, see Morss and Morss, *U.S. Foreign Aid*, pp. 71–72. On the relationships between U.S. advisers and Vietnamese counterparts, see Lewy, *America in Vietnam*, pp. 168–69; and Ronald H. Spector, *Advice and Support: The Early Years of the United States Army in Vietnam 1941–1960* (1983; reprint, New York: Free Press, 1985), pp. 291–95.

16. A summary discussion of participant training issues is provided in World Bank, *Report 1983*, pp. 103–6. On problems facing trainees after their overseas training, see, for example, "La formation agricole: Rapport sur une étude d'évaluation," *Série d'évaluation* no. 4 (Rome: Food and Agriculture Organization, 1980): 5, 38–40; and Craufurd D. Goodwin and Michael Nacht, *Decline and Renewal: Causes and Cures of Decay among Foreign-Trained Intellectuals and Professionals in the Third World* (New York: Institute of International Education, 1986), especially chaps. 3 and 4. On brain drain, see n. 7.

17. The reader is referred to the literature on institution building. An overview of this literature is provided in Joseph W. Eaton, ed., *Institution Building and Development: From Concepts to Application* (Beverly Hill, Calif.: Sage Publications, 1972); and in Melvin G. Blase, *Institution Building: A Source Book* (East Lansing, Mich.: Midwest Universities Consortium for International Activities, 1973). For a review of the approach, see Ingle, "Implementing Development Programs, pp. 31–34, 73; Rondinelli, "Development Management in AID," pp. 27–34; Morss and Morss, *U.S. Foreign Aid*, p. 38; and *Institutional Development: Improving Management in Developing Countries—Report on a Seminar Series* (Washington, D.C.: American Consortium for International Public Administration, 1986).

18. For an appraisal of the project management unit as an organizational alternative in integrated rural development efforts, see Honadle and VanSant, *Implementation for Sustainability*, pp. 12–15, 22, 40–41, 51–52, 79–80, 86, 100, 106. Summary discussions of project management experience in LDCs are provided in World Bank, *Report 1983*, pp. 88–100; Dennis A. Rondinelli, "Project as Instrument of Development Administration: A Qualified Defence and Suggestions for Improvement," *Public Administration and Development* 3, no. 4 (October–December 1983): 307–27; and Dennis A. Rondinelli, ed., *Planning Development Projects* (Stroudsberg, Pa.: Dowden, Hutchinson, and Ross, 1977).

19. For a review of incremental and comprehensive administrative reforms in LDCs, see William J. Siffin, "Two Decades of Public Administration in

Developing Countries," *Public Administration Review* 36 (January/February 1976): 61–71; World Bank, *Report 1983*, pp. 101–24; Marcus D. Ingle, "Implementing Development Programs," pp. 11–16; Edward W. Weidner, *Technical Assistance in Public Administration Overseas: The Case for Development Administration* (Chicago: Public Administration Service, 1964). See also literature concerning administrative reform in specific countries, for example, Arne F. Leemans, ed., *The Management of Change in Government* (The Hague: Institute of Social Studies, Martinus Nijhoff, 1976); Nguyen, "Culture and Technical Assistance in Public Administration," especially chap. 5; Roderick T. Groves, "Administrative Reform and the Politics of Reform: The Case of Venezuela," *Public Administration Review* 27, no. 5 (December 1967): 436–45; John D. Montgomery, *The Politics of Foreign Aid: American Experience in South East Asia* (New York: Praeger, 1962); and "Les projets d'assistance des Nations Unies aux pays francophones d'Afrique," *Development Administration Newsletter* (New York: Division of Development Administration, Department of Technical Cooperation for Development, United Nations, no. 71, November 1984–June 1985), pp. 15–16.

20. For a review of management issues confronting parastatals in LDCs, see World Bank, *Report 1983*, pp. 44–46, 74–87; V. V. Bhatt, "Institutional Framework and Public Enterprise Performance," *World Development* 12, no. 7 (1984): 713–21; Leroy P. Jones, ed., *Public Enterprise in Less-Developed Countries* (New York: Cambridge University Press, 1982); Jacob Meerman, "Cost Recovery in a Project Context: Some World Bank Experience in Tropical Africa," *World Development* 11, no. 6 (June 1983): 503–14; Abraham S. Waldstein, "Development for Whom?" in Stephen P. Reyna, ed., *Sahelian Social Development* (Abidjan: Regional Economic Development Services Offices/West Africa, USAID, 1980), pp. 507–603; P. Heller, "The Underfinancing of Recurrent Development Costs," *Finance and Development* 16, no. 1 (1979): 38–41; and *Compact for African Development*, pp. 6–10 passim. See also the literature on public enterprises in specific countries, for example, Nanda Lall Joshi, "Whither Public Enterprises?" *PRASHASAN (The Nepalese Journal of Public Administration)* 42 (March 1985): 1–5; D. P. Kaberuka, "Evaluating the Performance of Food-Marketing Parastatals," *Development Policy Review* 2 (November 1984), pp. 199–216; Tri Q. Nguyen, "Statutory and Administration Management Aspects of Parastatal Institutions," World Bank CAD/EAPD, Madagascar Public Sector Enterprises, subsector review, *Working Paper No. 1*, March 1982; Tri Q. Nguyen, "Case Study: The Sakay State Farm," World Bank CAD/EAPD, Madagascar Public Sector Enterprises, subsector review, *Working Paper No. 2*, May 1982. The very poor performance of public enterprises in Tanzania, a country admired by both the Communist and non-Communist worlds for its original and indigenous form of socialism under Julius Nyerere, is reported by Marc Yared in "Le Mwalimu s'en va," *Jeune Afrique* no. 1296 (6 November 1985): 9ff, especially 13, 14, 17, and 18.

21. The author does not know of any comprehensive study of the distribution of public servants in LDCs. Their concentration in the capital and large cities is reported here and there in many studies of LDC public administration. The reader is therefore referred to this literature. See, for example, Jean de Gaudusson, *L'administration malgache* (Paris: Éditions Berger-Levrault, 1976), p. 75; Dang, *Vietnam*, p. 180; and Morss, Crawford, and Owens, "Personnel Constraints," in Morss and Gow, *Implementing Rural Development Projects*, p. 70. As for former colonies in general, Rudolf von Albertini, *European Colo-*

nial Rule, 1880–1940—The Impact of the West on India, Southeast Asia, and Africa (Westport, Conn.: Greenwood Press, 1982), p. 492, points out that under colonial rule,

> central administrations tended to become somewhat muscle-bound, which hampered the transmission of impulses toward modernization to the local levels and increased the tendency toward bureaucratization of the capitals. After its Western-educated elites took over the administration, this tendency became stronger, and in the face of new development tasks the central administration ballooned out. The rural areas, on the other hand, remained underdeveloped administratively.

For an insightful analysis of cultural pressures to concentrate the elite in South Korea's capital, see Henderson, *Korea*, chap. 7.

In Vietnam, I once learned from Mr. T. T. Trach, director general of the Civil Service under the Diem administration, that no matter how strict the rules requiring civil servants to serve a minimum of time in the provinces, quite a few managed to transfer back to Saigon after a short while through "pulls" of some sort. Many areas away from the capital are, indeed, referred to as those where "monkeys cough and cranes sing" *(khi ho co gay)* or "ghosts are harmful and water poisonous" *(ma thieng nuoc doc)*, and Vietnamese popular wisdom advises people not to stay there long.

22. For a review of decentralization efforts in LDCs, see G. Shabbir Cheema and Dennis A. Rondinelli, eds., *Decentralization and Development* (Beverly Hill, Calif.: Sage Publications, 1983); Diana Conyers, "Decentralization: The Latest Fashion in Development Administration?" *Public Administration and Development* 3, no. 2 (April–June 1983): 97–109: "In comment on the decentralization efforts of the last decade there does seem to be an increasing feeling—both within the countries concerned and among international agencies, academics and other interested 'outsiders'—that many of the programmes are not living up to the initial expectations" (p. 106); Lenore Ralston, James Anderson, and Elizabeth Colson, *Voluntary Efforts in Decentralized Management: Opportunities and Constraints in Rural Development* (Berkeley: Institute of International Studies, University of California, 1983), pp. 18–21, provide an analysis of how the rural elites have usurped resources; Milton J. Esman and Norman T. Uphoff, *Local Organizations: Intermediaries in Rural Development* (Ithaca, N.Y. and London: Cornell University Press, 1984), chap. 6, pp. 181–202, discusses cultural decadence in analyzing vulnerabilities of rural local organizations); E. G. Vallianatos, *Fear in the Countryside: The Control of Agricultural Resources in the Poor Countries by Non peasant Elites* (Cambridge, Mass.: Ballinger, 1976); David K. Leonard and Dale Roger Marshall, eds., *Institutions of Rural Development for the Poor: Decentralization and Organizational Linkages* (Berkeley: Institute of International Studies, University of California, 1982); David D. Gow and Jerry VanSant, "Decentralization and Participation: Concepts in Need of Implementation Strategies," in Morss and Gow, *Implementing Rural Development Projects*, pp. 107–47. For a review of the literature, see Diana Conyers, "Decentralization and Development: A Review of the Literature," *Public Administration and Development* 4, no. 2 (April–June 1984): 187–97.

The explanation of the failures of attempts to decentralize used here is somewhat similar to Fred W. Riggs's in *Administration in Developing Countries*, pp. 341–46.

23. Morss and Gow, *Implementing Rural Development Projects.*

24. Ibid., p. xiv.

25. Morss, "Institutional Destruction," 40.

26. "Nigeria Set Debt Payment Ceiling," *Washington Post,* 5 January 1986, p. A22.

27. *Compact for African Development,* p. 3.

28. Morss and Morss, *U.S. Foreign Aid,* p. 66.

29. Ibid., footnote.

30. For further details on these nonproject forms of assistance, see World Bank, *Report 1985,* pp. 106–7.

31. Background materials serving as a basis for the analysis in this section on program and project approaches are Morss and Gow, *Implementing Rural Development Projects;* Morss and Morrs, *U.S. Foreign Aid;* Rondinelli, "Development Management in AID"; Honadle and VanSant, *Implementation for Sustainability;* World Bank, *Report 1985,* chap. 7; and Clive Crook, "The World Bank: A Change of Pace," *The Economist,* 27 September 1986, pp. 5–56.

32. Background materials serving as a basis for the analysis in this section on infrastructure, basic needs, and adjustment with growth are the same as those cited in n. 31.

33. *Compact for African Development,* p. 10.

34. For success stories, see, for example, Samuel Paul, *Managing Development Programs: The Lessons of Success* (Boulder, Colo.: Westview Press, 1982); and Guy Gran, "Learning from Development Success: Some Lessons from Contemporary Case Histories," *NASPAA Working Paper No. 9* (Washington, D.C.: National Association of Schools of Public Affairs and Administration, 1983).

Most, if not all, development assistance evaluation or research reports contain at least some bright spots in the overall dark picture. It is around these few lights that recommendations for improvement are made and hypotheses for success are advanced; such conditions are, in general, impossible to find in the LDC setting. This is understandable in light of the theme of effort and optimism that pervades the Western, especially U.S., expert milieu and also because most of the studies are funded directly or indirectly by government bureaucracies. If experts want to survive, they cannot swim against the tide. Thus, U.S. political science thinking has been demonstrated to reflect and support opinions and policies of top policymakers (see Gendzier, *Managing Political Change,* chap. 3). In the same vein, policy changes made at the top, from supporting infrastructure development to concerns with basic human needs have been echoed by the development expert community without reserve, as was the case with previously adopted changes (see Bagicha S. Minhas, "The Current Development Debate," in *Toward a New Strategy for Development: A Rothko Chapel Colloquium* [New York: Pergamon, 1979], pp. 75–96). Apparently, both professional idealism and pragmatism are responsible for the current deadlock in these fields of learning. (The crisis of modernization theory is pointed out by Hermassi in *The Third World,* pp. 194–95).

35. For an analysis of empirical evidence that improvement in health, nutrition, and education leads to unemployment and poverty unless there is accompanying economic growth, see Morss and Morss, *U.S. Foreign Aid,* pp. 51–52. For an analysis of relationships between population changes and development, see World Bank, *World Development Report 1984* (New York: Oxford University Press, 1984).

36. On capital flight and brain drain, see n. 5 and 7.
37. See n. 6 and 8.

CHAPTER 3. EVALUATING DEVELOPMENT: TO WIN THE WAR OR THE BATTLE?

1. For background on Vietnamese history, see Joseph Buttinger, *Vietnam: A Political History* (New York: Praeger, 1968); David G. Marr, *Vietnamese Anti-colonialism 1885–1925* (Berkeley and Los Angeles: University of California Press, 1971); and David G. Marr, *Vietnamese Tradition on Trial, 1920–1945* (Berkeley and Los Angeles: University of California Press, 1981). On relationships between the United States and Vietnam from colonial times until the end of World War II, see Spector, *Advice and Support*, part 1.

For a review of the regimes installed by the French from 1945 to 1954, see S. M. Bao Dai, *Le dragon d'Annam* (Paris: Plon, 1980), especially parts 3 and 4. The very low degree of both legitimacy and power enjoyed by the pro-French regimes is most clearly revealed in these memoirs by a most important witness of this period of Vietnamese history, former Emperor Bao Dai. In this book, he constantly refers to what the French called "Expérience Bao Dai" *(Bao Dai Experience)* as "Expérience française" (French experience). See also McAlister, Jr. and Mus, *The Vietnamese*, who show how Vietnamese communism fit the purposes of a national revolution and gained legitimacy in leading the war of resistance against the French and pro-French regimes; Philippe Devillers, *Histoire du Viêt-Nam de 1940 à 1952* (Paris: Editions du Seuil, 1952); Fall, *The Two Vietnams*, pp. 203–33. This period (1945 to 1954) is described by Fall as "the lost decade" in which France's reluctance to grant real independence to Vietnam prevented French-supported regimes from gaining enough legitimacy and power to deal with Vietnamese Communists. French policy hesitations and contradictions were summarized in the famous statement by François Mitterand, now France's president, quoted by Fall: "We have granted Vietnam 'full independence' eighteen times since 1949. Isn't it about time we did it just once, but for good?" (p. 221); and Milton Osborne, *Region of Revolt: Focus on Southeast Asia* (Pergamon Press Australia Pty Limited, 1970), pp. 92–108. On Dien Bien Phu, see Bernard B. Fall, *Hell in a Very Small Place: The Siege of Dien Bien Phu* (New York: J. B. Lippincott, 1967). On U.S. military aid to the French and French-installed regimes, see Spector, *Advice and Support*, part 2.

2. On the Ngo Dinh Diem regime, see Fall, *The Two Vietnams*, pp. 234–337, 396–400, and passim; Osborne, *Region of Revolt*, pp. 108–34; Dennis J. Duncanson, *Government and Revolution in Vietnam* (New York: Oxford University Press, 1968), pp. 204–341 and passim; and Douglas Pike, *Viet Cong: The Organization and Techniques of the National Liberation Front of South Vietnam* (Cambridge: M.I.T. Press, 1966), chap. 3. On Diem's fall, see Marguerite Higgins, *Our Vietnam Nightmare* (New York: Harper and Row, 1965). On the U.S. role in the coup that overthrew Diem, see William J. Rust, *Kennedy in Vietnam* (New York: Scribner's, 1985), chap. 9 and passim.

3. For accounts of the post-Diem regimes, see Guenter Lewy, *America in Vietnam*; Michael Maclear, *The Ten-Thousand-Day War: Vietnam—1945–1975* (New York: St. Martin's, 1981); Duncanson, *Government and Revolution*, chap. 7; Fall, *The Two Vietnams*, pp. 185–88. For analyses and accounts of the fall of South Vietnam, see Stephen T. Hosmer, Konrad Kellen, and Brian M.

Jenkins, *The Fall of South Vietnam: Statements by Vietnamese Military and Civilian Leaders* (Santa Monica, Calif.: Rand Corporation R-2208-OSD [HIST], 1978); Frank Snepp, *Decent Interval: An Insider's Account of Saigon's Indecent End* (New York: Random House, 1977); and David Butler, *The Fall of Saigon: Scenes from the Sudden End of a Long War* (New York: Simon and Schuster, 1985).

The importance of legitimacy cannot be overemphasized. Indeed, even many years after the fall of Saigon, when emotion has cooled and a more objective and impartial appraisal of the war can be made, there is very little recognition of the sacrifices, dedication, and heroic deeds on the part of Vietnamese anti-Communist nationalists, the South Vietnamese armed forces, and the South Vietnamese people, in general, in their fight for the country's freedom and independence in spite of a corrupt and inefficient leadership. Some radical and liberal media circles appear to continue to glorify the Vietnamese Communists and belittle and even condone the inhuman means they used to achieve their purposes. "Vietnam: a Television History" based on Stanley Karnow's *Vietnam: A History* (New York: Viking Press, 1983) and shown in 1984 on the PBS television network, is a case in point. See Nguyen Manh Hung, " 'Vietnam: A Television History' A Case Study in Perceptual Conflict Between the American Media and the Vietnamese Expatriates," *World Affairs* 147, no. 2 (Fall 1984): 71–84.

Some interesting issues of legitimacy of the South Vietnamese regimes have been pointed out by Pye in *Asian Power and Politics*. Given the Vietnamese tradition of unity and harmonious relationship, "the disciplined collective leadership of Hanoi was more properly legitimate than the would-be leaders of South Vietnam, who were chaotically contending over power and policy" (p. 65). Since Confucian leaders, including Ho Chi Minh,

> maintained their dignity and kept their distance from the common herd . . . One of the many mistakes Americans made . . . was to demand that South Vietnamese leaders mix with their own people, just as Americans do with theirs. To the Vietnamese such conduct lacked the dignity that was imperative for true authority. (p. 78)

4. For background on the Vietnamese anticolonialist revolutionary movement, see John T. McAlister, Jr., *Vietnam: The Origins of Revolution* (New York: Knopf, 1969); Marr, *Vietnamese Anticolonialism*; Marr, *Vietnamese Tradition on Trial*; Huynh Kim Khanh, *Vietnamese Communism 1925–1945* (Ithaca, N.Y.: Cornell University Press, 1983); and Spector, *Advice and Support*, pp. 5–17: American perceptions of this revolutionary movement were casual, unconcerned, and distorted, for example, in a report in 1930, Henry I. Waterman, U.S. consul general in Saigon, wrote that the VNQDD (a staunchly anticolonialist and anti-Communist nationalist party modeled after the Chinese Kuomingtang) was "communistic," and Thomas E. Ennis, a West Virginia history professor, described the Yen Bay uprisings led by the VNQDD as "controlled from Moscow" (pp. 14–15). (For an account of the U.S. government's similar ignorance of the situation in Korea and its total lack of preparation in dealing with this country's occupation after World War II, see Henderson, *Korea*, chap. 5.)

For studies illuminating how Vietnamese Communists integrated patriotism, nationalism, and proletarian internationalism with coercion, terrorism, deception, manipulation, and organizational ability to achieve a balance between legitimacy and power, see Hoang Van Chi, *From Colonialism to Communism: A Case History of North Vietnam* (New York: Praeger, 1964). Chi, who served under the Communist regime during its war of resistance against the French, relates its most arbitrary, ruthless, and inhuman use of power to achieve its socialist and Communist goals; Fall, *The Two Vietnams*, chaps. 5–9 and passim. Chapter 5 provides a vivid account of how the Vietnamese Communists managed to seize and maintain power until the start of the open war with the French, by outmaneuvering competing political parties, murdering many of the political parties' leaders, bribing Chinese warlords, compromising with the French, and courting the Americans. In Fall's words,

through the sheer energy and organizational ability of its Communist leadership, Vietnam had become a "people's democracy," in fact as well as in name—even while its territory was still occupied by Chinese Nationalist, British, and French military forces and American observers, and while the nearest Soviet Russian and Chinese Communist troops were still thousands of miles away. This was surely a unique feat among present-day Communist regimes, and yet another indication of how thoroughly bamboozled the West was about events in Southeast Asia. (p. 66)

See also Pike, *Viet Cong*, who attributes the growth of the National Liberation Front of South Vietnam as an arm of North Vietnam primarily to its organizational ability (power); Duncanson, *Government and Revolution*, chap. 4 and passim, who explains Communist success as resulting mainly from sophisticated use of techniques of manipulation, coercion, terrorism, and organization (power), as well as from the incapacity of South Vietnamese leadership to govern and the ineffectiveness of U.S. support; and Osborne, *Region of Revolt*, chaps. 7 and 8 and passim, who adds to the analysis the important role of changes in political and social consciousness and appeals of ideology (legitimacy). For a witness's account of how Ho Chi Minh manipulated former Emperor Bao Dai to gain legitimacy for the Communist regime during its earlier period, see Bao Dai, *Le dragon d'Annam*. For an insightful analysis of the Vietnamese Communist party's strategies and tactics of developing its legitimacy and power during the war of resistance against the French, see Paul Mus, *Sociologie d'une guerre* (Paris: Edition du Seuil, 1952). For a history of the Vietnamese Communist party from its birth until the takeover of South Vietnam, see Douglas Pike, *History of Vietnamese Communism, 1925–1976* (Stanford, Calif.: Hoover Institution Press, 1978). For an inside account of how the party manipulated the French-trained bourgeois intellectuals in South Vietnam to further its regime's legitimacy, see Truong Nhu Tang, *A Vietcong Memoir* (San Diego, Calif.: Hartcourt Brace Jovanovich, 1985). According to Tang, a founder of the National Liberation Front (NLF) and former minister of justice in the Provisional Revolutionary Government (PRG), the Alliance for National, Democratic, and Peace Forces was created in 1968 by the NLF to counterbalance the latter's increasing domination by the Communist party and the northern government. Alienated from Diem's South Vietnamese governments and generals, many neutral, non-Communist intellectuals reluctantly joined the alliance in spite of their wariness of the NLF and the party. It did not take long, however, for their suspicion to be dissipated by the exceptional treatment reserved for them by the Communist leadership, convinced as the latter were of the tactical need to establish the image of the

South's revolution as a broad-based movement that included southern nationalists of all backgrounds. Indeed, the alliance was at first treated as an equal partner in developing the strategy of resistance for the South together with the NLF and the Communist party headquarters branch for South Vietnam (COSVN). When a delegation of the alliance visited Hanoi in spring 1969, it was enthusiastically welcomed like that of a friendly country, and its president received honors reserved for a chief of state. Instead of receiving delegation members at the Presidential Palace, Ho Chi Minh came unannounced and without escorts to see them as a friend.

The honeymoon period did not last long, however. Conflicts began to develop soon afterward, and when southern intellectuals became aware that Communist cadres were tightening grips on the front and the alliance, no way out of the dilemma existed for them. And at the victory celebration on 15 May 1975 (only two weeks after the fall of Saigon), Tang learned that the Viet Cong network, including the NLF and the alliance, had already been disbanded.

On the situation in Vietnam after 1975, see Nguyen Long, *After Saigon Fell: Daily Life under the Vietnamese Communists* (Berkeley: Institute of East Asian Studies, University of California, 1981); Nguyen Van Canh, *Vietnam under Communism, 1975–1982* (Stanford, Calif.: Hoover Institution, Stanford University, 1983; Stephen J. Morris, "Vietnam under Communism," *Commentary*, 74, no. 3 (September 1982): 39–47; Brian Crozier, "Nine Years (or So) after," *National Review* 34 (10 December 1982): 1536. For an account of what happened to the National Liberation Front after the fall of Saigon, see Truong Nhu Tang, "How the Communists Betrayed the Vietnam Revolution," *Penthouse* 12 (April 1981): 64–69; Tang, *A Vietcong Memoir*, chaps. 21–24, and pp. 258–310. On the fate of the highlanders to whom North Vietnam had promised autonomous government after the country's liberation, see Gerald Cannon Hickey, *Free in the Forest: Ethnohistory of the Vietnamese Central Highlands 1954–1976* (New Haven and London: Yale University Press, 1982), pp. 284–92. On the Vietnamese, Cambodian, and Laotian refugees, see Barry Wain, *The Refused: The Agony of the Indochina Refugees* (New York: Simon and Schuster, 1981); Astri Suhrke, "Indochinese Refugees: The Law and Politics of First Asylum," in Gilburt D. Loescher and John A. Scanlan, eds., *The Global Refugee Problem: U.S. and World Response, Annals of the American Academy of Political and Social Science* 467, (May 1983); David W. Haines, ed., *Refugees in the United States: A Reference Handbook* (Westport, Conn.: Greenwood Press, 1985), chaps. 4, 7–9, and 12; and daily press reports. For an account of the situation in Vietnam after 1975 in general, the reader is referred to the literature and especially press reports on the occasion of the tenth anniversary of the fall of South Vietnam (30 April 1985).

For an analysis of how Communist Vietnam managed to increase its internal and external legitimacy by capturing U.S. liberal intellectuals through a strategy of political deception prior to 1975, see Morris, "Vietnam under Communism." Some of these intellectuals, whose books exerted a considerable influence on Western public opinion during the late 1960s and early 1970s, according to Morris, are George M. Kahin and John Wilson Lewis (*The United States in Vietnam*, 1967), who maintained that the National Liberation Front was not a tool of Hanoi; David Halberstam (*Ho*, 1971), who eulogized Ho Chi Minh at his death; and Frances Fitzgerald (*Fire in the Lake*, 1972), who concluded that Vietnamese Communists wanted to create a society with traditional Vietnamese values in which all people are able to participate. After demonstrating how the Communist totalitarian system had been applied to South Vietnam since 1975, Morris concluded that "It is now abundantly clear that the heroic image of the Vietnamese Communist revolution was a figment of the Western romantic imagination" (p. 47).

For an analysis of the Vietnamese concepts of authority, legitimacy, and power, see Pye, *Asian Power and Politics*, pp. 55–68 passim, 75–88 passim, 236–44, 246–47.

5. Lee, *Korea*, p. 128.

6. In Vietnamese, this Chinese teaching, which has become a proverb in Vietnam, is *Quan tu hoa nhi bat dong, tieu nhan dong nhi bat hoa.*

7. For a comprehensive summary study of South Korea, see Bunge, ed., *South Korea*. For an analysis of social and political-administrative changes from 1945 to the early part of the Park Chung Hee era, see Lee, *Korea*. For an analysis of Korean political culture and political development, see Henderson, *Korea*. For an account of the situation in Korea under and after Park Chung Hee, see Pak Chung Hui, *Korea Reborn: A Model for Development, Park Chung Hee* (Englewood Cliffs, N.J.: Prentice-Hall, 1979); Dae-Sook Suh and Chae-Jin Lee, eds., *Political Leadership in Korea* (Seattle: University of Washington Press, 1976); Harold C. Hinton, *Korea under New Leadership: The Fifth Republic* (New York: Praeger, 1983). For a favorable account of the relationship between Park Chung Hee's dictatorial leadership and Korea's successful accomplishments, see Michael Keon, *Korean Phoenix: A Nation from Ashes* (Englewood Cliffs, N.J.: Prentice-Hall International, 1977). For a balanced explanation of Korea's economic success as resulting not only from the contribution of foreign and domestic private investments but also from the crucial role of the public policy-making system, especially its bureaucratic and governmental components, as well as political stability and cultural revival, see L. L. Wade and B. S. Kim, *Economic Development of South Korea: The Political Economy of Success* (New York: Praeger, 1978). On Korea's creditworthiness, see Laxmi Nakarmi, "Korea's Foreign Debt: Why the Bankers Are Secure," *Business Korea* 2, no. 3 (September 1984): 17–25; and articles following in the cover story. On the equitable distribution of wealth resulting from measures that raised the position of farmers, see Vincent S. R. Brandt and Ji Woong Cheong, "Top-Down and Bottom-Up Rural Planning in South Korea," *Development Digest* 20, no. 2 (April 1982): 38–56. On cultural renewal, see Park Chung Hee, *Our Nation's Path: Ideology of Social Reconstruction* (Seoul, Korea: Hollym Corporation, 1970); and In-Joung Whang, *Management of Rural Change in Korea: The Saemaul Undong* (Seoul, Korea: Seoul National University Press, 1981), especially chap. 12.

For a comparative analysis of South Korea's economic performance, see Krauss, *Development without Aid*; and Lou, *Can the Third World Survive?* Wade and Kim, *Economic Development of South Korea*; and David Halberstam, "The Korean Challenge," *Washington Post*, 2 November 1986, *Parade Magazine*, p. 4ff. *Time Magazine*, 24 November 1986, p. 65, reported that "South Korea's Hyundai Excel has made a dazzling debut. The $4,995 subcompact has sold more than 130,000 units so far [in the U.S.] in 1986, a record for an imported auto's first year."

For an analysis of the Korean concepts of authority, legitimacy, and power, see Pye, *Asian Power and Politics*, pp. 55–90 passim, 216–28, and 244–47.

8. For a comprehensive study of Singapore, see Nena Vreeland et al., *Area Handbook for Singapore* (Washington, D.C.: U.S. Government Printing Office,

DA Pam 550-184, 1977); C. M. Turnbull, *A History of Singapore 1819–1975* (Kuala Lumpur and New York: Oxford University Press, 1977); and Alex Josey, *Singapore, Its Past, Present, and Future* (Singapore: Eastern University Press, 1979). For a political history of Singapore since 1945, see Richard Clutterbuck, *Conflict and Violence in Singapore and Malaysia, 1945–1983* (Singapore: Graham Brash [PTE] Ltd., 1984). On the relationship between power (authoritarianism) and success, see T. J. S. George, *Lee Kuan Yew's Singapore* (London: Andre Deutsch, 1973): "One of the first things Lee did on becoming prime minister was to call his parents and brothers around him and tell them that from then on they should expect no special consideration from him, that they were entirely on their own as ordinary citizens of the state" (p. 51). On Prime Minister Lee, see "The Philosopher King of Singapore," *CoEvolution Quarterly* no. 39 (Fall 1983): 62–65; Alex Josey, *Lee Kuan Yew* (Singapore: Asia Pacific Press, 1971). For an analysis of the Singaporean leadership's efforts to establish its regime's legitimacy, see Busch, *Legitimacy and Ethnicity*. On the People's Action party, see Cheng Lian Pang, *Singapore's People's Action Party: Its History, Organization, and Leadership* (Singapore and Kuala Lumpur: Oxford University Press, 1971); and Chan Heng Chee, *The Dynamics of One-Party Dominance: The PAP at the Grass Roots* (Singapore: Singapore University Press, 1976). On the significant role of foreign direct investment in Singapore, see Hafiz Mirza, *Multinationals and the Growth of the Singapore Economy* (New York: St. Martin's, 1986).

For a comparative analysis of Singapore's economic performance, see Lou, *Can the Third World Survive?* Krauss, *Development without Aid;* and Mirza, *Multinationals and Singapore,* especially table 1.2.

CHAPTER 4. DEVELOPMENT STRATEGY

1. For an analysis of cultural renewal and modernization in Japan, see Robert N. Bellah, "Religious Aspects of Modernization in Turkey and Japan," in Jason L. Finkle and Richard W. Gable, eds., *Political Development and Social Change,* 2d ed. (New York: Wiley, 1971), pp. 128–33; Robert N. Bellah, *Tokugawa Religion* (Glencoe, Ill.: Free Press, 1957); Robert E. Ward, "Political Modernization and Political Culture in Japan," in Claude E. Welch, Jr., ed., *Political Modernization,* 2d ed. (Belmont, Calif.: Duxbury Press, 1971), pp. 100–117; Y. Toriumi, "A New Role for Japan: The Meiji Revolution and Its Sequel," in Arnold Toynbee, ed., *Half the World: The History and Culture of China and Japan* (New York: Holt, Rinehart, and Winston, 1973), pp. 293–318; Pye, *Asian Power and Politics,* pp. 158–81, 186, 286–91, 328–44 passim; Bradley M. Richardson, *The Political Culture of Japan* (Berkeley: University of California Press, 1974); and Wei-Ming Tu, "Economic Growth in East Asia: Confucianism and Cultural Factors," *Wilson Center/Reports* (January 1985): 2–3.

Pye masterfully analyzes how South Korean leadership has used power and taken advantage of risk taking and other positive aspects of Korean culture to cope with the crisis of government legitimacy and successfully modernized the country, in *Asian Power and Politics,* especially pp. 55–90 passim, 216–28. For an analysis of Korea's success in generating rural development through a blend of military authoritarianism and Confucian moralism, see In-Joung Whang, *Management of Rural Change in Korea: The Saemaul Undong* (Seoul,

Korea: Seoul University Press, 1981); and Brandt and Cheong, "Rural Planning in South Korea," 39–43 and passim.

For an analysis of how cultures change at the tribal level through value renewal and an integration of homegrown and imported features, see Ward H. Goodenough, *Cooperation in Change* (New York: Russell Sage Foundation, 1963); Peter Farb, *Man's Rise to Civilization As Shown by the Indians of North America from Primeval Times to the Coming of the Industrial State* (New York: E. P. Dutton and Company, 1968); and Anthony F. C. Wallace, "Revitalization Movement in Development," in Richard J. Ward, ed., *The Challenge of Development* (Chicago: Aldine Publishing Company, 1967), pp. 448–54.

For an examination of a cultural regeneration movement in Sri Lanka, see Joanna Macy, *Dharma and Development: Religion as Resource in the Sarvodaya Self-Help Movement*, rev. ed. (West Hartford, Conn.: Kumarian Press, 1985); A. T. Ariyaratne, "Sarvodaya Shramadana in Sri Lanka," *Development Digest* 14, no. 1 (January 1976): 87–90; and David C. Korten, "Organizing for Rural Development: A Learning Process," *Development Digest* 20, no. 2 (April 1982): 12–14.

On cultural renewal in Singapore, see Nena Vreeland et al., *Area Handbook*, pp. 61–76; and Busch, *Legitimacy and Ethnicity.* A strategy of bringing about an African renaissance is proposed by Chinweizu in his *The West and the Rest of Us*, chap. 9.

2. The ambivalence of LDC intellectuals in choosing between native traditional culture and foreign modern culture, which results in a strong infusion of self-contradictions, is vividly described by Mary Matossian in "Ideology of Delayed Industrialization," in Finkle and Gable, *Political Development and Social Change*, pp. 113–22. On cultural confusion in Africa, see: Chinweizu, *The West and the Rest of Us*, chaps. 14 and 15.

3. A review of the history of China and Vietnam, for example, reveals that the more successfully the people of these countries managed to live up to ideal cultural values, the better off they were. The reader can test this assumption against the history of other countries.

For Vietnam, see Joseph Buttinger, *The Smaller Dragon: A Political History of Vietnam* (New York: Praeger, 1958); Buttinger, *Vietnam*; Le Thanh Khoi, *Le Viêt-Nam. Histoire et civilisation* (Paris: Les Editions de minuit, 1955); and Tran-Trong-Kim, *Viet-Nam Su-Luoc*, summary history of Vietnam (N.p.: Song Moi, 1978, originally published by the Ministry of Education, Republic of Vietnam, 1971).

The moral foundation of the Vietnamese and Chinese way of life has been based on Confucianism harmonized with Taoism and Buddhism; see Chan, "The Path to Wisdom," pp. 95–130; and Dang, *Viet-Nam*, pp. 51–59. Stability, peace, happiness, and prosperity prevailed when rulers' policies succeeded in promoting these values more through moral persuasion than coercion. Rulers who adopted such policies during their rule, include Ly Thanh Tong (1054–72), Tran Thanh Tong (1258–78), Tran Nhan Tong (1279–93), and Le Thanh Tong (1460–97).

Anarchy, war, and misery prevailed when these moral values were violated. This is illustrated in the reigns of such kings as Le Long Dinh (1005–09); Le Uy Muc (1505–09), Le Tuong Duc (1510–16), who were debauched, cruel, and ineffectual.

Among the great kings who made heavy use of power when required by circumstances, for example, after a period of foreign domination, war and/or social anarchy, were Dinh-Tien-Hoang (968–80), Le-Thai-To (1428–33), and Minh-Mang (1820–41).

The country was not in good shape, however, under generous but weak (lacking power) rulers, such as Emperors Thieu-Tri (1841–47) and Tu-Duc (1847–83).

For China, see Rene Grousset, *The Rise and Splendour of the Chinese Empire* (Berkeley and Los Angeles: University of California Press, 1953); Henri Cordier, *Histoire générale de la Chine et de ses relations avec les pays étrangers depuis les temps les plus anciens jusqu'à la chute de la dynastie mandchoue*. 4 vols. (Paris: Librairie Paul Gouthner, 1920); and D. C. Twitchett, " 'The Middle Kingdom': Chinese Politics and Society from the Bronze Age to the Manchus," in Toynbee, *Half the World*, pp. 31–78.

The era of Emperor Yao, Fang Hiun (2357–2208 B.C.), and Emperor Chouen (or Shun), Keou Wang (2255–2208 B.C.), during the period of legendary history, and that of the early Chou dynasty (1134–770 B.C.) have been considered by later historians and writers on politics as golden ages in China and models for later dynasties. This humanist model of government stresses reliance on authority to be earned by an effort to gain legitimacy. In contrast, the last emperor of the Chang (or Shang or Yin) dynasty, Tcheou Sin (or Chou-hsin, 1154–1123 B.C.), who made the heaviest use of power to pursue negative purposes, lost his throne.

During the period of the warring states, power was relied on to the greatest extent by the Ch'in (or Ts'in) kings to defeat all competing state dynasties and unify China under the Ch'in dynasty. Influenced like his predecessors by the legalist school, which advocated power to achieve the absolutism of king and state, the famous Ch'in emperor, Shih-huang-ti (or Ts'in Che Houang Ti, 246–210 B.C.), through incredibly drastic measures succeeded in expanding and unifying the Chinese empire under one centralized government. Excessive reliance on sheer power could not endure too long, however. Shih huang-ti's son and successor, a cruel and incompetent youth, was forced to commit suicide amid general revolt after three years of disorder, making the Ch'in dynasty the shortest in Chinese history. After a short period of anarchy, central government control was reestablished by Liu Pang, who founded the Han dynasty.

A return to humanist government was attempted under the Hans, who lasted from 202 B.C. to A.D. 220. The dynasty's authority and legitimacy was greatly enhanced under its first rulers, who won support of the Confucian literati and the people by adopting moral and religious principles of the times. One of the greatest representatives of these principles, Hsiao-wen-ti (180–157 B.C.), constantly promoted the Confucian code of conduct. Another great Han emperor, Wu-Ti, whose reign was exceptionally long (140–87 B.C.), made use of the literati to serve his policy of professionalization of the bureaucracy and neutralization of the nobility. Chinese history in later years until modern times consisted roughly of a succession of long and short dynasties whose destiny depended on greater or lesser, good or bad emperors who succeeded or failed in integrating legitimacy, authority, and power along these models to rule over this vast empire.

Later emperors who achieved stability, strength, and prosperity by emphasizing governmental legitimacy included T'ang T'ai-tsung (626–49), T'ang Hsuan-tsung (712–56), Sung T'ai-tsu (960–76), Yuan Shih-tsu (Kublai Khan,

1260–94), K'ang-hsi-ti (1662–1722), and Ch'ien-lung-ti (1736–96). Among the debauched, cruel, weak, or ineffectual rulers who destroyed their regimes' legitimacy and brought internal dissensions, revolts, war, and misery, were Shih Hu (334–49); emperors of the Liu Sung dynasty in general (420–79); emperors of the Ch'i dynasty in general (479–502); Yuan Shun-ti (Toghan Temur, 1333–68); in general, emperors of the Ming dynasty after Yung-le-ti's rule (1424–1644); in general, emperors of the Manchu (Ch'ing) dynasty from 1796 to 1912.

It is interesting to note that the basis of governmental legitimacy in China until modern times was a syncretism of Confucianism, Buddhism, and Taoism with a predominance of Confucianism. Rulers who violated this balance by emphasizing Buddhism or Taoism (which promotes a passive way of life) at the expense of Confucianism (which advocates an active attitude toward life) usually courted trouble for themselves and the ruling dynasties. Such was the case, for example, of Buddhist-oriented emperors Liang Wu-ti (502–49) and T'ang Chung-tsung (683–90, 705–10), and Taoist-oriented emperor Sung Hui-tsung (1100–1126).

4. These were General Nguyen Khoa Nam, commander of IV Corps at the fall of South Vietnam and his deputy, General Le Van Hung, and General Pham Van Phu, former commander of III Corps. See Butler, *The Fall of Saigon*, p. 488. Their suicides are reported by Butler as follows:

That evening (April 30, 1975) general Le Van Hung, the deputy commander in the Mekong delta, made a short, moving speech to his staff and then killed himself in his bedroom. (Two of his children later walked across Cambodia to Thailand. His wife lived as a hunted woman in Saigon for several years, but eventually escaped in a fishing boat).
On the morning of May 1, Hung's superior, MR4 Commander General Nguyen Khoa Nam, also killed himself. Expatriate nationalist Vietnamese generally feel that Phu died in disgrace but that Hung and Nam should be honored as heroes who died rather than surrender or run. (p. 488)

In *Decent Interval,* Snepp describes Phu's death as follows:

At the DAO compound itself, another Vietnamese army notable was paying a last call on General Smith. He stood before the American, in a neatly pressed dress uniform, campaign medals glittering on his chest. Then General Pham Van Phu, the man who had surrendered the highlands without a fight and had abandoned his command to destruction, executed a slow formal salute, turned on his heel, and walked out. He had asked General Smith to evacuate some of his family. He had requested nothing for himself. A short while later Phu put a bullet through his head. (pp. 503–4)

According to Vietnamese boat people, those who committed suicide shortly after the fall of Saigon also included Brigadier General Le Nguyen Vy, commandant of the Fifth Infantry Division, Brigadier General Tran Van Hai, commandant of the Seventh Infantry Division, and Senator Tran Chanh Thanh.

5. For a review of Confucian values that influenced the Vietnamese way of life, see Nguyen, "Culture and Technical Assistance in Public Administration," pp. 140–59, 160–97 passim; Pierre Huard and Maurice Durand, *Connaissance du Viêt-Nam* (Paris: Imprimerie nationale, 1954). On Chinese values and ways of life, see Francis L. K. Hsu, *Americans and Chinese: Two Ways of Life* (New

York: Henry Schuman, 1953); Francis L. K. Hsu, *Clan, Caste, and Club* (Princeton, N.J.: Van Nostrand, 1963). The reader should be warned that this literature sometimes confuses achieved behavior with ideal values.

6. This story was taught in Vietnamese elementary schools attended by students of this author's generation.

7. Translated from the Chinese phrase well known in Vietnam and vietnamized as *Phap bat vi than.*

8. Translated from a Vietnamese popular song that has become a proverb, *Thuong em anh de trong long; Viec cong anh cu phep cong anh lam.*

9. Translated from a classic Vietnamese poem that has become a popular, *Phep cong la trong niem tay sa nao.*

10. That was the case with the rule of such Vietnamese emperors as Ly Thanh Tong (1054–72), Tran Thanh Tong (1258–78), Tran Nhan Tong (1279–93), and Le Thanh Tong (1460–97). See Kim, *Viet-Nam Su-Luoc*, vol. 1, pp. 99–100, 128–30, 131–36, and 255–64, respectively. See also n. 3.

11. These drastic means were used in Vietnam by Emperor Le Thai To (1428–33), who, after leading a successful and most bloody revolution against the Chinese conquerors, had to deal with negative forces in a culture in decay following two decades of Chinese domination. In this way, he managed to restore order and consolidate the legitimacy of his rule and the Le dynasty, which endured the longest of all dynasties in Vietnamese history (360 years, 1427–1788); and by Emperor Dinh Bo Linh (968–80), who had to consolidate his newly established dynasty following twenty-three years of anarchy and internal war during the period of the Twelve Warlords (Kim, *Viet-Nam Su-Luoc*, vol. 1, pp. 250, and 86–87, respectively).

The Tran dynasty (1225–1400) was founded by very ruthless and questionable means, for example, plotting to bury alive all members of the Ly imperial family to prevent the latter from restoring the Ly dynasty. Yet, through determined and effective use of power in serving the country's interest, the Tran dynasty succeeded in building up its legitimacy and became one of the greatest, if not the greatest, dynasties Vietnam has ever had. Indeed, under the Tran kings, the Vietnamese managed to repell three successive invasions of the Mongols in the North (Kim, *Viet-Nam Su-Luoc*, pp. 115–87).

In China, Li Shih-min (T'ang T'ai-tsung, 626–49), who killed his two rival brothers as well as all their wives and children in order to avoid vendettas and pacify the empire, became one of China's greatest emperors in terms of courage, intelligence, humanism, and accomplishments. (Grousset, *The Rise and Splendour*, chap. 17. See also n. 3.

12. For an analysis of the positive and negative sides of Confucianism and their impact on development efforts of China, Japan, Korea, and Vietnam, see Pye, *Asian Power and Politics*, pp. 55–89 passim and chap. 12.

McAlister and Mus pointed out in *The Vietnamese*, p. 30, that a non-Western culture can be described as positive or negative depending on the observer's emphasis and purpose. Oscar Lewis, "The Culture of Poverty," *Scientific American* 215 (October 1966): 19, makes the same points.

For a discussion of the concept of world culture, see Lucian W. Pye, *Politics, Personality, and Nation Building: Burma's Search for Identity* (New Haven: Yale University Press, 1962), pp. 10–15; and also his *Asian Power and Politics*, pp. 2, 12, 342; and Harold D. Lasswell, "The Emerging International Culture," in Richard J. Ward, ed., *Challenge of Development* (Chicago: Aldine Publishing Company, 1967), pp. 489–95.

The fact that modern management technology is strongly influenced by national cultural values now appears to be confirmed and recognized. See, for example, the seminal study by Hofstede, *Culture's Consequences*. Just as recently, part of the development community has tried to develop management systems that are responsive to, and congruent with, the values, needs, and resources of each specific country. See, for example, Mendoza, "The Transferability of Western Management Concepts and Programs," pp. 61–71. In my opinion, this promising change in approach may not lead anywhere without a cultural renewal movement backed by positive leadership, as proposed in this book, because attempts to introduce this change at the micro level will be negated by the vicious cycle confronting the whole system.

13. For an analysis of how Japan has transformed its centralized feudalism into a modern bureaucratic state, see Pye, *Asian Power and Politics*, pp. 158–81 and passim.

14. This emphasis on the leadership variable appears to go against the attitude of most practitioners of development administration. Indeed, two authorities on development management have recently commented that "the key role of leadership is often ignored because it is seen as a nonreplicable factor that eludes analysts, planners, and donor designers." See Honadle and VanSant, *Implementation for Sustainability*, p. 118, n. 3. This confirmed the author's experience.

The crucial role of political leadership in the development of Third-World countries has been documented in a quantified study by Taketsugu Tsurutani in *Politics of National Development: Political Leadership in Transitional Societies* (New York: Chandler Publishing Company, 1973).

15. This neglect of *political* institution building appears to be a main reason why LDCs have had to rely excessively and apparently eternally on strong leadership. Lucian W. Pye has observed that most East and Southeast Asian leaders have refused to step down at the proper time, and he explains this phenomenon as a remnant of traditional cultural values (*Asian Power and Politics*, p. 225). There were, however, cases where Oriental emperors and kings gracefully abdicated in favor of others; and leaders' refusals to step down, whether in Asia or elsewhere in the Third World seem to derive rather from the failure to develop the legitimacy of the political institution than from traditional values. The situation of LDC power wielders as tiger riders (described in chap. 1) has made it very difficult, if not impossible, for them to afford the luxury of letting power escape their hands.

The succession crisis can be solved only when the political system has reached a high degree of legitimacy or institutionalization, as is the case in most Western countries or Japan. A Vietnamese popular saying describes the power wielder's situation, "In thrusting a spear, one has to follow through with it" (*Dam lao thi phai theo lao*), or "It's a pity the hands are already dipped in indigo" (*Tiec thay tay da nhung cham*).

Cases of graceful resignations of LDC power wielders have occurred only when incumbents felt sufficiently secure to leave office, for example, Tungku Abdul Rahman of Malaysia, Leopold Sedar Senghor of Senegal, and Julius Nyerere of Tanzania. In South Vietnam, Nguyen Van Thieu grudgingly resigned only after having realized the imminent danger to his life if he clung to power and having secured a way to leave the country. In his resignation speech, Thieu solemnly swore to continue to support the new government as a citizen and to support it in the fight against communism. A couple of days later, he clandestinely fled with his wife to Taiwan in a U.S. military plane, his children having already been abroad. This does not seem to differ from the way Haiti's Duvalier and the Philippines' Marcos stepped down recently. It is thus very important for the foreign observer to empathize with the tiger-rider situation of the LDC power wielder in studying Third-World politics.

16. On civil service compensation in LDCs, see World Bank, *Report 1983*, pp. 111–12. That "today, an illiterate maid easily can earn twice the starting salary of a university graduate or teacher, and many wives working as secretaries in private firms bring home bigger paychecks than their husbands employed by the government," as reported recently by *Washington Post* 29 January 1985, p. A14, is not something unusual in LDCs. This is confirmed by the author's experience as a government employee in South Vietnam. The reader is referred to literature on each specific country. See, for example, Djunaedi Hadisumarto, "The Indonesian Civil Service and Its Reform Movements" (Ph.D. diss., University of Southern California, 1974), p. 32.

For a summary review of price control policies in LDCs, see World Bank, *Report 1983*, pp. 57–63. The policy of subsidies in many countries has reached the point of absurdity. In Egypt, for example, a country that received nearly US $10 billion in economic assistance betwen 1975 and mid-1984, government subsidies have led to "an economy in which farmers feed bread instead of fodder to their cattle because it is cheaper, and buy cheap flour from the city for their village bakeries rather than growing wheat themselves" *Washington Post*, 28 January 1985, p. A16.

17. Political institutionalization has been strongly advocated by Samuel P. Huntington in "Political Development and Political Decay," in Claude E. Welch, Jr., ed., *Political Modernization: A Reader in Comparative Political Change* (Belmont, Calif.: Wadsworth Publishing Company, 1967), pp. 207–46. Administrative institutionalization has also been urged by the institution-building school (see n. 17, chap. 2). Attempts to bring reforms incrementally along these lines have apparently failed because of the lack of support of cultural renewal and positive leadership at the macro level.

18. Empirical facts that tend to support the rationale of this section are the most successful cases of modernization are found among countries that could accommodate the free enterprise system of the free world (the so-called Gang of Four: Singapore, Hongkong, South Korea, and Taiwan); the heavier and heavier reliance of Communist LDCs on Soviet aid to cope with the pressure of Western powers and other countries (Afghanistan, Vietnam, Cuba, Angola, Ethiopia); and the unsuccessful development efforts of those LDC regimes that have adopted a version of socialism without being Communist, in hope of benefiting from the best of both worlds (India in the 1950s and 1960s, Tanzania, Madagascar, Burma, Algeria, Ghana, and so on).

For a comparison of the growth rate and income distribution between private-sector-oriented economies and non-Communist public-sector-oriented economies, see Krauss, *Development without Aid*, pp. 3–8, 70–76, chap. 2, and passim; Lal, *The Poverty of "Development Economics"*; and John Greenwald, "A New Age of Capitalism: As Socialism Falters, Free Enterprise Is on the Move around the Globe," *Time Magazine*, 28 July 1986, pp. 28ff. For a comparative analysis of the successful economic performance of the Gang of Four, see Lou, *Can the Third World Survive?* and Krauss, *Development without Aid*.

On Communist LDCs' dependence on Soviet aid, the reader is referred to the literature. For Vietnam, for example, see Crozier, "Nine Years (or So) after," p.

1536. Between 1975 and 1982, Soviet subsidies to Vietnam totaled between US $1.5 to 2 billion a year; yet in 1981, Vietnam's PCI was only US $153, down from $241 in 1976, the first year after the war ended.

For the case of non-Communist socialist developing countries, see Jagdish N. Bhagwati and Padma Desai, *India Planning for Industrialization: Industrialization and Trade Policies since 1951* (New York: Oxford University Press, 1970), cited by Pye, *Asian Power and Politics*, p. 394, n. 5. India seems to have the worst of both worlds by adopting half-way measures between central planning and the market allocation. Hans Dieter Seibel and Ukandi G. Damachi, *Self-Management in Yugoslavia and the Developing World* (New York: St. Martin's, 1982). It is interesting to note that attempts by certain countries to adopt some features that may lead to the Yugoslavian model, which the authors advocate as a viable third way between the capitalist and state-socialist models for the Third World because of its successful combination of democracy, egalitarianism, and efficiency, have had scant success (see chaps. 14 and 15). For Burma, see Pye, *Asian Power and Politics*, p. 5 and passim. For Tanzania, see Yared, "Le Mwalimu s'en va," pp. 9ff: Former President Julius Nyerere, in his resignation speech late in 1985, recognized the disastrous performance of Tanzania's *ujamaa* socialism, which had been the subject of so many praiseworthy comments in Tanzania as well as overseas, in these terms: "The country is much poorer than 10 years ago . . . I have not been able to fulfill the mission that I assigned myself in 1962: to overcome poverty, hunger and disease; only ignorance has been eradicated. I cannot continue to lead a country which is obligated to beg for food" (p. 13–14) (translation by present author from French.) The gap between rich and poor has been widening (p. 13). Neighbor Kenya, which has adopted the free enterprise system, achieved a PCI of US $340 against US $240 for Tanzania (p. 14).

19. The fact that Western donor countries' taxpayers, power wielders, media, and development agencies are bound by their cultures and take the market model for granted, is something too obvious to require evidence. Leading international organizations that provide support to LDC development efforts are also strongly influenced by this model. Because they are funded mainly by the United States, Japan, France, Great Britain, and other Western countries, their staffs are mainly composed of Americans, British, French, and others who have graduated from Western universities. See, for example, van de Laar, *The World Bank and the Poor*, chap. 4; and Borgin and Corbett, *The Destruction of a Continent*, pp. 25–45. Since the market model, which has been dominating the world for centuries, is deeply rooted in the unconscious and subconscious of Western peoples, attempts to change or avoid it to suit the particular conditions of LDCs have proven futile. Indeed, Burma, which chose to isolate itself from both the Communist and non-Communist worlds to follow its Burmese path to socialism, has seen its economy stagnate, a decline in the standard of living, and a black market that "had grown to such proportions and was so successful in providing consumer goods that the Burmese peasants once again became interested in producing for the market, and consequently the country had a surprising 6 percent a year growth in GNP" by the early 1980s (Pye, *Asian Power and Politics*, p. 5).

20. The Vietnamese phrase for the people's will is heaven's will, is *Y dan la y troi*; the Chinese phrase *Thien y dan tam*, a teaching by Mencius, a leader of the Confucian school. This does not seem to be different from the Latin phrase *vox populi, vox dei*.

"One must use people just like using wood" is translated from a popular Vietnamese saying borrowed from a Chinese teaching, *Dung nhan nhu dung moc.*

"The King must behave as King . . ." is translated from a Chinese phrase well known in Vietnam, *Quan quan, than than, phu phu, tu tu.*

"To eliminate a tyrant . . ." is translated from a Chinese teaching also well known in Vietnam, *Tru bao quoc chi quan nhuoc tru doc phu*, which was a statement by Mencius. (These are Chinese characters written in Vietnamese after the romanization of the Vietnamese language in the early twentieth century.)

Other proverbs that reflect the ideals of democratic government include "Justice knows no partiality" *(Phap bat vi than)*; "The people matter most, next the national institutions, and lastly the king" *(Dan vi quy, xa tac thu chi, quan vi khinh)*; "The power of the emperor stops at the village gate" *(phep vua thua le lang)*.

According to the *Book of Documents* (Shu-ching), one of the canonical books of orthodox Confucianism, "Heaven's mandate could be taken away, should the king either break the pattern of accepted moral conduct expected by Heaven, or treat his people with undue harshness," and "the exercise of power in accordance with moral ethical norms meeting Heaven's approval, not the use of coercive force, was the way the mandate could be kept. Loss of mandate by a reigning dynasty was the justification claimed for rebellion and for its replacement by a new royal house." (Twitchett, " 'The Middle Kingdom'," p. 56.)

In the same vein, democratic features can also be found in other traditional cultures. For example, according to Yadh Ben Achour, the justice of the Madhalim, an Islamic institution particularly well established in the tenth century under the Abbassid dynasty, was governed by the same general principles as the modern administrative justice imported from France by various Islamic countries, such as Egypt, Syria, Tunisia, and Lebanon. The adoption of the French model has thus responded to a real culturally rooted need and cannot be considered as simply mimicry. See Achour, "Justice des Madhalim et justice administrative moderne," *International Review of Administrative Sciences* 51, no. 2 (1985): 109–19.

21. See the literature on Chinese and Vietnamese history cited in n. 3. The rule of succession by designation in the emperor's will of any of his children, grandchildren, or nephews was applied under the Nguyen dynasty in Vietnam. Succession by merit was advocated by Confucius, who urged rulers to imitate the legendary Chinese emperors Yao and Shun (Chouen), who transmitted their thrones to virtuous ministers but not to their own sons. In Vietnam, Le Hoan, the commander-in-chief of the armed forces was elected by his troops to succeed Emperor Dinh Tien Hoang in place of the latter's six-year-old son, to defend the country against an imminent invasion by China. Hoan became Emperor Le Dai Hanh and succeeded in defeating the Chinese and later making peace with them. Ly Cong Uan, founder of the Ly dynasty was elected by the mandarins of the court to succeed Emperor Le Long Dinh in place of the latter's young son. When the first Tran emperor felt old and weak, he abdicated in favor of the heir apparent and remained as a tutor and adviser to his successor. This precedent became institutionalized under the Tran dynasty (1293–341). Chinese emperor T'ang Kao-tsu abdicated in favor of his son Li Shih-min (T'ang T'ai-tsung), who became one of the greatest rulers of China.

Emperor T'ang Jui-tsung, who had great moral qualities but did not feel endowed with the strength needed to cope with a critical situation, handed over power to his son Li Lung-chi (T'ang Hsuan-tsung), who was to have one of the most brilliant reigns in Chinese history's great age.

In China, the professional civil service began under the Ch'in dynasty (221–213 B.C.), and the examination system assumed its final form under the early T'ang (midseventh century). Both have been strong features of the Vietnamese government system since the Dinh dynasty (968–80).

22. See literature cited in n. 3.

As regards the historian mandarin institution, Twitchett indicates in " 'The Middle Kingdom'," p. 53, that:

> More than in the case of any other culture, the modern historian of China is dependent upon a complex, highly developed native histriographical tradition. This tradition has a number of features which dictate the sort of knowledge which we have of China's past. Firstly, it is official history, written "for the record" by servants of the state. Above all it is "political history." It is essentially a record of the exercise of dynastic power by successive royal houses, and of the conduct of their administration. It is dydactic history, applying the model of orthodox ethic and morality to the events of the past, destined to provide models of political conduct, *both good and bad*, for future rulers and for the officials through whom they would in turn rule. (emphasis added)

In Vietnam the three positions of queen, heir apparent, and premier were abolished under the Nguyen dynasty until the last emperor (Kim, *Viet-Nam Su-Luoc*, vol. 2, p. 171 and passim). The council of senior mandarins who shared policy making with the king and the censorate and historian mandarin were constant features of almost all established dynasties in China and Vietnam. For China, see Charles O. Hucker, *China's Imperial Past: An Introduction to Chinese History and Culture* (Stanford, Calif.: Stanford University Press, 1975), pp. 49–57, chaps. 6 and 11, and passim.

23. The misuse and maladaptation of political and administrative institutional models borrowed from the West have been documented in previous chapters, especially 1 and 2.

24. The reader is referred to literature on political parties. Their crucial role as an integrating mechanism has been strongly emphasized, for example, by Robert K. Merton in his *Social Theory and Social Structure* (New York: Free Press, 1968), pp. 125–36, on the latent functions of the political machine.

25. The reader is referred to literature on communism. For a review of Communist parties in the world, see Richard F. Staar, ed., *Yearbook on International Communist Affairs 1985: Parties and Revolutionary Movements* (Standford, Calif.: Hoover Institution Press, 1985). For China, see, for example, Herbert F. Schurmann, *Ideology and Organization in Communist China* (Berkeley: University of California Press, 1966). For Vietnam, see Khanh, *Vietnamese Communism 1925–1945*. On the role of Communist parties in LDCs, see Edward Taborsky, *Communist Penetration of the Third World* (New York: R. Speller, 1973), especially pp. 123–68.

26. The reader is referred to literature on Third-World political parties. See, for example, Samuel P. Huntington, *Political Order in Changing Societies* (New Haven: Yale University Press, 1968), pp. 397–461; Almond and Coleman, *The Politics of the Developing Areas* (Princeton: Princeton University Press,

1960), passim (see index, *party systems*); Jason L. Finkle and Richard W. Gable, eds., *Political Development and Social Change*, 2d ed. (New York: Wiley, 1971), chap. 14; Wriggins, *The Ruler's Imperative*, chap. 6; and Fred R. von der Mehden, *Politics of the Developing Nations* (Englewood Cliffs, N.J.: Prentice-Hall, 1964), pp. 53–76.

27. It is to be noted that most LDC leaders have attempted to develop common denominators based on traditional cultural themes, such as Nehru's democratic collectivism; Senghor's Negritude and African socialism; Nyerere's "communitarianism"; Sekou Toure's "communaucracy" and democratic dictatorship; Nasser's democratic, socialist, cooperative democracy; Sukarno's guided democracy; Ayub Khan's basic democracy; and Nkrumah's African personality; see Paul E. Sigmund, Jr., ed., *The Ideologies of the Developing Nations* (New York: Praeger, 1963). Most if not all of these attempts failed to further development. Apparently several reasons already discussed contributed to these failures: (1) The party lacked positive leadership and an effective organization that could help in using power to increase the new system's legitimacy; in this situation, efforts to revive the traditional culture became mere rhetoric contradicted by daily negative behavior of party members, making it impossible to break the vicious cycle. (2) The system of indigenous "socialism" developed by top LDC leadership, which is an eclectic borrowing from both Western liberalism and Communist collectivism, with the purpose of benefiting from the best of both, has resulted in half-way measures. The adoption makes it more difficult to achieve a balance between legitimacy (internalized control) and power (externalized control) at the local as well as international levels. These LDCs are then left with the worst of both worlds. On the use and misuse of ideology, see Wriggins, *The Ruler's Imperative*, chap. 7; also see n. 18.

28. For a review of the People's Action party (P.A.P.) of Singapore, see Vreeland, *Area Handbook*, pp.; 96–102 and passim; Pang, *Singapore's People's Action Party*; and Chee, *The Dynamics of One-Party Dominance*.

29. This is the current situation in many of the LDCs that have benefited most from Western aid. For a strong argument for balanced development between the public and private sectors, see Lorand Dabasi-Schweng, "The Influence of Economic Factors," in Martin Kriesberg, ed., *Public Administration in Developing Countries* (Washington, D.C.: Brookings Institution, 1965), pp. 18–32; and Krauss, *Development without Aid*. According to Krauss, the cart-before-the-horse economics advocated by "European social-democrats and American liberals" is responsible for the creation through foreign aid of a burdensome, ineffective, and inefficient public sector in recipient LDCs (pp. 16–45). He argues that the poor do benefit from economic growth because it facilitates the rapid expansion of public consumption (pp. 40–41) and concludes that "foreign aid allows big government to pursue policies that damage the competitive sectors of the economy and thus its economic base" (p. 190).

30. The World Bank's *Report 1983* (p. 111) confirmed that "Singapore and Malaysia, where public sector salaries are regularly adjusted for changes in the cost of living, are two of the few developing countries that appear to have maintained parity [between both sectors]." On the effectiveness and integrity of the Singaporean civil service, see Vreeland, *Area Handbook*, pp. 86–88. This writer was amazed to learn, through an interview in the early 1970s with the leadership of the business department, University of Singapore, that the majority of graduates of the honored year (fifth year following completion of the

bachelor's program) preferred to and did work for government agencies because of higher job prestige and pay. On the effective, symbiotic relationship between politics and administration or between the P.A.P. and the civil service, see Seah Chee Meow, "The Singapore Bureaucracy and Issues of Transition," Department of Political Science, University of Singapore, *Occasional Paper Series* no. 12 (February 1975).

31. For further elaboration on real life application of the law of comparative advantage, see Krauss, *Development without Aid*, especially chaps. 3 and 5.

32. Multinational corporations (MNCs) have been strongly criticized by many Third-World countries and international and national donor institutions for their questionable practices, such as bribery, "legal" land stealing, taking excessive profits, capital-intensive production methods, collaboration with racist regimes or colonial administrations, and exploiting the world at will. A balanced view of MNCs is presented by Loeher and Powelson in *Threat to Development*, chap. 4; there is a favorable view of MNCs by Krauss in *Development without Aid*, chap. 4 and passim. My view is that in order for symbiotic relationships between foreign private capital and domestic capital to work for the benefit of both sides and both the developed and developing worlds, the role of donor institutions should be as supplement, mediator, or arbiter, but not as substitutes for the MNCs.

33. The attempt to increase the standard of living of all, rich and poor alike, by economic growth (expanding the size of the pie) has proven to benefit the poor more than attempting to improve the standard of living of the poor alone via redistribution of a state economic pie. See, for example, Krauss, *Development without Aid*, especially pp. 34–41. This is the case especially of Singapore and South Korea, where economic development has made the income gap between rich and poor much less pronounced than in the LDCs that follow the socialist paths.

34. The term legal system is used here in the broadest sense possible, including substantive laws derived from the Constitution and legislative organizations as well as regulations issued by executive and administrative authorities, legal institutions, the legal profession, and legal culture.

35. For an explanation of the low level of legal compliance, see Riggs, *Administration in Developing Countries*, pp. 57–60, 199, 232–34, and 381; and Lucian W. Pye, *Aspects of Political Development* (Boston: Little, Brown and Company, 1966), chap. 6.

Modernization seems to bring with it even more lawlessness. In Cairo, the capital city of Egypt, which has recently been one of the most privileged recipients of U.S. aid, "80 percent of the house-building today is being done without licenses, inspection or planning" and the mobilization of thousands of additional policemen failed "to get cars off the sidewalks, prevent double and triple parking and force pedestrians to wait at red lights and stop jaywalking"; see David B. Ottaway, "Cairo Seems to Fight Chaos with Chaos," *Washington Post*, 29 January 1985, p. A14. This situation appears to be little different from the one experienced by this writer in Saigon, South Vietnam in the 1960s and 1970s.

36. The reader is referred to literature on specific LDC politics. Violations of the law by power wielders are commonplace: election rigging, abuses, oppression, corruption, embezzlements. In Saigon, South Vietnam campaigns on campaigns involving thousands of civil and military policemen failed to deal with the city's vehicular anarchy and notorious black market at Ham Nghi

Boulevard because, among other reasons, powerful officials and their relatives, police and military officer's wives, were themselves violators of the law.

37. Examples of arbitrary, unjust, absurd and unenforceable laws abound in LDCs. See the literature on development administration, in particular, that is cited in n. 16. Many other examples can be cited; for example,

Peruvian law makes it impossible to dismiss workers (in both the public and private sectors). Although the company (a state-owned freeze-drying plant) offered its staff a bonus over and above required severance pay to leave, for more than six months after the plant was shut down a small group of workers continued to report for work each day to receive their wages. Until all the staff had left, the assets could not be sold. (World Bank, *Report 1983*, p. 85)

It is also a well-known fact that in many LDCs, laws and regulations are often promulgated without provision for enforcement or designation of enforcement agencies. For Madagascar, for example, see Nguyen, "Parastatal Institution." Madagascar law also made it practically impossible to dismiss public or private sector employees by requiring clearance through the labor inspectorate before dismissal could take place.

38. The legal vicious cycle is borne out by the literature cited in n. 35–37. The following examples taken from the writer's personal experience may be more useful to the Western reader who has never been part of LDC culture. In the late 1950s, as chief of the Bureau of General Administration of the Provincial Government of Gia-Dinh, the province surrounding Saigon, he was assigned the task of prosecuting housing builders who violated building laws and regulations. Before court, the prosecuting judge, who was supposed to provide assistance to the prosecution never cared to do anything. Only exceptionally was he present on his bench; if there, he did not speak at all. Most of the time, he was not physically present but left only his cape on his table. The trial judge, after hearing from both sides, the prosecutor and the defendant and/or his attorney, usually gave a nominal fine regardless of the prosecutor's request. The rate of the fine set by an old law was, as a result of galloping inflation, about one-tenth to one-fifth of the cost of obtaining a building permit, not including the amount needed to speed up the process or to circumvent legal obstacles. Whenever authorization to remove the building was granted because of imminent public danger it might cause, the defendant's appeal to the higher court would delay the process for years. Once the authorization became final, enforcement of the court's decision still remained very doubtful: "Big shots" intervened politically; the building was rented or nominally sold to a disabled veteran who appealed to his association for help against the police; or friends, colleagues, or relatives of policemen in charge of the enforcement intervened to obtain interminable delays of grace until the matter was finally forgotten. And if all these means did not work, interested parties resorted to outright bribes. After all, administrative authorities had the right not to enforce a court decision on the ground that enforcement might lead to social disturbance. Moreover, the provincial police force, which reported to the province chief on "administrative" matters but to the director general of police of the central government on "technical" matters, ended up becoming practically free to use its discretionary power to enforce the court's decision. The final results were that practically all housing constructed without a permit endured forever. This author's appeal to higher authorities to change the system got nowhere. Nobody really cared.

In the late 1960s, when this writer was a participant trainee in the United States, his wife was trying to save and borrow money to build a house on a 400-square-meter lot they owned on Truong Minh Gian Street, Saigon. The land happened to be occupied by a squatter who managed to build a hut overnight and settle there with his family. Vietnamese law made it impossible to dislodge a tenant or squatter without court authorization. It took years and years to obtain this authorization, required before confronting the difficulty of obtaining police assistance in enforcing it. When this writer returned to Vietnam in 1969, instead of a hut, he saw a complex of townhouses. It was impossible to know which townhouse was built on his land. Only many months later, his attorney managed to discover that the owner of the house built on his land had bought it from a developer who apparently had hired a disabled veteran to squat on the land. The owner, who bought the house with the full knowledge that it had been built without permit and on other people's land, was brought to court. In 1975, the issue was still pending in the appeal court of Saigon, and it was not known how many more years it would take that court to hear the case. In the meantime, the attorney continued to collect his fees. Fortunately, the land owner was relieved of the long headache when Saigon fell and a barge took him and his family away from his homeland to start anew as refugees in the United States.

39. See Hinton, *Korea under New Leadership*, pp. 38 and 53. On strong measures taken by Ayub of Pakistan, see Wriggins, *The Ruler's Imperative*, pp. 181–82.

40. Vietnamese popular wisdom that suggests that "one has to be firm in order to withstand the storm" *(Co cung moi dung dau gio)* and "one must hit the snake right on its head" *(Danh ran phai danh dang dau)* seems to be of universal application.

Unsuccessful attempts to suppress petty legal violations by small fish while leaving big fish untouched, abounded in South Vietnam. Among other examples witnessed by this writer were traffic violations, constructions without permit, and the notorious open black market on Ham Nghi Boulevard in Saigon.

41. Most of these constraints have been reviewed in previous chapters. The reader is referred to the literature for others. For example, for ecological constraints, see Udo Ernst Simonis, "Environmental Crisis: The Missing Dimension in the North South Dialogue," *Economics* (Tubingen) 30 (1984): 48–64; Clare Oxby, "Settlement Schemes for Herders in the Subhumid Tropics of West Africa: Issues of Land Rights and Ethnicity," *Development Policy Review* 2, no. 2 (November 1984): 217–33. For urban problems, see Bryant and White, *Managing Development*, chap. 12; and Joan M. Nelson, *Access to Power Politics and the Urban Poor in the Developing Nations* (Princeton: Princeton University Press, 1979); Blaine Harden, "World Oil Glut, Oddly Easing Squalor in Lagos," *Washington Post*, 21 October 1985, front page and p. A22. For a summary review of constraints confronting African countries, see *Compact for African Development: of the Committee on African Development Strategies*, pp. 6–10.

CHAPTER 5. PROPOSED CHANGES IN DEVELOPMENT ASSISTANCE POLICY

1. This appears to have been the case in Angola, Ethiopia, Afghanistan, Yemen, People's Democratic Republic (PDR), Grenada (before the armed intervention by the United States), Nicaragua, and Laos.

2. This seems to have been the case in Kuomingtang's, China, Cuba, Vietnam, Kampuchea (Cambodia), and Iran (which has become not Communist but staunchly anti-West).

3. The reader is referred to the literature on the aftermath of the Vietnam War.

4. The reader is referred to literature on the fall of pro-American regimes, such as Batista's Cuba, Chang Kai Chek's China, Long Nol's Kampuchea, and Shah Pahlavi's Iran. On the collapse of Thieu's South Vietnam, see Hosmer, Kellen, and Jenkins, *The Fall of South Vietnam*. Note, in particular, the contribution of the BBC and VOA in precipitating the collapse (p. 103, n. 21). Also see Snepp, *Decent Interval*; and Butler, *The Fall of Saigon*.

5. See Morss, "Institutional Destruction," p. 466; Anne Colamosca, "Exploiting the Third World Is Getting Hard: White Man's Burden," *New Republic*, 4 April 1981, pp. 12–15; Maurice Bertrand, "Must We Convert Multilateral Aid? Reshaping the Tool," *Development Forum* 14 (May 1986), front page f; "Only the Right Kind of Help Can Help," book review of *Does Aid Work?* by Robert Cassen and Associates, *Economist*, 27 September 1986, p. 98, points out that

> When aid goes wrong, it is often the case of too many cooks. A typical poor country may have 30 different official aid agencies at work on its economy, plus twice as many charities and other non-governmental organizations. The result is a mess. In Kenya, for example, the water-supply system uses 18 different makes of pump. This proliferation of donors creates an administrative burden that is too heavy for many poor countries, especially in Africa.

Also see Borgin and Corbet, *The Destruction of a Continent*, chap. 4, especially pp. 71–72.

6. See chap. 2, section "From Program to Project and then from Project Back to Program" on development agencies' ambivalence between the flexible and the rigid project approaches. The current tendency is to allow for some experimentation, flexibility, adaptation, and social learning. David C. Korten, whom this writer considers to embody U.S. effort-optimism, has been a leading advocate of learning through experimentation. In a critical review of donor experience with the rigid blueprint approach, he advocated and defended the learning-process approach as an alternative in these terms:

> Stage 1 investments, designed to produce knowledge of how to be relevant to key beneficiary needs, would represent very high risks for the funding agency—i.e., they would represent a sort of venture capital commitment. Only 10 to 20 percent of programs funded for stage 1 might be expected to merit stage 2 support, especially as the funding agency is itself learning how to spot promising leads and support them in appropriate ways. But if as many as one out of 10 turned out eventually to be a BRAC, and NDDB, or a national agency such as the NIA with a new nation-wide capacity to manage effectively a $100 million-a-year program in a way that worked in support of farmer organization and initiative, it would be a very favorable return on investment, and a substantial improvement over current funding agency performance. ("Organizing for Rural Development," p. 29)

In the same vein, a leading authority on development management research, in a thorough review of donors' experience, concluded that "a more flexible, adaptive, experimental and responsive set of planning and implementation procedures must be used to facilitate and promote social learning when projects are addressed to the uncertain and complex problems of human development"; or that "development is still an uncertain, complex and risky venture, characterized by rapid change and extreme diversity. The task of improving development administration must be approached with realism, flexibility, and, above all, humility" (Rondinelli, "Project as Instrument of Development Administration," p. 325). Also see "Develpoment Management in AID," p. 174.

More philosophically, two authorities who combine both theory and practice of development administration drew the following conclusion from field experience: "Development is essentially a creative and artistic social endeavor, not a technical procedure or a political dictate" (Honadle and VanSant, *Implementing for Sustainability*, p. 118. In a series of seminars on institutional development in LDCs recently organized by the American Consortium for International Public Administration (ACIPA), a group of experienced development experts also cautioned us to "avoid overoptimism and high expectations; public management is not a precise science and technical assistance is a high-risk enterprise" (ACIPA, *Institutional Development: Improving Management in Developing Countries—Report on a Seminar Series* [Washington, D.C.: ACIPA,, 1986], p. iv). The reader is invited to look for similar statements in the literature to find out to what extent the field has gone back to square one. See, for example, Bryant and White, *Managing Develoment*, p. 294; and Salahuddin Md. Aminuzzaman, "Design of Integrated Rural Development Programmes: Some Ideas and Issues," *International Review of Administrative Sciences* 51, no. 4 (1985): 311–17; and comments by Saleh A. Al-Hathloul that follow Aminuzzaman's article on pp. 318–22.

7. See n. 8, chap. 2 on confluence of interests between donor and donee bureaucracies.

On the general tendency of bureaucracies and bureaucrats to displace organizational goals and become self-serving, see Anthony Down, *Inside Bureaucracy* (Boston: Little Brown and Company, 1967). For development aid bureaucracies, see van de Laar, *The World Bank and the Poor*, pp. 209–48; Thomas S. Loeber, *Foreign Aid: Our Tragic Experiment* (New York: W. W. Norton and Company, 1961), especially chaps. 3 and 4; Gow and VanSant, "Decentralization and Participation," p. 142, n. 45; Morss and Morss, *U.S. Foreign Aid*, pp. 67–72, 104–5. In these authors' words, "Sadly, the missionary zeal has gone out of the U.S. foreign aid program. Foreign aid officers no longer show the enthusiasm that was present in the earlier days; they have been reduced to being lackluster bureaucrats whose major concern is following regulations" (pp. 104–5). Also see Borgin and Corbett, *The Destruction of a Continent*, chaps. 3, 4, and 9. For an analysis of major issues confronting the international civil service of the U.N. system, see Henri Reymond and Sidney Mailick, "The International Civil Service Revisited," *Public Administration Review* 46, no. 2 (March/April 1986): 135–43.

8. *Newsweek International*, 26 November 1984, p. 55.

For a summary appraisal of donors' and donees' mistakes in using aid, see *Compact for African Development*, pp. 8–10. For a critical appraisal of international staffs' and experts' qualifications and performance, see Borgin and Corbett, *The Destruction of a Continent*, chap. 3.

9. For an empirical test of the controversial dependency theory literature,

which denounced the subservient dependence of LDCs on Western imperialist countries, see Mahler, *Dependency Approaches to International Political Economy.* This quantified study in general confirmed a major part of what had been maintained in the literature. Lucian W. Pye maintained, however, that "by the mid-1980s empirical research in Latin America had eroded confidence in the relevance of dependency theory" (*Asian Power and Politics*, p. 348, n. 13). For a critical review of dependency theory, see I. M. D. Little, ed., *Economic Development—Theory, Policies, and International Relations* (New York: Basic Books, 1982), cited by Lal, *The Poverty of "Development Economics,"* p. 43, n. 2. What is more important, in my opinion, appears to be the perception and belief of Western and Third-World intellectuals, especially in Latin America, reflected in dependency literature rather than its empirical validation. The negative consequences of this belief has been pointed out recently by a retired AID official who had served as mission director in five Latin American countries (Harrison, *Underdevelopment Is a State of Mind*, p. 162).

10. On refugees, and legal and illegal immigrants from the Third World, see Richard D. Lamm and Gary Imhoff, *The Immigration Timebomb: The Fragmenting of America* (New York: Truman Talley Books/E. P. Dutton, 1985); Haines, ed., *Refugees in the United States*; Milton D. Morris, *Immigration: The Beleaguered Bureaucracy* (Washington, D.C.: Brookings Institution, 1985); Neal R. Peirce, "Immigration Perils at the Border," *Public Administration Times 9*, no. 1 (1 January 1986): 2; Wain, *The Refused*; Michael R. Marrus, *The Unwanted: European Refugees in the Twentieth Century* (New York: Oxford University Press, 1985), pp. 347, 354–55, 367–71; Alfred Zanker et al., "Europe's Immigration Battles," *U.S. News & World Report*, 31 March 1986, pp. 25–27; "Europe's Racial Timebomb," *World Press Review 32*, no. 12 (December 1985): pp. 27–29; John Nielsen, "Rising Racism on the Continent," *Time Magazine*, 6 February 1984, pp. 40ff. The reader is also referred to frequent press reports on the conflict between church and state in the United States on smuggling and providing sanctuary to refugees in disregard of the law.

11. This policy has been denounced as neocolonialism, especially by the neo-Marxist or dependency school. For a review of literature produced by this school, see Hermassi, *The Third World*, pp. 30–40. For a book that vividly illustrates the practical application of this policy of neocolonialism, see Gould, *Bureaucratic Corruption and Underdevelopment in the Third World*. See also n. 9.

12. Krauss, *Development without Aid*, pp. 54, 190.

13. For a discussion along the same line of the dilemma created by the Baker and Bradley approaches, see Hobart Rowen, "The Dilemma of Mexican Aid," *Washington Post*, 17 August 1986, p. K1f.

14. On Soviet institutions concerned with training LDC cadres (Communist University of the Toilers of the East [KUTV], Sun Yat-sen University, the Lenin Institute, the Patrice Lumumba Friendship University, International School of Marxism-Leninism), see Xenia Joukoff Eudin and Robert C. North, *Soviet Russia and the East 1920–1927: A Documentary Survey* (Stanford, Calif.: Stanford University Press, 1957), pp. 84–89, 173–174; Joseph Stalin, "The Political Tasks of the University of the Peoples of the East," in Alvin Z. Rubinstein, ed., *The Foreign Policy of the Soviet Union* (New York: Random House, 1960), pp. 364–68; Branko Lazitch, "Les Ecoles de cadres du Comintern," in Jacques Freymond, ed., *Contributions à l'histoire du Comintern* (Genève: Librairie Droz, 1965), pp. 233–57; Dominique Desanti, *L'interna-*

tionale communiste (Paris: Payot, 1970), chap. 12; Brian Crozier, *Strategy of Survival* (New Rochelle, N.Y.: Arlington House, Publishers, 1978), pp. 146–47; R. A. Ulyanovsky, *The Comintern and the East* (Moscow: Progress Publishers, 1979), pp. 286, 468, 469; Alfred Burmeister, *Dissolution and Aftermath of the Comintern: Experiences and Observations, 1937–1947* (New York: Research Program on the USSR, 1955), mimeographed series no. 77. On Soviet training of cadres for Communist Vietnam, see Khanh, *Vietnamese Communism 1925–1945*, pp. 76, 173, 175–77, 176 (nn. 77, 78).

15. On the persecution of LDC patriot revolutionaries, the reader is referred to literature on colonialism.

The shortage of generalist political cadres in non-Communist LDCs is in no way surprising if one takes into account the fact that the United States, which has provided the most help in participant training for the Third World, is a country of specialists. The lack of well-rounded, broad-gauged politicians has been pointed out by Gabriel A. Almond as one important weakness of U.S. diplomacy (*American People and Foreign Policy* [New York: Praeger, 1960], chap. 7).

On the lack of generalists in public administration, see Robert A. Dahl, "The Science of Public Administration," *Public Administration Review* 7, no. 1 (1947): 13–14. Dahl's contention that there is little room for the generalist professional administrator in the U.S. bureaucratic environment seems to be confirmed by the apparently dim future of the recently introduced Senior Executive Service of the federal government. See, for example, Peter Smith Ring and James L. Perry, "Reforming the Upper Levels of the Bureaucracy: A Longitudinal Study of the Senior Executive Service," *Administration & Society* 15, no. 1 (May 1983): 119–44. Wendell G. Schaeffer points out that public administration education in the United States has focused on training staff specialists, and questions its relevance to students of the Third World. ("The Formation of Managers for Developing Countries," *International Review of Administrative Sciences* 51, no. 3 (1985): 239–47).

Moreover, there does not appear to be any need for extensive research to find that political science training in U.S. universities is less relevant to LDC participants than Moscow's *agitprop* school or University of the Toilers of the East, attended by Ho Chi Minh and other Communist followers. In a critical review of literature on political development Irene L. Gendzier, *Managing Political Change*, points out that U.S.

> development doctrine is deeply rooted in contemporary political thinking and that it is more revealing of a particular dimension of American political thinking than it is of Third World societies in transition. (p. 197)

> Policy-oriented social scientists specializing in Political Development were generally blunt about the purpose of their studies. They made clear their thinking on Development as a process of historic proportions that was beyond the capacity of most Third World statesmen to control, let alone to implement. (p. 59)

In their opinion, there was little experience in guiding development processes, "The social sciences were overly specialized, narrow, and unfit to deal with the processes involved in Development . . . No social science discipline is yet very skilled in dealing with these processes of complex interaction as they proceed through time" (p. 60).

Colonial policies, in general, left newly independent countries with practically no political cadres. Dennis J. Duncanson observes that "Vietnam counts among her own intellectuals an abundance of technical talents, thanks to her Chinese and her French traditions; but so far she has produced relatively few political leaders and no ideas on government" (*Government and Revolution*, p. 379). The Committee on African Development Strategies points out that "at independence, colonial powers left African economies for the most part dependent upon a few commodity exports. New African regimes started out with few workable political institutions and had little training to run them" (*Compact for African Development*, p. 9). Rudolf von Albertini observes that in European colonies, "The central administrative cadres and the technical branches were primarily European and to an extent floated above the traditional society. The natives shared administrative duties only in very subaltern positions, acting more as order followers than as active participants in the apparatus of rule" (*European Colonial Rule, 1880–1940*, p. 493).

16. The reader is referred to literature on Third-World politics. On political conjunctures when society is controlled by negative leadership, according to a popular Vietnamese saying, during periods of decadence, monsters predominate and insects take the place of human beings.

17. It appears that without an improvement in the coordinating capacity of the recipient country or an agreement among donor countries at the highest political level, the perennial issue of coordination among aid agencies can hardly be solved at professional levels. Indeed, the problem has been raised off and on for decades without any solution in view. For discussion and analysis of the issue, see, for example, I. M. D. Little and J. M. Clifford, *International Aid: A Discussion of the Flow of Public Resources from Rich to Poor Countries* (Chicago: Aldine Publishing Company, 1965, 1966), chap. 13 and pp. 198–202; Jacob J. Caplan, *The Challenge of Foreign Aid* (New York: Praeger, 1967), chap. 16; Nihal Kappagoda, *The Cost of Foreign Aid to Developing Countries* (Ottawa, Canada: International Development Research Center, 1978); Organisation for Economic Cooperation and Development, *Development Co-operation: 1981 Review*, pp. 37ff; and Gerald Holtham and Arthur Hazlewood, *Aid and Inequality in Kenya: British Development Assistance to Kenya* (London, 1976), pp. 104, 184–89, cited by Sperber in "The Efficiency-Reducing Effects of Official Development Aid"; Borgin and Corbett, *The Destruction of a Continent*, pp. 66–72; Bertrand, "Must We Convert Multilateral Aid?"; *Compact for African Development*, p. 10; and ACIPA, *Institutional Development*, pp. v, vi, and 13–14.

18. For further details on research approaches to development, see Hermassi, *The Third World*, pp. 16–40.

19. Pye, *Asian Power and Politics*, p. 344.

20. Country studies by the Foreign Area Studies, American University, entitled Area Handbook or Country Study provide comprehensive background information. With further in-depth research on strategic areas suggested in the present study—leadership, value system, legitimation, comparative advantages—macro development strategies for each country can be developed without adding much to research cost.

21. For further application of the theory of comparative advantage, see Krauss, *Development without Aid*, chap. 5 and passim. On U.S. firms' efforts to deal with expensive labor by importing parts from overseas ("hollowing out" manufacturing companies) and moving service jobs overseas, see "Singing the

Shutdown Blues," *Time Magazine*, 23 June 1986, pp. 58 ff; and "Have Data, Will Travel," Ibid., p. 60.

22. On multinationals, see n. 32, chap. 4.

23. Hermassi, *The Third World*, p. 39.

24. It is important to note that foreign assistance in these areas was not neglected, especially as far as U.S. aid to Latin American countries, South Vietnam, and Shah Pahlavi's Iran were concerned. The failure of assistance efforts to contribute to establishing viable polities in terms of legitimacy and power balance, has drawn heavy criticism that has made foreign aid shy away from politically sensitive areas and concentrate on the so-called development institutions. What is advocated here, as elsewhere, should not be considered separately, but as part of a comprehensive aid package aimed at creating viable recipient regimes.

25. For a discussion by a group of development experts of what constitutes a favorable environment for free enterprise, see "The Requisite Environment for Privatization," in ACIPA, *Institutional Development*, pp. 97–106.

26. See Hinton, *Korea under New Leadership*, p. 75; and Nakarmi, "Korea's Foreign Debt," cited in n. 7, chap. 3.

27. See Bunge, ed., *South Korea*, especially p. xx and chap. 3; and Hinton, *Korea under New Leadership*, p. 33 and chap. 3.

28. On the role of the World Bank and the IMF in development assistance, see Crook, "The World Bank, pp. 58ff; George Russell, "Easing into an Era: Barber Conable Aims to Reshape Priorities at the World Bank," *Time Magazine*, 14 July 1986, pp. 44f; The World Bank, *Report 1985*, pp. 105–7; and van de Laar, *The World Bank and the Poor*. For a critical appraisal of the World Bank and the IMF from a leftist author, see Cheryl Payer, *The World Bank: A Critical Analysis* (New York and London: Monthly Review Press, 1982); and Cheryl Payer, *The Debt Trap: The IMF and the Third World* (New York and London: Monthly Review Press, 1974). For critical analysis of these two institutions by a rightist author, see Krauss, *Development without Aid*, pp. 165–73.

SELECT BIBLIOGRAPHY

Achour, Yadh Ben. "Justice des Madhalim et justice administrative moderne." *International Review of Administrative Sciences* 51, no. 2 (1985): 109–19.

Albertini, Rudolf von. *European Colonial Rule, 1880–1940—The Impact of the West on India, Southeast Asia, and Africa.* Westport, Conn.: Greenwood Press, 1982.

Almond, Gabriel A., and James S. Coleman. *The Politics of the Developing Areas.* Princeton: Princeton University Press, 1960.

American Consortium for International Public Administration (ACIPA). *Institutional Development: Improving Management in Developing Countries—Report on a Seminar Series.* Washington, D.C.: ACIPA, 1986.

Aminuzzaman, Salahuddin Md. "Design of Integrated Rural Development Programmes: Some Ideas and Issues." *International Review of Administrative Sciences* 51, no. 4 (1985): 311–17.

Ariyaratne, A. T. "Sarvodaya Shramadana in Sri Lanka." *Development Digest* 14 (January 1976): 87–90.

Bank, Arthur, and Robert Textor. *A Cross-Polity Survey.* Cambridge, Mass.: M.I.T. Press, 1963.

Bao Dai, S. M. *Le dragon d'Annam.* Paris: Plon, 1980.

Bellah, Robert N. "Religious Aspects of Modernization in Turkey and Japan." In *Political Development and Social Change,* 2d ed., edited by Jason L. Finkle and Richard W. Gable. New York: Wiley, 1971, pp. 128–33.

———. *Tokugawa Religion.* Glencoe, Ill.: Free Press, 1957.

Bertrand, Maurice. "Must We Convert Multilateral Aid? Reshaping the Tool." *Development Forum* 14 (May 1986).

Bhagwati, Jagdish N., and Padma Desai. *India Planning for Industrialization: Industrialization and Trade Policies since 1951.* New York: Oxford University Press, 1970.

Bhatt, V. V. "Institutional Framework and Public Enterprise Performance." *World Development* 12, no. 7 (1984): 713–21.

Blase, Melvin G. *Institution Building: A Source Book.* East Lansing, Mich.: Midwest Universities Consortium for International Activities, 1973.

Borgin, Karl, and Kathleen Corbet. *The Destruction of a Continent: Africa and International Aid.* San Diego, Calif.: Harcourt Brace Jovanovich, 1982.

Brandt, Vincent S. R., and Ji Woong Cheong. "Top-Down and Bottom-Up Rural Planning in South Korea." *Development Digest* 20, no. 2 (April 1982): 38–56.

Bryant, Coralie, and Louise G. White. *Managing Development in the Third World.* Boulder, Colo.: Westview Press, 1982.

Bunge, Frederica M., ed. *South Korea: A Country Study.* 3d ed. Washington, D.C.: Foreign Area Studies, American University, 1982.

Bunge, Frederica M., and Rinn-Sup-Shinn, eds. *China: A Country Study.* Washington, D.C.: Foreign Area Studies, American University, 1981.

Burmeister, Alfred. *Dissolution and Aftermath of the Comintern: Experiences and Observations, 1937–1947.* New York: Research Programs on the USSR, 1955. Mimeographed series no. 77.

Busch, Peter A. *Legitimacy and Ethnicity: A Case Study of Singapore.* Lexington, Mass.: Lexington Books, D. C. Heath and Company, 1974.

Butler, David. *The Fall of Saigon: Scenes from the Sudden End of a Long War.* New York: Simon and Schuster, 1985.

Buttinger, Joseph. *The Smaller Dragon: A Political History of Vietnam.* New York: Praeger, 1958.

———. *Vietnam: A Political History.* New York: Praeger, 1968.

Canh, Nguyen Van. *Vietnam under Communism, 1975–1982.* Stanford, Calif.: Hoover Institution, Stanford University, 1983.

Caplan, Jacob J. *The Challenge of Foreign Aid.* New York: Praeger, 1967.

Carino, Ledivina V. "The Politicization of the Philippine Bureaucracy: Corruption or Commitment?" *International Review of Administrative Sciences* 51, no. 1 (1985): 13–18.

Cathie, John. *The Political Economy of Food Aid.* New York: St. Martin's, 1982.

Chan, Wing-Tsit. "The Path to Wisdom: Chinese Philosophy and Religion." In *Half the World: The History and Culture of China and Japan,* edited by Arnold Toynbee. New York: Holt, Rinehart and Winston, 1973. Pp. 95–130.

Chapman, Christopher. *Third-World Politics: An Introduction.* Madison: University of Wisconsin Press, 1985.

Chee, Chan Heng. *The Dynamics of One-Party Dominance: The PAP and the Grass Roots.* Singapore: Singapore University Press, 1976.

Cheema, G. Shabbir, and Dennis A. Rondinelli, eds. *Decentralization and Development.* Beverly Hill, Calif.: Sage Publications, 1983.

Chi, Hoang Van. *From Colonialism to Communism: A Case History of North Vietnam.* New York: Praeger, 1964.

Chinweizu. "Africa in the Eighties." *Africa* 125 (January 1982): 54–55.

———. *The West and the Rest of Us: White Predators, Black Slavers, and the African Elite.* New York: Vintage Books, 1975.

Clutterbuck, Richard. *Conflict and Violence in Singapore and Malaysia, 1945–1983.* Singapore: Graham Brash (PTE) Ltd., 1984.

Colamosca, Anne. "Exploiting the Third World Is Getting Hard: White Man's Burden." *New Republic,* 4 April 1981, pp. 12–15.

Compact for African Development, Report of the Committee on African Development Strategies. Lawrence S. Eagleburger and Donald F. McHenry, cochairmen. A joint project of the Council on Foreign Relations and the Overseas Development Council, December 1985.

Conyers, Diana. "Decentralization and Development: A Review of the Literature." *Public Administration and Development* 4 (April–June 1984): 187–97.

————. "Decentralization: The Latest Fashion in Development Administration?" *Public Administration and Development* 3 (April–June 1983): 97–109.

Cordier, Henri. *Histoire générale de la Chine et de ses relations avec les pays étrangers depuis les temps les plus anciens jusqu'à la chute de la dynastie mandchoue.* 4 vols. Paris: Librairie Paul Gouthner, 1920.

Crook, Clive. "The World Bank: A Change of Pace." *Economist,* 27 September 1986, pp. 5–56.

Crozier, Brian. "Nine Years (or So) after." *National Review* 34 (10 December 1982): 1536.

————. *Strategy of Survival.* New Rochelle, N.Y.: Arlington House, Publishers, 1978.

Dahl, Robert A. "The Science of Public Administration." *Public Administration Review* 7, no. 1 (1947).

Damachi, Ukandi G. *Self-Management in Yugoslavia and the Developing World.* New York: St. Martin's, 1982.

Dang, Nghiem. *Vietnam: Politics and Public Administration.* Honolulu: East-West Center Press, 1966.

David, Steven R. *Defending Third-World Regimes from Coups d'Etat.* Lanham, Md.: University Press of America and the Center for International Affairs, Harvard University, 1985.

————. *Third-World Coups d'Etat and International Security.* Baltimore: Johns Hopkins University Press, 1987.

Davis, Stanley M. "Politics and Organizational Underdevelopment in Chile." In *Comparative Management: Organizational and Cultural Perspectives,* edited by Stanley M. Davis. Englewood Cliffs, N.J.: Prentice-Hall, 1971. Pp. 188–209.

Desanti, Dominique. *L'internationale communiste.* Paris: Payot, 1970.

Dettman, Paul R. "Leaders and Structures in 'Third-World' Politics: Contrasting Approaches to Legitimacy." In *Analyzing the Third World: Essays from Comparative Politics,* edited by Norman W. Provizer, Cambridge, Mass.: Schenkman Publishing Company, 1978. Pp. 408–32.

Devillers, Philippe. *Histoire du Viêt-Nam de 1940 à 1952.* Paris: Edition du Seuil, 1952.

Diederich, Bernard. *Somoza—and the Legacy of U.S. Involvement in Central America.* New York: E. P. Dutton, 1981.

Down, Anthony. *Inside Bureaucracy.* Boston: Little, Brown and Company, 1967.

"Dragon Ladies under Siege." *People,* 3 March 1986.

Duncanson, Dennis J. *Government and Revolution in Vietnam.* New York: Oxford University Press, 1968.

Dwivedi, O. P. "Ethics and Values of Public Responsibility and Accountability." *International Review of Administrative Sciences* 51, no. 2 (1985): 61–66.

Easton, David. *A Framework for Political Analysis.* Englewood Cliffs, N.J.: Prentice-Hall, 1965.

————. "An Approach to the Analysis of Political Systems." *World Politics* 9 (1957): 383–400.

————. *The Political System.* New York: Knopf, 1953.

Eaton, Joseph W., ed. *Institution Building and Development: From Concepts to Application.* Beverly Hill, Calif.: Sage Publications, 1972.

Esman, Milton J. "Foreign Aid: Not by Bread Alone." *Public Administration Review* 31 (January/February 1971): 92–100.

Esman, Milton J., and John D. Montgomery. "Systems Approaches to Technical Cooperation: The Role of Development Administration." *Public Administration Review* 29 (September/October 1969): 507–39.

Esman, Milton J., and Norman T. Uphoff. *Local Organizations: Intermediaries in Rural Development.* Ithaca, N.Y. and London: Cornell University Press, 1984.

Etzioni, Amitai. *Modern Organization.* Englewood Cliffs, N.J.: Prentice-Hall, 1964.

Eudin, Xenia Joukoff, and Robert C. North. *Soviet Russia and the East 1920–1927: A Documentary Survey.* Stanford, Calif.: Stanford University Press, 1957.

"Europe's Racial Timebomb." *World Press Review* 32 (December 1985): 27–29.

"An Exodus of Capital Is Sapping the LDC Economies: It Has Also Created a Tremendous Distortion of Global Money Flows." *Business Week,* 3 October 1983, 132–34.

Fall, Bernard B. *Hell in a Very Small Place: The Siege of Dien Bien Phu.* New York: J. B. Lippincot, 1967.

————. *The Two Vietnams: A Political and Military Analysis.* 2d rev. ed. New York: Praeger, 1967.

Fanon, Frantz. "The Pitfalls of National Consciousness." In *Comparative Management: Organizational and Cultural Perpectives,* edited by Stanley M. Davis. Englewood Cliffs, N.J.: Prentice-Hall, 1971. Pp. 40–70.

————. *The Wretched of the Earth.* New York: Grove Press, 1966.

Farb, Peter. *Man's Rise to Civilization As Shown by the Indians of North America from Primeval Times to the Coming of the Industrial State.* New York: E. P. Dutton and Company, 1968.

Finkle, Jason L., and Richard W. Gable, eds. *Political Development and Social Change.* 2d ed. New York: Wiley, 1971.

Food and Agriculture Organization. "La formation agricole: Rapport sur une étude d'évaluation." *Série d'évaluation,* no. 4. Rome: Food and Agriculture Organization, 1980.

Frank, Andre Gunder. *Capitalism and Underdevelopment in Latin America.* New York and London: Monthly Review Press, 1969.

————. *Latin America: Underdevelopment or Revolution.* New York and London: Monthly Review Press, 1969.

Friedrich, Carl Joachim. *Man and His Government.* New York: McGraw-Hill, 1963.

"From the Professional Stream: Currents and Sounding." *Public Administration Review* 40, no. 5 (September/October 1980): 407–33.

Gamer, Robert E. *The Developing Nations: A Comparative Perspective,* Boston: Allyn and Bacon, 1976.

Gaudusson, Jean de. *L'administration malgache.* Paris: Edition Berger-Levrault, 1976.

Gendzier, Irene L. *Managing Political Change: Social Scientists and the Third World.* Boulder, Colo. and London: Westview Press, 1985.

George, T. J. S. *Lee Kuan Yew's Singapore.* London: Andre Deutch, 1973.

Gerth, H. H., and C. Wright Mills, eds. *From Max Weber: Essays in Sociology.* New York: Oxford University Press, 1946.

Ghosh, Pradip K., ed. *Appropriate Technology in Third-World Development,* Westport, Conn.: Greenwood Press, 1984.

Goodenough, Ward H. *Cooperation in Change.* New York: Russel Sage Foundation, 1963.

Goodwin, Craufurd D., and Michael Nacht. *Decline and Renewal: Causes and Cures of Decay among Foreign-Trained Intellectuals and Professionals in the Third World.* New York: Institute of International Education, 1986.

Gould, David J. *Bureaucratic Corruption and Underdevelopment in the Third World: The Case of Zaire.* New York: Pergamon, 1980.

Gow, David D., and Jerry VanSant. "Decentralization and Participation: Concepts in Need of Implementation Strategies." In *Implementing Rural Development Projects: Lessons from AID and World Bank Experiences,* edited by Elliott R. Morss and David D. Gow. Boulder, Colo.: Westview Press, 1985.

Gran, Guy. "Learning from Development Success: Some Lessons from Contemporary Case Histories." *NASPAA Working Paper No. 9.* Washington, D.C.: National Association of Schools of Public Affairs and Administration, 1983.

Greene, Graham. *The Quiet American.* New York: Modern Library, 1955.

Greenwald, John. "A New Age of Capitalism: As Socialism Falters, Free Enterprise Is on the Move around the Globe." *Time Magazine,* 28 July 1986.

Grousset, Rene. *The Rise and Spendour of the Chinese Empire.* Berkeley and Los Angeles: University of California Press, 1953.

Groves, Roderick T. "Administrative Reform and the Politics of Reform: The Case of Venezuela." *Public Administration Review* 27 (December 1967): 436–45.

Gurtow, Melvin, and Ray Maghroori. *Roots of Failure: United States Policy in the Third World.* Westport, Conn.: Greenwood Press, 1984.

Haines, David W., ed. *Refugees in the United States: A Reference Handbook.* Westport, Conn.: Greenwood Press, 1985.

Halberstam, David. "The Korean Challenge." *Washington Post,* 2 November 1986, *Parade Magazine,* pp. 4ff.

Harari, Denise. *The Role of the Technical Assistance Expert: An Inquiry into the Expert's Identity Motivations and Attitudes.* Paris: Development Centre, Organization for Economic Cooperation and Development, 1974.

Harden, Blaine. "World Oil Glut, Oddly Easing Squalor in Lagos." *Washington Post,* 21 October 1985.

Harrison, Lawrence E. *Underdevelopment Is a State of Mind: The Latin American Case.* Lanham, Md.: Center for International Affairs, Harvard University and the University Press of America, 1985.

"Have Data, Will Travel." *Time Magazine,* 23 June 1986, p. 60.

Heady, Ferrel. *Public Administration: A Comparative Perspective.* 3d ed. New York and Basel: Marcel Dekker, 1984.

Hee, Park Chung. *Our Nation's Path: Ideology of Social Reconstruction.* Seoul, Korea: Hollym Corporation, 1970.

Heller, P. "The Underfinancing of Recurrent Development Costs." *Finance and Development* 16, no. 1 (1979): 38–41.

Henderson, Gregory. *Korea: The Politics of the Vortex.* Cambridge: Harvard University Press, 1968.

Henry, James S. "Where the Money Went." *New Republic,* 14 April 1986, pp. 20–23.

Hermassi, Elbaki. *The Third World Reassessed.* Berkeley: University of California Press, 1980.

Hickey, Gerald Cannon. *Free in the Forest: Ethnohistory of the Vietnamese Central Highlands 1954–1976.* New Haven and London: Yale University Press, 1982.

Higgins, Marguerite. *Our Vietnam Nightmare.* New York: Harper and Row, 1965.

Hinton, Harold C. *Korea under New Leadership: The Fifth Republic.* New York: Praeger, 1983.

Hofstede, Geert. *Culture's Consequences: International Differences in Work-Related Values.* Beverly Hill, Calif.: Sage Publications, 1980.

Honadle, George, Jerry M. Silverman, and Donald R. Mickelwait. "Technical Assistance Shortcomings." In *Implementing Rural Development Projects— Lessons from AID and World Bank Experiences,* edited by Elliott R. Morss and David D. Gow. Boulder, Colo.: Westview Press, 1985.

Honadle, George, and Jerry VanSant. *Implementing for Sustainability: Lessons from Integrated Rural Development.* West Hartford, Conn.: Kumarian Press, 1985.

Hope, Kempe Ronald. "Politics, Bureaucratic Corruption, and Maladministration in the Third World." *International Review of Administrative Sciences* 51, no. 1 (1985): 1–6.

Hosmer, Stephen T., Konrad Kellen, and Brian M. Jenkins. *The Fall of South Vietnam: Statements by Vietnamese Military and Civilian Leaders.* Santa Monica, Calif.: Rand Corporation R-2208-OSD (HIST), 1978.

Hsu, Francis L. K. *Americans and Chinese: Two Ways of Life.* New York: Henry Schuman, 1953.

———. *Clan, Cast, and Club.* Princeton, N.J.: Van Nostrand, 1963.

Huard, Pierre, and Maurice Durand. *Connaissance du Viêt-Nam.* Paris: Imprimerie nationale, 1954.

Hucker, Charles O. *China's Imperial Past: An Introduction to Chinese History and Culture.* Stanford, Calif.: Stanford University Press, 1975.

Hui, Pak Chung. *Korea Reborn: A Model for Development, Park Chung Hee.* Englewood Cliffs, N.J.: Prentice-Hall, 1979.

Hung, Nguyen Manh. " 'Vietnam: A Television History' A Case Study in Perceptual Conflict between the American Media and the Vietnamese Expatriates." *World Affairs* 147, no. 2 (Fall 1984): 71–84.

Huntington, Samuel P. "Political Development and Political Decay." In *Polit-*

ical Modernization: A Reader in Comparative Political Change, edited by Claude E. Welch, Jr. Belmont, Calif.: Wadsworth Publishing Company, 1967. Pp. 207–46.

————. *Political Order in Changing Societies*. New Haven: Yale University Press, 1968.

Ingle, Marcus D. "Implementing Development Programs: A State-of-the-Art Review." Washington, D.C.: Agency for International Development, 1979 (contract AID/ta-147-612). Mimeographed.

Jackson, Henry F. "The African Crisis: Drought and Debt." *Foreign Affairs* 63, no. 5 (Summer 1985): 1082–94.

Jackson, Robert H., and Carl G. Rosberg. *Personal Rules in Black Africa: Prince, Autocrat, Prophet, Tyrant*. Berkeley: University of California Press, 1982.

Jackson, Tony, and Deborah Eade. *Against the Grain: The Dilemma of Project Food Aid*. Oxford, U.K.: OXFAM, 1982.

Jones, Edwin. "Politics, Bureaucratic Corruption, and Maladministration in the Third World: Some Commonwealth Caribbean Considerations." *International Review of Administrative Sciences* 51, no. 1 (1985): 19–23.

Jones, Leroy P., ed. *Public Enterprise in Less Developed Countries*. New York: Cambridge University Press, 1982.

Josey, Alex. *Lee Kuan Yew.* Singapore: Asia Pacific Press, 1971.

————. *Singapore, Its Past, Present, and Future*. Singapore: Eastern University Press, 1979.

Joshi, Nanda Lall. "Whither Public Enterprises?" *PRASHASAN (The Nepalese Journal of Public Administration)* 42 (March 1985): 1–5.

Jreisat, Jamil. "Building Administrative Capacity for Action: The Arab States." *SICA Occasional Paper Series*. 2d ser., no. 8. Austin: Institute of Latin American Studies, University of Texas at Austin and the Section on International and Comparative Administration, 1985.

Kaberuka, D. P. "Evaluating the Performance of Food-Marketing Parastatals." *Development Policy Review* 2 (November 1984): 199–216.

Karnow, Stanley. *Vietnam: A History.* New York: Viking Press, 1983.

Keon, Michael. *Korean Phoenix: A Nation from Ashes*. Englewood Cliffs, N.J.: Prentice-Hall International, 1977.

Khanh, Huynh Kim. *Vietnamese Communism 1925–1945*. Ithaca, N.Y.: Cornell University Press, 1983.

Khoi, Le Thanh. *Le Viêt-Nam. Histoire et civilisation*. Paris: Les Editions de minuit, 1955.

Kim, Tran Trong. *Viet-Nam Su-Luoc*. Summary history of Vietnam. 2 vols. N.p.: Song Moi, 1978. Originally published by the Ministry of Education, Republic of Vietnam, 1971.

Korten, David C. "Organizing for Rural Development: A Learning Process." *Development Digest* 20 (April 1982): 3–30.

Koteen, Jack. "Key Problems in Development Administration." In *Administrative Issues in Developing Economies*, edited by Kenneth J. Rothwell. Lexington, Mass.: Lexington Books, 1972. Pp. 47–67.

Krauss, Melvyn B. *Development without Aid—Growth, Poverty, and Government.* New York: McGraw-Hill, 1983.

Laar, Aart van de. *The World Bank and the Poor.* Boston: Martinus Nijhoff, 1980.

Lal, Deepak. *The Poverty of "Development Economics."* Cambridge: Harvard University Press, 1985.

Lamm, Richard D., and Gary Imhoff. *The Immigration Timebomb: The Fragmenting of America.* New York: Truman Talley Books/E. P. Dutton, 1985.

Lasswell, Harold D. "The Emerging International Culture." In *Challenge of Development,* edited by Richard D. Ward. Chicago: Aldine Publishing Company, 1967. Pp. 489–95.

Lazitch, Branko. "Les Ecoles de cadres du Comintern." In *Contributions à l'histoire du Comintern,* edited by Jacques Freymond. Genève: Librairie Droz, 1965. Pp. 233–57.

Lee, Hahn Been. *Korea: Time, Change, and Administration.* Honolulu: East-West Center Press, 1968.

Leemans, Arne F., ed. *The Management of Change in Government.* The Hague: Institute of Social Studies, Martinus Nijhoff, 1976.

Leonard, David K., and Dale Roger Marshall, eds. *Institutions of Rural Development for the Poor: Decentralization and Organizational Linkages.* Berkeley: Institute of International Studies, University of California, 1982.

"Les projets d'assistance des Nations Unies aux pays francophones d'Afrique." *Development Administration Newsletter* 71 (November 1984–June 1985): 15–16.

Lewis, Oscar. "The Culture of Poverty." *Scientific American* 215 (October 1966): 19–25.

Lewy, Guenter. *America in Vietnam.* New York: Oxford University Press, 1978.

Lindenberg, Marc, and Benjamin Crosby. *Managing Development: The Political Dimension.* West Hartford, Conn.: Kumarian Press, 1981.

Lipset, Seymour Martin. *Political Man: The Social Bases of Politics.* Garden City, N.Y.: Anchor Books, Doubleday and Company, 1959.

———. *The First New Nation: The United States in Historical and Comparative Perspective.* New York: Basic Books, 1963.

Little, I. M. D. and J. M. Clifford. *International Aid: A Discussion of the Flow of Public Resources from Rich to Poor Countries.* Chicago: Aldine Publishing Company, 1965, 1966.

Loeber, Thomas S. *Foreign Aid: Our Tragic Experiment.* New York: W. W. Norton and Company, 1961.

Loehr, William, and John P. Powelson. *Threat to Development: Pitfalls of the NIEO.* Boulder, Colo.: Westview Press, 1983.

Long, Nguyen. *After Saigon Fell: Daily Life under the Communists.* Berkeley: Institute of East Asian Studies, University of California, 1981.

Lou, Jacques. *Can the Third World Survive?* Baltimore: Johns Hopkins University Press, 1983. Originally published in France, 1980.

McAlister, John T., Jr., and Paul Mus. *The Vietnamese and Their Revolution.* New York: Harper and Row, 1970.

Maclear, Michael. *The Ten-Thousand-Day War: Vietnam—1945–1975.* New York: St. Martin's, 1981.

Macy, Joanna. *Dharma and Development: Religion as Resource in the Sarvodaya Self Help Movement,* 2d ed. West Hartford, Conn.: Kumarian Press, 1985.

Mahler, Vincent A. *Dependency Approaches to International Political Economy: A Cross-National Study.* New York: Columbia University Press, 1980.

Marr, David G. *Vietnamese Anticolonialism 1885–1925.* Berkeley and Los Angeles: University of California Press, 1971.

———. *Vietnamese Tradition on Trial, 1920–1945.* Berkeley and Los Angeles: University of California Press, 1981.

Marrus, Michael R. *The Unwanted: European Refugees in the Twentieth Century.* New York: Oxford University Press, 1985.

Matossian, Mary. "Ideology of Delayed Industrialization." In *Political Development and Social change,* 2d ed., edited by Jason L. Finkle and Richard W. Gable. New York: Wiley 1971. Pp. 113–22.

Meerman, Jacob. "Cost Recovery in a Project Context: Some World Bank Experience in Tropical Africa." *World Development* 11, no. 6 (June 1983): 503–14.

Mehden, Fred R. von der. *Politics of the Developing Nations.* Englewood Cliffs, N.J.: Prentice-Hall, 1964.

Memmi, Albert. *Portrait du colonisé précédé du portrait du colonisateur.* Paris: Payot, 1973.

Mendoza, Gabino A. "The Transferability of Western Management Concepts and Programs: an Asian Perspective." In *Education and Training for Public Sector Management in Developing Countries,* edited by Joseph E. Black, James S. Coleman, and Lawrence D. Stifel. New York: Rockefeller Foundation, March 1977, Pp. 61–71.

Meow, Seah Chee. "The Singapore Bureaucracy and Issues of Transition." Department of Political Science, University of Singapore. *Occasional Paper Series* no. 12 (February 1975).

Merton, Robert K. *Social Theory and Social Structure.* New York: Free Press, 1968.

Minhas, Bagicha S. "The Current Development Debate." In *Toward a New Strategy for Development: A Rothko Chapel Colloquium.* New York: Pergamon, 1979. Pp. 75–96.

Mirza, Hafiz. *Multinationals and the Growth of the Singapore Economy.* New York: St. Martin's, 1986.

Montgomery, John D. *The Politics of Foreign Aid: American Experience in South East Asia.* New York: Praeger, 1962.

Moris, Jon. "The Transferability of Western Management Concepts and Programs: An East African Perspective." In *Education and Training for Public Sector Management in Developing Countries,* edited by Joseph E. Black, James S. Coleman, and Lawrence D. Stifel. New York: Rockefeller Foundation, March 1977. Pp. 73–83.

Morris, Milton D. *Immigration: The Beleaguered Bureaucracy.* Washington, D.C.: Brookings Institution, 1985.

Morris, Stephen J. "Vietnam under Communism." *Commentary* 74, no. 3 (September 1982): 39–47.

Morss, Elliott R. "Institutional Destruction Resulting from Donor and Project Proliferation in Sub-Saharan Countries." *World Development* 12, no. 4 (1984).

Morss, Elliott R., and David D. Gow, eds. *Implementing Rural Development Projects: Lessons from AID and World Bank Experiences.* Boulder, Colo.: Westview Press, 1985.

Morss, Elliott R., Paul R. Crawford, and Gene M. Owens. "Personnel Constraints." In *Implementing Rural Development Projects—Lessons from AID and World Bank Experiences,* edited by Elliott R. Morss and David D. Gow. Boulder, Colo.: Westview Press, 1985. Pp. 65–81.

Morss, Elliott R., and Victoria Morss. *U.S. Foreign Aid: An Assessment of New and Traditional Strategies.* Boulder, Colo.: Westview Press, 1982.

Murrell, Kenneth L. "The Managerial Infrastructure in Economic Development: Its Importance and How to Analyze It." *SICA Occasional Papers Series.* 2d ser., no. 12. Austin: Institute for Latin American Studies, University of Texas at Austin and the Section on International and Comparative Administration, 1986.

Mus, Paul. *Sociologie d'une guerre.* Paris: Edition du Seuil, 1952.

Nakarmi, Laxmi. "Korea's Foreign Debt: Why the Bankers Are Secure." *Business Korea* 2, no. 3 (September 1984): 17–25.

Nelson, Joan M. *Access to Power Politics and the Urban Poor in the Developing Nations.* Princeton: Princeton University Press, 1979.

Nguyen, Tri Q. "Culture and Technical Assistance in Public Administration: A Study of What Can Be Transferred from the United States to Vietnam." Ph.D. diss., University of Southern California, January 1970.

———. "Statutory and Administration Management Aspects of Parastatal Institutions." World Bank CAD/EAPD, Madagascar Public Sector Enterprises, subsector review, *Working Paper No. 1,* March 1982.

———. "Case Study: The Sakay State Farm." World Bank CAD/EAPD, Madagascar Public Sector Enterprises, subsector review, *Working Paper No. 2,* May 1982.

Nielsen, John. "Rising Racism on the Continent." *Time Magazine,* 6 February 1984.

Olowu, Dele. "Bureaucratic Corruption and Public Accountability in Nigeria: An Assessment of Recent Developments." *International Review of Administrative Sciences* 51 (1985): 7–12.

———. "Bureaucratic Performance in Developed and Developing Countries: A Review of Recent Literature and Developments." *Public Administration Review* 44, no. 5 (September/October 1984): 453–58.

Osborne, Milton. *Region of Revolt: Focus on Southeast Asia.* Pergamon Press Australia Pty Limited, 1970.

Ottaway, David B. "Cairo Seems to Fight Chaos with Chaos." *Washington Post,* 29 January 1985.

Oxby, Clare. "Settlement Schemes for Herders in the Subhumid Tropics of West Africa: Issues of Land Rights and Ethnicity." *Development Policy Review* 2, no. 2 (November 1984): 217–33.

Pang, Cheng Lian. *Singapore's People's Action Party: Its History, Organization, and Leadership.* Singapore and Kuala Lumpur: Oxford University Press, 1971.

Pauker, Guy J. *Sources of Instability in Developing Countries.* Santa Monica, Calif.: Rand Corporation, 1973.

Paul, Samuel. *Managing Development Programs: The Lessons of Success.* Boulder, Colo.: Westview Press, 1982.

Payenne, Andre. "Plugging the Brain Drain—A Third-World Call for Western Reparations." *World Press Review* (August 1985): 33–34.

Payer, Cheryl. *The Debt Trap: The IMF and the Third World.* New York and London: Monthly Review Press, 1974.

———. *The World Bank: A Critical Analysis.* New York and London: Monthly Review Press, 1982.

Peirce, Neal R. "Immigration Perils at the Border." *Public Administration Times* 9, no. 1 (1 January 1986): 2.

"The Philosopher King of Singapore." *CoEvolution Quarterly* 39 (Fall 1983): 62–65.

Pike, Douglas. *Viet Cong: The Organization and Techniques of the National Liberation Front of South Vietnam.* Cambridge: M.I.T. Press, 1966.

Pye, Lucian W. *Asian Power and Politics: The Cultural Dimension of Authority.* Cambridge, Mass.: Belknap Press, 1985.

———. *Aspects of Political Development.* Boston: Little, Brown and Company, 1966.

———. *Politics, Personality, and Nation Building: Burma's Search for Identity.* New Haven: Yale University Press, 1962.

Ralston, Lenore, James Anderson, and Elizabeth Colson. *Voluntary Efforts in Decentralized Management: Opportunities and Constraints in Rural Development.* Berkeley: Institute of International Studies, University of California, 1983.

Richardson, Bradley M. *The Political Culture of Japan.* Berkeley: University of California Press, 1974.

Rigby, T. H., and Ferenc Feher, eds. *Political Legitimation in Communist States.* New York: St. Martin's, 1982.

Riggs, Fred W. *Administration in Developing Countries: The Theory of Prismatic Society.* Boston: Houghton Mifflin, 1964.

———. *Thailand: The Modernization of a Bureaucratic Polity.* Honolulu: East-West Center Press, 1966.

Ring, Peter Smith, and James L. Perry. "Reforming the Upper Levels of the Bureaucracy: A Longitudinal Study of the Senior Executive Service." *Administration & Society* 15, no. 1 (May 1983): 119–44.

Rondinelli, Dennis A. "Development Management in AID: A Baseline Review of Project and Program Management Assistance in the U.S. Agency for International Development." Washington, D.C.: Technical Cooperation Project, National Association of Schools of Public Affairs and Administration, 1984. Mimeographed.

———. *Development Projects as Policy Experiments: An Adaptive Approach to Development Administration.* London and New York: Methuen, 1983.

———. "Project as Instrument of Development Administration: A Qualified Defence and Suggestions for Improvement." *Public Administration and Development* 3, no. 4 (October–December 1983): 307–27.

————, ed. *Planning Development Projects.* Stroudsberg, Pa.: Dowden, Hutchinson and Ross, 1977.

"The Requisites Environment for Privatization." In *Institutional Development: Improving Management in Developing Countries—Report on a Seminar Series.* Washington, D.C.: American Consortium for International Public Administration, 1986.

Ross, Harold, and Jan Bouwmeesters. *Management in the Developing Countries: A Field Survey.* Geneva: United Nations Research Institute for Social Development, 1972.

Rowen, Hobart. "The Dilemma of Mexican Aid." *Washington Post,* 17 August 1986.

Rozman, Gilbert, ed. *The Modernization of China.* New York: Free Press, 1981.

Russakoff, Dale. "The Philippines: Anatomy of a Looting." *Washington Post,* 30 March 1986.

Russel, George. "Easing into an Era: Barber Conable Aims to Reshape Priorities at the World Bank." *Time Magazine,* 14 July 1986.

Rust, William J. *Kennedy in Vietnam.* New York: Scribner's, 1985.

Sangmeister, Harmut. "The Economic and Social Situation of the Least Developed Countries (LLDCs)." *Economics* (Tübingen) 30 (1984): 129–41.

————. "World Development Indicators." *Development and Cooperation* 1 (1983).

Schaeffer, Wendell G. "The Formation of Managers for Developing Countries." *International Review of Administrative Sciences* 15, no. 3 (1985): 239–47.

Schurmann, Herbert F. *Ideology and Organization in Communist China.* Berkeley: University of California Press, 1966.

Shaukat, Ali. *Nation-Building Development and Administration: A Third-World Perspective.* Urdu Bazar, Lahore, Pakistan: S. Aziz Shah Bukhari, Aziz Publishers, 1979.

Siffin, William J. "Two Decades of Public Administration in Developing Countries." *Public Administration Review* 36 (January/February 1976): 61–71.

Sigmund, Paul E., Jr., ed. *The Ideologies of the Developing Nations.* New York: Praeger, 1963.

Simonis, Udo Ernst. "Environmental Crisis: The Missing Dimension in the North South Dialogue." *Economics* (Tübingen) 30 (1984): 48–64.

"Singing the Shutdown Blues." *Time Magazine,* 23 June 1986.

Snepp, Frank. *Decent Interval: An Insider's Account of Saigon's Indecent End.* New York: Random House, 1977.

Spector, Ronald H. *Advice and Support: The Early Years of the United States Army in Vietnam 1941–1960.* 1983. Reprint. New York: Free Press, 1985.

Sperber, Herbert. "The Efficiency-Reducing Effects of Official Development Aid." *Intereconomics* (March/April 1983): 84–89.

Spitzberg, Irving J., Jr., ed. *Exchange of Expertise: The Counterpart System in the New International Order.* Boulder, Colo.: Westview Press, 1978.

Staar, Richard F., ed. *Yearbook on International Communist Affairs 1985: Parties and Revolutionary Movements.* Stanford, Calif.: Hoover Institution Press, 1985.

Stalin, Joseph. "The Political Tasks of the University of the Peoples of the

East." In *The Foreign Policy of the Soviet Union*, edited by Alvin Z. Rubinstein. New York: Random House, 1960. Pp. 364–68.

Suh, Dae-Sook, and Chae-Jin Lee, eds. *Political Leadership in Korea*. Seattle: University of Washington Press, 1976.

Suhrke, Astri. "Indochinese Refugees: The Law and Politics of First Asylum." In *The Global Refugee Problem: U.S. and World Response*, edited by Gilburt D. Loescher and John A. Scanlan. The *Annals of the American Academy of Political and Social Science* 467 (May 1983).

Sullivan, Marianna P. *France's Vietnam Policy: A Study in French-American Relations*. Westport, Conn.: Greenwood Press, 1978.

Taborsky, Edward. *Communist Penetration of the Third World*. New York: R. Speller, 1973.

Tang, Truong Nhu. *A Vietcong Memoir*. San Diego, Calif.: Hartcourt Brace Jovanovich, 1985.

———. "How the Communists Betrayed the Vietnam Revolution." *Penthouse* 12 (April 1981): 64–69.

Tannenbaum, Frank. "The Influence of Social Conditions." In *Public Administration in Developing Countries*, edited by Martin Kriesberg. Washington, D.C.: Brookings Institution, 1965. Pp. 33–42.

Taylor, Charles L., and David A. Jodice. *World Handbook of Political and Social Indicators*. 3d ed., 2 vols. New Haven and London: Yale University Press, 1983.

Thomas, Evan. "The U.N. Midlife Crisis." *Time Magazine*, 28 October 1985.

Time Magazine, 16 January 1984. Special issue on "Africa's Woes: A Continent Gone Wrong."

Toriumi, Y. "A New Role for Japan: The Meiji Revolution and Its Sequel." In *Half the World: The History and Culture of China and Japan*, edited by Arnold Toynbee. New York: Holt, Rinehart, and Winston, 1973. Pp. 293–318.

Tsurutani, Taketsugu. *Politics of National Development: Political Leadership in Transitional Societies*. New York: Chandler Publishing Company, 1973.

Tu, Wei-Ming. "Economic Growth in East Asia: Confucianism and Cultural Factors." *The Wilson Center/Reports* (January 1985).

Turnbull, C. M. *A History of Singapore 1819–1975*. Kuala Lumpur and New York: Oxford University Press, 1977.

Turnbull, Colin M. *The Lonely African*. Garden City, N.Y.: Anchor Books, 1963.

———. "The Lonely African." In *Comparative Management: Organizational and Cultural Perspectives*, edited by Stanley M. Davis. Englewood Cliffs, N.J.: Prentice-Hall, 1971. Pp. 32–40.

Twitchett, D. C. " 'The Middle Kingdom': Chinese Politics and Society from the Bronze Age to the Manchus." In *Half the World: The History and Culture of China and Japan*, edited by Arnold Toynbee. New York: Holt, Rinehart, and Winston, 1973. Pp. 31–78.

"The Two Faces of Third-World Debt: A Fragile Financial Environment and Debt Enslavement." *Monthly Review* 35, no. 8 (January 1984): 1–10.

Ulyanovsky, R. A. *The Comintern and the East.* Moscow: Progress Publishers, 1979.

UNCTAD Secretariat. *The Reverse Transfer of Technology, Its Dimensions, Economic Effects, and Policy Implications: A Study.* New York: United Nations, 1975.

U.S. General Accounting Office. *Financial Management Problems in Developing Countries Reduce the Impact of Assistance.* Report to the administrator, Agency for International Development, GAO/NSIAD -85-19, 5 November 1984.

Vallianatos, E. G. *Fear in the Countryside: The Control of Agricultural Resources in the Poor Countries by Nonpeasant Elites.* Cambridge, Mass.: Ballinger, 1976.

VanSant, Jerry, and Paul R. Crawford. "Coping with Political, Economic, Environmental, and Institutional Constraints." In *Implementing Rural Development Projects: Lessons from AID and World Bank Experiences,* edited by Elliott R. Morss and David D. Gow. Boulder, Colo.: Westview Press, 1985.

Vreeland, Nena, Glenn Dana, Geoffrey B. Hurwitz, Peter Just, and R. S. Shinn. *Area Handbook for Singapore.* Washington, D.C.: U.S. Government Printing Office, DA Pam 550-184, 1977.

Wade, L. L. and B. S. Kim. *Economic Development of South Korea: The Political Economy of Success.* New York: Praeger, 1978.

Wagley, Charles. "The Dilemma of the Latin American Middle Class." In *Comparative Management: Organizational and Cultural Perspectives,* edited by Stanley M. Davis. Englewood Cliffs, N.J.: Prentice-Hall, 1971. Pp. 144–50.

Wain, Barry. *The Refused: The Agony of the Indochina Refugees.* New York: Simon and Schuster, 1981.

Waldo, Dwight, ed. "A Symposium—Comparative and Development Administration: Retrospect and Prospect." *Public Administration Review* (November/December 1976): 615–54.

Waldstein, Abraham S. "Development for Whom?" In *Sahelian Social Development,* edited by Stephen P. Reyna. Abidjan: Regional Economic Development Services Offices/West Africa, USAID, 1980. Pp. 507–603.

Wallace, Anthony F. C. "Revitalization Movement in Development." In *The Challenge of Development,* edited by Richard J. Ward. Chicago: Aldine Publishing Company, 1967. Pp. 448–54.

Ward, Robert E. "Political Modernization and Political Culture in Japan." In *Political Modernization,* 2d ed., edited by Claude E. Welch, Jr., Belmont, Calif.: Duxbury Press, 1971. Pp. 100–117.

Whang, In-Joung. *Management of Rural Change in Korea: The Saemaul Undong.* Seoul, Korea: Seoul National University Press, 1981.

Weber, Max, and Kemper Fullerton. "The Protestant Ethic and the Spirit of Capitalism." In *Culture and Management,* edited by Ross Weber. Homewood, Ill.: Richard D. Irvin, 1969. Pp. 91–112.

Weidner, Edward W. *Technical Assistance in Public Administration Overseas: The Case for Development Administration.* Chicago: Public Administration Service, 1964.

Willner, Ann Ruth. *The Spellbinders: Charismatic Political Leadership.* New Haven: Yale University Press, 1984.

World Bank. *Debt and the Developing World: Current Trends and Prospects; an Abridged Version of World Debt Tables.* 1983–84 ed. Washington, D.C.: World Bank, 1984.

——. *World Development Report 1983.* New York: Oxford University Press, 1983.

——. *World Development Report 1984.* New York: Oxford University Press, 1984.

——. *World Development Report 1985.* New York: Oxford University Press, 1985.

Wraith, Ronald, and Edgar Simpkins. *Corruption in Developing Countries.* New York: W. W. Norton and Company, 1964.

Wriggins, W. Howard. *The Ruler's Imperative: Strategies for Political Survival in Asia and Africa.* New York: Columbia University Press, 1969.

Yared, Marc. "Le Mwalimu s'en va." *Jeune Afrique* no. 1296 (6 November 1985).

Zanker, Alfred, Robin Knight, Richard Z. Chesnoff, and Douglas Stanglin. "Europe's Immigration Battles." *U.S. News & World Report,* 31 March 1986, pp. 25–27.

INDEX